Christopher Winn has been a freelance writer and trivia collector for over twenty years. He has worked with Terry Wogan and Jonathan Ross, and sets quiz questions for television as well as for the *Daily Mail* and *Daily Telegraph*. He is the author of the bestselling *I Never Knew That* series of books and was the Associate Producer for a TV series by ITV about Great Britain. He is married to artist Mai Osawa, who illustrates all of his books.

CHRISTOPHER WINN

I Never Knew That About
About
THE ENGLISH

ILLUSTRATIONS BY
Mai Osawa

EBURY
PRESS

3 5 7 9 10 8 6 4 2

Ebury Press, an imprint of Ebury Publishing,
20 Vauxhall Bridge Road,
London SW1V 2SA

Ebury Press is part of the Penguin Random House group of companies
whose addresses can be found at global.penguinrandomhouse.com

Penguin
Random House
UK

First published by Ebury Press in 2008
This edition published by Ebury Press in 2016

www.eburypublishing.co.uk

A CIP catalogue record for this book is available from the British Library

ISBN 9781785033926

Printed and bound in Great Britain by Clays Ltd, St Ives PLC

MIX
Paper from
responsible sources
FSC® C018179

Penguin Random House is committed to a sustainable future
for our business, our readers and our planet. This book is
made from Forest Stewardship Council® certified paper.

For Uncle Peter

CONTENTS

————◆•••◆————

◀ Essex ▶

First Town ✦ *Biggest Keep* ✦ *Captain of the Mayflower* ✦ *Fine Words*
✦ *Triangular Tower* ✦ *First in Brick* ✦ *Jam Today*
ESSEX FOLK
95

◀ Gloucestershire ▶

Dark Deeds ✦ *Birthplace of Modern Conservation*
Biggest Norman Tower ✦ *Cheese Rolling* ✦ *Champagne*
✦ *Manors Houses*
GLOUCESTERSHIRE FOLK
103

◀ Hampshire ▶

First English Capital ✦ *Longest Cathedral* ✦ *St Swithun's Day*
✦ *Manners Maketh Man* ✦ *A Great Hall* ✦ *The Round Table*
✦ *England's Oldest Charity* ✦ *Weights and Measures*
✦ *The English National Game*
HAMPSHIRE FOLK
III

◀ Herefordshire ▶

Cider Country ✦ *Member for Cider* ✦ *Biggest Vat* ✦ *Wassailing*
HEREFORDSHIRE FOLK
121

◀ Hertfordshire ▶

First Garden City ✦ *First New Town* ✦ *House of Fun* ✦ *Paper Trail*
✦ *Royal Spin*
HERTFORDSHIRE FOLK
127

◀ Huntingdonshire ▶

Cromwell Country ✦ *Presidential Ancestors* ✦ *A Unique Community*
HUNTINGDONSHIRE FOLK
137

─────◄ Kent ►─────

The Oldest English Church ✦ *Oldest School* ✦ *Biggest Norman Crypt*
✦ *Primate of All England* ✦ *Maidstone* ✦ *First in Flight* ✦ *Staple Drink*
✦ *Cockles and Winkles*

KENT FOLK

143

─────◄ Lancashire ►─────

House of Lancaster ✦ *Scousers* ✦ *Mersey Beat* ✦ *Liver Building* ✦ *Two Cathedrals*
✦ *Gladstone and Hitler* ✦ *Hotpot* ✦ *Greatest Steeplechase*

LANCASHIRE FOLK

151

─────◄ Leicestershire ►─────

Unspeakable ✦ *An English Sport* ✦ *Red Cheese*

LEICESTERSHIRE FOLK

161

─────◄ Lincolnshire ►─────

A Precious Piece of Architecture ✦ *Tallest Building in the World* ✦ *Angel Choir*
✦ *Polygonal Parliament* ✦ *An Old Town* ✦ *First Tank* ✦ *An English Order*
✦ *A Princess of Wales*

LINCOLNSHIRE FOLK

167

─────◄ Middlesex ►─────

World's Oldest Film Studios ✦ *Ealing Comedies* ✦ *The Longitude Problem*
✦ *Early Cartoonist* ✦ *G and T*

MIDDLESEX FOLK

177

─────◄ Norfolk ►─────

The First English Holiday Camp ✦ *Early English Brickwork* ✦ *Paston Letters*
✦ *First Steeplechase* ✦ *Norfolk Terrier*

NORFOLK FOLK

185

Contents

Contents

PREFACE

THE ENGLISH are a remarkable and singular people. They owe much to being an island race and much to the beauty and landscape of their island. They owe much to all those who have settled in England and fallen in love with this uncommon land. Celts, Romans, Jutes, Angles, Saxons, Danes, Jews, Normans, Huguenots, Flemings and Walloons – the English have borrowed something from all these peoples, and have forged the disparate elements together in a very English way, be it in language, customs, identity or character.

In return the English have given much back. The English language, the language of Shakespeare, more widely spoken than any other, 'Parliamentary' democracy, 'the worst form of government except all the others that have been tried,' according to Winston Churchill, cricket, football, rugby, the Industrial Revolution, railways, the pub, the class system, Georgian architecture, *Alice in Wonderland*, afternoon tea.

This book travels to every corner of England to discover the people and the flavour that each has contributed to England and the English. You cannot pin down or define the English, you can only listen to their stories, learn something of their ways and enjoy the experience.

THE ENGLISH COUNTIES

T HE ENGLISH CHARACTER is defined by county as much as by anything. A Yorkshireman is instantly recognisable from a Cornishman, a Geordie from a Man of Kent, by accent, by outlook, by appearance.

Hence, *I Never Knew That About the English* is divided into the 39 historic English counties and the Vale of the White Horse – counties that come down to us from the dawn of England, that have moulded their inhabitants, conferred distinctive characteristics and blessings upon them, presented them with different challenges and loyalties.

The story of the English people is intertwined with the English counties, and the bureaucrats have sought in vain to separate them. I would not dare to try – nor would I wish to.

Bedfordshire

Houghton House – John Bunyan's 'House Beautiful'.

◄ BEDFORDSHIRE FOLK ►

Admiral Byng ✦ Samuel Whitbread ✦ John Howard ✦ Harold Abrahams
✦ John Le Mesurier ✦ Ronnie Barker ✦ Arthur Hailey ✦ Paul Young
✦ Monty Panesar

Thomas Tompion
1639–1713

England's Father Time, THOMAS TOMPION, was born in a small thatched cottage beside the huge green at ICKWELL GREEN, near Biggleswade. He was the son of the village blacksmith and worked in his father's smithy until he was 25. In the 17th century, blacksmiths were the most proficient engineers of their day, and it was in the smithy that Tompion learned the precision skills he was later to put to good use as a clockmaker's apprentice in London.

In 1671 Tompion joined the recently formed Worshipful Company of Clockmakers, and was later elected Master. In 1676 Charles II commissioned him to make two clocks for the new Royal Observatory, demanding that they should be accurate enough for astronomers to make calculations by them, and that they should only need to be wound once a year. These helped the first Astronomer Royal, John Flamsteed, to prove that the earth spins on its axis at a uniform rate.

Tompion was the first watchmaker to join the Royal Society, and created the first English watches with balance springs, which were much more accurate than earlier watches. He also designed and improved on various types of escapements, or devices to control the rotational movement of wheels, inventing a cylinder escapement that allowed the first flat watches to be made. He was

THE FIRST MANUFACTURER KNOWN TO PUT SERIAL NUMBERS ON HIS PRODUCTS.

Tompion was a prolific and innovative watchmaker, producing not just watches but the finest mantel and grandfather clocks in the world. Modern clocks and watches owe much of their design to the techniques he perfected. Known as the Father of English Clockmaking, he is buried in Westminster Abbey.

Close to Tompion's cottage, with an upturned horseshoe picked out in brick above the door, is his father's old smithy, now restored and used as a changing room by the local football club.

Tompion's Clocks

Tompion's timepieces were so well built that many examples survive and are still working, over 300 years after they were made.

The British Museum has a number of his creations, including his greatest masterpiece, the 'MOSTYN', a year clock made for William and Mary and possibly 'the most valuable clock in the world'.

ICKWELL & OLD WARDEN F.C.

The Pump Room in Bath boasts one of Tompion's finest clocks, donated to the city by Tompion himself in 1709 and in full working order. It still only needs winding once a month.

St Mary's Church at Northill, where Tompion was christened, has a famous one-handed clock made by Tompion on the church tower.

John Bunyan
1628–88

J ohn Bunyan's THE PILGRIM'S PROGRESS, published in 1678, tells of the adventures of a young man called Christian, burdened down with sins, who must flee the worldly City of Destruction and journey through a land of dangers and temptations towards the heavenly Celestial City. Bunyan uses simple language, colourful characters and vivid visual imagery to make his story widely accessible, and *The Pilgrim's Progress* was carried all over the world by English missionaries and explorers, making Bunyan THE FIRST BEST-SELLING NOVELIST IN THE ENGLISH LANGUAGE. It has been translated into over 200 languages, more than any other book apart from the Bible, and is probably the most widely read religious novel ever written.

Bunyan was born, the son of a tinker, in a small cottage outside Elstow, an attractive village on the outskirts of Bedford. He was a boisterous, energetic boy who enjoyed playing tipcat, a form of rounders, on the village green and had a reputation for being disobedient and rebellious.

In 1644, during the Civil War, he joined the Parliamentary army dreaming of excitement, and his dream came alarmingly true when a soldier who had just replaced him at the siege of Leicester was shot dead. Bunyan began to think that maybe God was keeping him for some deeper purpose.

He returned home to Elstow and reluctantly settled down to be a tinker like his father. The family was poor and Bunyan found village life frustrating, but marriage to a local girl, Mary, mellowed him somewhat. When their daughter was born blind, Bunyan was convinced this was the result of his former life, and he decided to turn from his wicked ways and embrace the Christianity of Cromwell's Puritan England.

At the Restoration, Charles II attempted to suppress the Puritans, and Bunyan was flung into Bedford gaol for preaching without a licence.

Elstow Abbey Church, where John Bunyan rang the church bells

Refusing to compromise, he spent the next 12 years in and out of gaol. While inside he made shoelaces for his blind daughter to sell at the gaol gate, so that his wife and four children could buy food, and fashioned himself a flute out of the leg of his prison stool, with which he could entertain his fellow inmates. It was during his third period of imprisonment in 1672 that he began writing the great Christian epic that would make him famous.

After his release from gaol Bunyan became a Congregational pastor in Bedford and continued to publish books and travel around the countryside preaching. He died of a cold in London in 1688 and is buried in Bunhill Fields.

The village green at Elstow where Bunyan used to play tipcat and where the annual Elstow Fair was held remains largely unchanged. At one end of the green is the lovely timber-framed Moot Hall, built in the 15th century by the nuns of Elstow Abbey as a market stall for the fair, and for use as a courthouse and schoolroom. It is now a museum in his memory.

Elstow Abbey was founded in the 11th century by Judith, niece of William the Conqueror, and became the third largest in England. All that is left is the magnificent church with its detached bell tower where, as a young man, Bunyan would ring the bells, all the while gazing upwards nervously in case they fell down on his head as a punishment from God.

Inside the main body of the church are the Norman font where Bunyan was baptised and where he later brought his blind daughter Mary to be christened, the balustrade where he would kneel for Communion, and the seat he used when attending services.

In the floor of the north aisle of the church is one of only two brasses in all England to portray an abbess.

Maypole Dancing

Ickwell Green is famous for its Mayday celebrations, which have been held on the green for over 400 years, and is one of the only villages in England to have a permanent maypole.

Maypole dancing takes place on village greens all over England on May Day, and is a celebration of fertility, new life and the start of the growing season. In the 16th century the young people of the village would go out and gather up garlands of spring flowers and hawthorn branches, as referred to in the rhyme 'Here we go gathering nuts (or knots) in May'. The hawthorn, which blossoms in May, is also known as the May Tree and is symbolic of fertility.

In earlier, pagan days a hawthorn branch was stuck in the ground, and the young people would attach a strip of their clothing to it as an offering to the country spirits for an abundant harvest of both crops and children. Then they would dance around it in celebration, weaving intricate patterns with the ribbons and pay court to Flora, the goddess of flowers, as represented by the May Queen, the 'fairest maid' in the village, who would be seated on a throne wearing a crown of flowers.

The hawthorn was eventually replaced by the maypole and strips of clothing by brightly coloured ribbons.

The custom of having children dance around the maypole was introduced by John Ruskin in 1881.

The tallest maypole ever known stood outside St Mary-le-Strand in London and was 143 ft (44 m) tall.

Morris Dancing

Morris dancing is also associated with May Day, although it is performed at other times of year as well, and is traditionally danced by the men of the village. Based on a pagan ritual, the actual Morris dance is derived from a style of 'Moorish' dancing introduced into Europe by the Moors in the 15th century, and taken up enthusiastically by the Tudor court in England.

The dancers wear jingles attached to their legs and dress in white, with differently coloured belts and jackets depending which part of the country they are in. Six or eight dancers wielding sticks line up facing each other and go through a variety of dances to the accompaniment of, in earlier times, a pipe and tabor, in more modern times a violin or accordion.

By the end of the 19th century Morris dancing had virtually died out. In 1899 the musician and teacher Cecil Sharp happened to witness a special performance in Oxford, which inspired him to tour the country researching the various forms of Morris dancing that survived. In 1911 he founded the English Folk Dance Society, and this led a revival in the popularity of Morris dancing and the folk music that accompanies it.

Well, I never knew this
about
BEDFORDSHIRE FOLK

Admiral Byng
◄ 1704–57 ►

JOHN BYNG was born at SOUTHILL PARK, fourth son of a distinguished admiral, the 1st Viscount Torrington.

He enlisted in the Navy at 14, and thanks in part to his illustrious father's influence, rose quickly through the ranks. In 1756, by now an admiral, Byng was sent by a dithering government to reinforce the British garrison on the island of Minorca against the French.

Byng's squadron was small and ill-equipped, and before he could land the relief force, a French fleet appeared. There followed an inconclusive sea-fight, during which the French were repulsed, but a number of the English ships were damaged. Byng judged that his scant relief force was insufficient to repel a French attack on the fort, and rather than abandon them on the island to suffer inevitable rout and capture, he sailed back to Gibraltar for repairs and to treat the wounded, leaving Minorca to fall to the French.

The English government, appalled by what they saw as an embarrassing defeat, summoned Admiral Byng back to England for court martial. They refused to accept that their own indecision and lack of preparation were partly to blame and tried to whip up resentment against Byng, leaking stories that he was a coward and a liar.

Byng was cleared of cowardice, but found guilty of not having 'done his utmost against the enemy, either in battle or pursuit'. This carried the death penalty, and on 14 March 1757 he was shot on the quarterdeck of the HMS *Monarch*, in Portsmouth Harbour. The brutality of the execution shocked the public. The French author Voltaire, arriving in Portsmouth on the very day of the killing, was so disgusted by the whole episode, which had been closely followed throughout Europe, that he was moved to write in his novel *Candide*: 'In this country they see fit to shoot an admiral from time to time to encourage the others' – *'pour encourager les autres'*.

Admiral John Byng was carried home to Southill, where he was laid to rest beside his father in the Torrington vaults in All Saints Church.

Samuel Whitbread
◄ 1720–96 ►

SAMUEL WHITBREAD was born in the village of CARDINGTON, the son of a Bedfordshire farmer. At the age of 16 he was apprenticed to a London brewer by his widowed mother, and at 22 he laid the foundations of his industrial empire when he used his inheritance to invest in a small brewery. At this time ale was being promoted as a healthy alternative to the demon gin, and the business flour-

To The Perpetual Disgrace
of PUBLICK JUSTICE
The Honble JOHN BYNG Esqr
Admiral of the Blue
Fell a MARTYR to
POLITICAL PERSECUTION
March 14th in the Year 1757 when
BRAVERY and LOYALTY
were Insufficient Securities
For the
Life and Honour
of a
NAVAL OFFICER

ished. In 1750 Whitbread built his own brewery in London's Chiswell Street, the first purpose-built, large-scale brewery in the country, which soon grew into THE BIGGEST BREWERY IN BRITAIN.

Whitbread was one of the first people to make a fortune through 'trade', which was much looked down upon by 18th-century society, but he was also one of the first great philanthropists, who believed in using the fruits of his success for the benefit of all. Whitbread ran his business with a concern for the welfare of his workforce, and his greatest contribution to the industrial society of which he was a pioneer was the template he created for honest business practice and good relations between management and workers.

In 1768 Whitbread was elected MP for Bedford, a post he held for over 20 years, and he was THE FIRST MAN TO SPEAK OUT IN PARLIAMENT AGAINST SLAVERY. In 1795 he bought nearby Southill Park from the Byng family, and his descendants still live there today.

Samuel Whitbread is buried in St Mary's Church in Cardington.

John Howard
◄ 1726–90 ►

JOHN HOWARD was born in London but would often visit Cardington,

where his grandmother had a farm, and became firm friends with Samuel Whitbread. In 1756 he came to live in Cardington and his fine house still stands close to the church. Independently rich, Howard travelled far and wide and was once imprisoned by a French privateer and forced to endure appalling conditions, an incident which sparked his interest in the plight of those in prison.

In 1773 he became High Sheriff of Bedfordshire and set off on a tour of the county's gaols. He was horrified by what he found. They were filthy, overcrowded and diseased. Men and women were herded together like

John Howard's statue in Bedford

cattle. The innocent had to pay their gaoler for their release, which they usually were unable to do, and so were kept unjustly confined. Howard raised all these issues in Parliament and sponsored several bills for reform. He carried on his crusade all over Britain and then on the Continent. In 1790, having prophetically left his affairs in order, he travelled to Russia to visit military hospitals, contracted typhus there, and died. He is buried in Russia beneath a simple tombstone which reads, 'Whosoever thou art, thou standest at the grave of thy friend'.

John Howard of Cardington was held in such esteem that a statue of him was placed in St Paul's Cathedral – the first time a commoner had ever received such an honour. THE HOWARD LEAGUE FOR PENAL REFORM is named in his honour.

Born in Bedford

HAROLD ABRAHAMS (1899–1978), winner of the gold medal for the 100 metres at the 1924 Olympics in Paris, a feat immortalised in the 1981 Oscar-winning film *Chariots of Fire*.

JOHN LE MESURIER (1912–83), actor, best remembered for his role as Sergeant Wilson in the BBC sitcom *Dad's Army*.

RONNIE BARKER (1929–2005), comic actor, known for his starring roles in *The Two Ronnies, Porridge* and *Open All Hours* for the BBC. He was also a prolific writer who sent in material under the fictitious name Gerald Wiley, so that it would be 'judged on merit'.

Born in Luton

ARTHUR HAILEY (1920–2004), best-selling author of novels such as *Hotel* and *Airport*.

PAUL YOUNG, pop singer and the first voice heard on the 1984 Band Aid single 'Do They Know It's Christmas?', born 1956.

MONTY PANESAR, cricketer and the first Sikh to represent England, or any nation other than India, at Test cricket, born 1982.

Berkshire

HOUSE OF WINDSOR ✦ WINDSOR CASTLE
✦ OLDEST ORDER OF CHIVALRY ✦ ST GEORGE'S CHAPEL
✦ WINDSOR TOWN ✦ ENGLAND'S PATRON SAINT
✦ THE FIRST ENGLISH MINIMUM WAGE

St George's Chapel, Windsor.
Spiritual home of the Order of the Garter.

◄ BERKSHIRE FOLK ►

Jack O'Newbury ✦ Sir John Soane ✦ Hugo Lofting ✦ Mike Oldfield
✦ Tracy Edwards ✦ Sir William Herschel ✦ Sir Stanley Spencer

The House of Windsor

The name of WINDSOR has reverberated throughout the history of the English people as a principal centre of the English monarchy for over 1,000 years. In 1917, during the Great War against Germany, George V chose this very English name as the new family name for the English royal family, to replace the Germanic sounding Saxe-Coburg-Gotha.

The first castle at Windsor, a motte and bailey, was built by William the Conqueror in 1070, to take advantage of a strategic bluff above the River Thames and guard the western approaches to London. Putting a round tower on the motte, or mound, fed conveniently into the local belief that this was the site of King Arthur's Round Table, helping William to wrap himself in the mantle of that legendary predecessor. The walls of the castle today enclose the same area and follow the same shape as William's original castle, which Henry II rebuilt in stone and expanded in 1170.

Windsor Castle, the English monarchy's weekend cottage, is now THE OLDEST AND LARGEST OCCUPIED CASTLE IN THE WORLD. It offers a fairytale vision of towers and turrets and battlements from wherever you view it – a fitting first glimpse of England for the millions who fly over it on their way into Heathrow. As one awe-struck tourist was heard to gasp, 'It's real dandy – but why the heck did they build it so close to the airport?'

Order of the Garter

E DWARD III was born at Windsor in 1312, and amongst his many ambitions, two were paramount. To press his claim for the throne of France, and to create a court based on the Arthurian knightly values of chivalry and valour. In 1348 he initiated THE FIRST AND MOST PRES-TIGIOUS ENGLISH ORDER OF CHIVALRY, THE NOBLE ORDER OF THE GARTER, consisting of the monarch, his son the Black Prince, and 24 of his most courageous and trust-worthy knights. The Order was based on King Arthur's Knights of the Round Table – and was intended as a mark of royal favour and a reward for loyalty.

The symbol of the Garter was derived from an item of military dress, and the Order's motto referred to Edward's claim to the French throne. There is, however, a much more romantic and memorable tale of how the Order came by its name and motto. During a dance at Windsor, Joan, Countess of Salisbury, a noted beauty rumoured to be the King's mistress, dropped one of her garters. To cover her embarrassment, Edward picked it up and tied it around his own leg, much to the shock and amusement of the assembled court. 'Honi soit qui mal y pense,' he said, and this became the motto of the Order – 'Shame on him who thinks evil of this'.

To strengthen the knightly theme, Edward proclaimed St George, who was patron saint of soldiers, to be the patron saint of the Order. Edward was a renowned warrior king and had just achieved a great victory against the French at the Battle of Crecy in 1346, and thus the chival-rous St George was a highly appro-priate choice for the furtherance of his aims.

St George's Chapel
Subsequently, the magnificent chapel at Windsor, begun by Edward IV and completed by Henry VIII, was dedi-cated to St George and became the spiritual home of the Order of the Garter.

Today the Order of the Garter, which is still in the sole gift of the monarch, consists of 26 Companions and a number of royals. Every June, members process in their robes to St George's Chapel for a service.

Windsor Town

T he town that grew up under the mighty castle walls is one of England's show towns and has some stories of its own to tell. In 1597 William Shakespeare stayed at Windsor's Garter Inn and there wrote

The Merry Wives of Windsor for Queen Elizabeth I.

WINDSOR GUILDHALL was built in 1689 by Sir Christopher Wren, whose father was Dean of Windsor. He modelled his design on the old market hall that was being replaced, which had open arcades, but the good burgesses of Windsor didn't trust the slender columns supporting the upper floors and insisted he put in some more. Wren complied, but those with a keen eye will spot that the extra columns don't actually reach the floor above.

As well as the Royal Family, Windsor gives its name to a brown soup, the perfect knot for a tie, and a kind of chair.

Windsor is also the reason why Berkshire is THE ONLY ENGLISH COUNTY WITH THE PREFIX 'ROYAL'. Reading football club are nicknamed the Royals.

St George, Patron Saint of England

◆◆◆◆

ST GEORGE was born in Cappadocia, in what is now Turkey, around AD 280. He joined the Roman army at the age of 17 and rose rapidly through the ranks to become a military tribune, while his valour and strength made him a favourite of the Emperor Diocletian.

They were restless times for the Roman Empire, and Diocletian decided to try and restore order by reviving the pagan gods and traditions of old Rome. This involved persecuting other religions that were threatening the authority of the Emperor, particularly Christianity, which Diocletian suppressed with ruthless cruelty.

St George, who had become a convert to Christianity, used his position to try and temper the worst excesses of the persecution, rescuing Christians from execution and helping many to escape to safety. Eventually, in AD 303, he confronted Diocletian in the city of Nicomedia, then the eastern capital of the Roman Empire, and condemned the Emperor for his injustice and brutality.

Diocletian had St George cast into prison and tortured, but the saint would not renounce his faith, and on 23 April he was dragged through the streets and beheaded. His body was laid to rest at his mother's home at Lydda in Palestine, while his head was later taken to be buried in Rome, where Constantine, the first Christian Emperor, had a church in St George's name built over the grave.

The legend of St George and the Dragon, as documented by Jacobus de Voragine, Bishop of Genoa, in his *Golden Legends*, originates from St

George's time as a soldier in North Africa, when he was stationed near Silene in Libya. The town was being terrorised by a large beast akin to a crocodile with wings, which had settled on a nearby lake. To keep the creature satisfied the townsfolk had sacrificed all their animals and then their young maidens, until only the King's daughter was left. When her turn came she was tethered outside the town walls and left to her fate. As the dragon approached, St George appeared, riding on a white charger, and fought the monster to a standstill, finally cutting off its head with a single blow. He was rewarded by the jubilant King with a bag of gold, which he then distributed amongst the poor.

The story is an allegory for the triumph of good over evil, and as St George's fame spread across Europe he became a symbol of valour and Christian values. His connection with England begins during the Crusades, when he is said to have appeared to the English Crusaders, riding under the banner of a red cross and inspiring them in battle. Hence the English knights adopted the red cross, on a white or silver background, as an emblem, and it became recognised as the Cross of St George.

St George is mentioned in the writings of the Venerable Bede, and the earliest physical reference to him in England is carved in stone above the south door of an early Norman church at Fordington, in Dorset. In 1222 the Council of Oxford dedicated 23 April, the date of his martyrdom, as St George's Day.

After 1348, when Edward III made St George the patron saint of his chivalrous new Order of the Garter, the English began to regard him as their own. Shakespeare has Henry V exhort his troops before the Battle of Agincourt with the words 'Cry God for Harry, England and St George!' and indeed, in 1415, the soldier saint was made patron saint of England to celebrate the English victory at Agincourt.

John Cabot flew the pennant of the Cross of St George when he sailed to discover Newfoundland in 1497, and it was also flown by great English explorers such as Sir Francis Drake and Sir Walter Raleigh. In 1620 the St George's flag flew from the *Mayflower* as it sailed into Plymouth, Massachusetts.

Today the flag of St George is recog-

nised throughout Christendom as the flag of the Church of England, and is also sported by followers of the England football and rugby teams.

In 2005 police in Oldham fined 20-year-old football supporter Neil Prendergast £30 for having a cross of St George sticker over the European Union flag on his car number plate.

In the late 18th century there was devastating poverty amongst agricultural workers due to land enclosures, inflation caused by the war with France, and the move towards industrialisation. Across the country, riots were fermenting and in 1795 Berkshire magistrates met in Speenhamland to announce the SPEENHAMLAND ACT. This was a revolutionary system which set wages according to the price of wheat and the number of children in the family. If a farmer couldn't afford the wage, then the shortfall was subsidised from the poor relief fund – it was the first time poverty had been tackled with wage subsidies for farm workers, rather than by the creation of monstrous workhouses.

However, farmers soon began to employ only workers who qualified for the subsidy, and those who weren't indigent became unemployable, leading to a collapse in the labour market, and a huge burden on the relief funds.

The First English Minimum Wage

❧

On the western outskirts of Newbury lies SPEEN, once known as Speenhamland, which was the scene of the FIRST ATTEMPT IN ENGLISH HISTORY TO APPLY A MINIMUM WAGE.

Shaw House

❧

Lying unexpected and lovely to the east of Newbury is SHAW HOUSE, one of the finest Elizabethan houses in England, built by a Newbury clothier called Thomas Dolman. English history was almost drastically altered here in 1644, when Charles I was using the

house as his headquarters during the second Battle of Newbury. On the morning of the battle, a Roundhead soldier, spotting Charles dressing by a window, fired his musket at the King, missing him by a whisker. The place where the bullet struck the wall can still be seen.

Well, I never   knew this *about*
BERKSHIRE FOLK

Jack O'Newbury

Although John Lombe of Derby is rightly credited with building England's first mechanical factory, and Richard Arkwright England's first factory complex, it is a Berkshire lad from Newbury who gave them both the idea.

Newbury today is best known for traffic jams and horse-racing, but this prosperous old town actually deserves a prominent place in history as the home of ENGLAND'S FIRST FACTORY OWNER. In the late 15th century, an apprentice clothier called John Winchcombe, better known as JACK O'NEWBURY, in good entrepreneurial style married the boss's daughter, and used her money to build up a huge clothing business. Eventually he had over 200 weavers working for him in one building, along with areas for drying and stretching the cloth, and retail outlets selling the finished product. This was the first time that all stages of manufacture had ever been brought together under one roof – the first factory building. There is nothing left of the factory, but some of Jack's house remains near the River Kennet, and the beautiful Jacobean Cloth Hall, now the town museum, is a reminder of the wealth brought to Newbury by Jack and the cloth trade.

Bells, the first record produced by Richard Branson's Virgin record company.

TRACY EDWARDS, yachtswoman, born in READING in 1962. Skippered the first all-female crew to sail around the world.

Born in Berkshire

SIR JOHN SOANE (1753–1837), architect, born in GORING-ON-THAMES. Best known for designing the Bank of England (demolished in 1920) and for his house, now a museum, at Lincoln's Inn Fields in London.

HUGH LOFTING (1886–1947), author of the Dr Doolittle books, born in MAIDENHEAD.

MIKE OLDFIELD, musician, born in READING in 1953. Composed *Tubular*

Buried in Berkshire

SIR WILLIAM HERSCHEL (1738–1822), German-born astronomer, is buried at St Laurence's Church in Upton, SLOUGH. Discovered Uranus in 1781. Built a famous telescope in the back garden of his house in Slough, Observatory House (now demolished).

SIR STANLEY SPENCER (1891–1959), painter, was born and buried in COOKHAM.

England's traditional source of wealth was WOOL, and even today the focal point of the House of Lords is the 'WOOLSACK', a seat of stuffed wool on which the Lord Chancellor sits as a reminder of what underpinned England's prosperity. (The Woolsack is now stuffed with wool from Commonwealth countries.) The great wool merchants of old proclaimed their wealth by building magnificent 'wool' churches, most commonly found in the Cotswolds and East Anglia. St Nicholas's church in Newbury, built by Jack O'Newbury around 1500, is a fine example of a wool church.

Buckinghamshire

---❖❖❖---

CHILTERN HUNDREDS ✦ AN ENGLISH INVENTION
✦ FREEDOM OF CONSCIENCE ✦ GREATEST ENGLISH POEM
✦ HELLFIRE ✦ ENGLISH HYMNAL ✦ PANCAKE RACE

Jordans Quaker Meeting House, built in 1688. Burial place of William Penn, the founder of Pennsylvania.

---◀ BUCKINGHAMSHIRE FOLK ▶---

John Hampden ✦ George and William Grenville ✦ Benjamin Disraeli
✦ Sir George Gilbert Scott ✦ Major George Howson
✦ Herbert Austin ✦ Roald Dahl

Chiltern Hundreds

Buckinghamshire has always been at the forefront of British politics, particularly the Chilterns, which have even lent their name to a political procedure. To resign as a Member of Parliament is forbidden, but an MP who wishes to step down between elections may apply for the 'STEWARDSHIP OF THE CHILTERN HUNDREDS'. The Chilterns were once plagued by ruffians and highwaymen, and so a Steward was appointed by the Crown to impose law and order. Anyone who held an office paid for by the Crown was prohibited from sitting as an MP, and thus, by applying for the post, an MP would effectively disqualify himself from sitting in the House.

Bletchley Park

During the Second World War, BLETCHLEY PARK, a Victorian mansion now on the edge of Milton Keynes, was very much in the front line. In 1939 a small group of mathematicians and crossword puzzle enthusiasts were assembled here, in total secrecy, with orders to crack Germany's Enigma code. To begin with, using knowledge smuggled in by the Poles of how the Enigma worked, mathematician ALAN TURING, regarded as the founder of modern computer science, developed an apparatus that could decipher a large number of Enigma machines at one time, and this proved key in helping the team to unravel the code. This feat allowed England to monitor German plans for bombing raids and U-boat attacks, and shortened the war by two years, according to Winston Churchill.

In order to process messages even faster, Alan Turing's lecturer from Cambridge, PROFESSOR MAX NEWMAN, and engineer TOMMY FLOWERS, using Turing's theories on computation as a basis, designed and built 'COLOSSUS', the world's first

programmable electronic computer. It is to them that we owe the computers that run the world today, and yet for a long time the invention of the computer was credited to the Americans – because Colossus and Bletchley Park remained covered by the 30-year rule of the Official Secrets Act until 1974.

Bletchley Park was ENGLAND'S FIRST GOVERNMENT LISTENING POST, and forerunner of today's GCHQ at Cheltenham. The mansion itself was saved from demolition and is now run as a museum, complete with a working model of Colossus, in memory of the vital work done there and its contribution to winning the Second World War.

Jordans

Tucked away down an undulating country lane near Beaconsfield is JORDANS, a hidden place of supreme importance to English freedoms both at home and overseas.

There is a Tudor farmhouse, a barn made with timbers from the *Mayflower*, one of the earliest Quaker meeting-houses, and the simple graves of men and women who fought for the freedom of English people to think for themselves.

Amongst those lying here is THOMAS ELLWOOD (1639–1713), a leading Quaker who learnt young what it meant to question authority. On becoming a Quaker, as a young man, he refused to take off his hat at meal times in case that signified a deference to his father which should be shown only to God, whereupon his father confiscated all Thomas's hats and beat him roundly for such impudence. Ellwood went on to edit the journals of George Fox (1624–91), founder of the Society of Friends, and read for John Milton, who was going blind (*see* Milton's Cottage).

Another Quaker buried here is WILLIAM PENN (1644–1718), the son of a famous admiral, and the founder of the State of Pennsylvania.

The Quakers' belief that every individual has a personal relationship with God and should be free to worship God without the intervention of priests, brought them into conflict with the Church authorities, and many Quakers, including Penn, were persecuted and imprisoned.

In 1670 William Penn's father died, leaving him a considerable fortune and a debt of £16,000 owed by Charles II. In lieu of the debt Penn was granted land in the American colonies, and he founded Pennsylvania, named in honour of his father, as a place where those fleeing persecution in England could live and worship freely by their own or Quaker principles. He named the principal settlement Philadelphia, which is Greek for 'brotherly love'. And in the tiny meeting-house at Jordans, in 1701, William Penn wrote his CHARTER OF PRIVILEGES, Pennsylvania's original constitution. With its emphasis on human rights, religious freedom and the inclusion of ordinary citizens in the law-making process, it was a template for the American Constitution.

By virtue of his friendship with James II, Penn persuaded the King to issue a Declaration of Indulgence, allowing everyone in England to worship God in their own way, and thereafter persecution of all religious sects ceased. Some of the more fundamentalist groups disapproved, suspecting the Catholic King of merely trying to gain freedom for the Roman Catholic religion, which they despised, but William Penn believed in freedom for all, not just his own, and he would not back down. He remains one of the most courageous and influential fighters for freedom of conscience in English history.

In 2005 Jordans Meeting House, built in 1688, suffered a serious fire, but has since been restored as near as possible to its original state.

Milton's Cottage

Not far away from Jordans, in the village of CHALFONT ST GILES, is a pretty timber-framed brick cottage – the last and only remaining home of JOHN MILTON. He rented it from his friend and reader Thomas Ellwood, and came here in 1665 to escape the plague and finish his epic poem PARADISE LOST, about man's fall from grace. When he

showed the poem to Thomas Ellwood, Ellwood replied, 'Thou hath said much here about Paradise Lost, but what hast thou to say about Paradise Found?' And so Milton wrote *Paradise Regained*, about Satan's unsuccessful temptation of Jesus in the desert.

It is largely for these two works that Milton is regarded as one of the greatest poets in the English language. Thomas Jefferson conceded that he was greatly influenced by the style and ideas of Milton when he was writing the American Declaration of Independence.

Milton's Cottage now houses a museum in his memory.

West Wycombe

The picture book village of WEST WYCOMBE, slumbering on the old London to Oxford coach road, is kept safe by the National Trust. It consists of a street lined with timbered houses, a grand Palladian mansion with park and, forming a prominent landmark on top of a steep hill, the distinctive church of St Laurence. Crowning the 14th-century church tower is a golden ball with seating for six where, in the 18th century, SIR FRANCIS DASHWOOD and his friends would meet and play cards, drink and sing 'jolly songs very unfit for the profane ears of the world below'.

In fact, in the world 300 ft (90 m) directly below, profanity and worse was a regular occurrence, for here, in caves dug out of the chalk, would meet the infamous Hellfire Club. Sir Francis Dashwood, who owned West Wycombe, was a wealthy London merchant with a wide circle of friends centred on Frederick, Prince of Wales, who made up 'The Knights of St Francis of Wycombe', or the Hellfire Club. In the 1750s Dashwood had mined the hill below the church for material to make the straight stretch of road into High Wycombe that you can see from the hill. The Hellfire Club, which used to meet in Medmenham Abbey a few miles away, began to gather in the caves, which reached quarter of a mile (0.4 km) into the hillside. The meetings, for which the men were dressed in white flowing robes, were secret, lasted all night and gained a reputation as wild, Bacchanalian orgies – especially as only ladies of 'a cheerful and lively disposition' were invited.

In 1763, as so often happens, rough-house led to tears, and the club was disbanded. One night at Medmenham Abbey, Sir Henry Vansittart, Governor of Bengal, brought along as his guest a baboon from India. John Wilkes, the cross-eyed radical, journalist and MP for Aylesbury, thought what fun it would be to dress the animal up as the Devil and conceal it in a box. At just the right moment he let it out and the

poor creature sprang from the box on to the back of the Earl of Sandwich, First Lord of the Admiralty, who cried out in terror, 'Spare me gracious Devil, thou knowest I was only fooling, I am not half as wicked as I pretended!' The Earl and the baboon both fled from the chapel. The baboon was never seen again, while the Earl retired into private life to do Good Works. The Hellfire Club limped on as a pale imitation before finally closing in 1774.

The church is often open and it is sometimes possible to climb into the golden ball. There are daily tours into the caves, which can also be hired for dinner parties, wedding receptions or other entertainments.

English Hymnal

The hymn 'AMAZING GRACE', which became a No. 1 hit for the Royal Scots Dragoon Guards in 1972, was written in the 1760s by slave-trader turned hymn-writer JOHN NEWTON, while he was a curate in the north Buckinghamshire village of Olney. His great friend, who also lived in Olney, was poet WILLIAM COWPER, whose most famous work was the comic ballad THE DIVERTING HISTORY OF JOHN GILPIN. Together they wrote the *Olney Hymns,* a collection of nearly

350 hymns, including 'God Moves in a Mysterious Way' and 'How Sweet the Name of Jesus Sounds'.

Pancake Race

Olney is famous for its annual Shrove Tuesday PANCAKE RACE, dating back to 1445. Apparently it began when a harassed housewife, hearing the church bells, rushed off to church still clutching her frying pan. Those taking part must be women over 18 who have lived in Olney for over three months. They must wear the clothing of a traditional housewife and run 400 yards from the market-place to the church, while tossing pancakes. The winner gets a kiss from a bell ringer and a silver cup.

Well, I never   *knew this*
about
BUCKINGHAMSHIRE FOLK

John Hampden
◄ 1594–1643 ►

HAMPDEN HOUSE, hidden in the hills near Princes Risborough, was the ancestral home of England's greatest parliamentarian, JOHN HAMPDEN, a cousin of Oliver Cromwell. In 1637 Hampden refused to pay the King's Ship Tax, originally levied on ports but extended by the extravagant Charles I to include inland areas as well. Hampden's defiance of the King on a point of principle – that the King could only raise taxes through Parliament – made him a hero, and he was one of the five MPs the King tried to arrest in Parliament in January 1642. The King took the Speaker's

chair and asked Speaker Lenthall if the men he wanted were there, to which the Speaker answered, 'May it please your Majesty, I have neither eyes to see, nor tongue to speak in this place, but as the House is pleased to direct me...' 'I see my birds have flown,' replied the King.

This incident lit the fuse of the English Civil War, and resulted in the Monarch being banned from the House of Commons for evermore. It is the origin of the ceremony during the State Opening of Parliament, when Black Rod goes to the Commons, on behalf of the Monarch, to summon MPs for the Queen's Speech, and has the door slammed in his face in a gesture that symbolises the Commons' independence.

Hampden was killed at the Battle of Chalgrove Field in 1643 and is buried amongst his ancestors in the lovely old church next to Hampden

House. He was the staunchest architect of parliamentary democracy and the greatest defender of its privileges. As one commentator said, 'Never Kingdom received a greater loss in one subject.'

George and William Grenville

In Wotton Underwood lies the prime minister whose actions sparked the American War of Independence. GEORGE GRENVILLE (1712–70), whose family were once Dukes of Buckingham, introduced the Stamp Act in 1765. This stipulated that the American colonies should bear some of the cost of 'defending, protecting and securing the British colonies and plantations'. Every document in America was made subject to a stamp duty, in one of the

first attempts to impose taxes on goods imported into the colonies. The colonies, who had no voice in the British Parliament, naturally protested, calling for 'no taxation without representation'. They were ignored, and thus were sown the seeds of rebellion.

In Burnham church, nestling amongst the beech trees, lies George Grenville's son WILLIAM WYNDHAM GRENVILLE (1759–1834), who also had a profound effect on the United States, for he was the prime minister under whose 'Ministry of all the Talents' the Slave Trade was abolished in 1807.

Benjamin Disraeli
◄ 1804–81 ►

Queen Victoria's favourite prime minister, and England's first and only Jewish-born prime minister, BENJAMIN DISRAELI lived at Hughenden Manor near High Wycombe, and is buried in a vault in the church next door, beneath a memorial erected for him by the Queen herself.

Sir George Gilbert Scott
◄ 1811–78 ►

SIR GEORGE GILBERT SCOTT was born in the village of GAWCOTT, just south of Buckingham. He restored over 500 English churches and left us with some fine English icons – the

Martyrs' Memorial in Oxford, the Albert Memorial in London, for which he was knighted by a grateful Queen Victoria, and most spectacular of all, the immense gothic St Pancras Station, now restored as the terminal for the Channel Tunnel railway.

His grandson, SIR GILES GILBERT SCOTT (1880–1960), designed England's biggest cathedral at Liverpool, Battersea and Bankside power stations – the latter is now the Tate Modern – and the original red telephone box.

Poppies

Sleeping in the churchyard at HAMBLEDEN is war hero MAJOR GEORGE HOWSON MC, the man who brought us the Remembrance Day poppy. Disabled in the First World War, he founded the Disabled Society specifically to find work for disabled war veterans like himself. In 1921 the British Legion started to sell poppies to help ex-servicemen, and Major Howson designed an artificial poppy that could be made by someone who had lost the use of a hand. He set up a workshop for five disabled veterans off the Old Kent Road, but this quickly outgrew its premises, and in 1922 he founded the Poppy Factory in Richmond, Surrey, which still produces millions of poppies every year.

HERBERT AUSTIN, 1st Baron Austin (1866–1941), founder of Austin Cars, was born in LITTLE MISSENDEN. In 1906 Austins became the first cars to be manufactured at the Longbridge plant, in Birmingham. In the 1930s Austin was Britain's biggest car manufacturer, producing the iconic Austin Seven.

ROALD DAHL (1916–90), children's author, is buried in GREAT MISSENDEN, location of the Roald Dahl Museum and Story Centre. He is remembered for stories such as *Willy Wonka and the Chocolate Factory* and *The Big Friendly Giant.*

Cambridgeshire

THE MOST BEAUTIFUL MILE IN THE WORLD
✦ CAMBRIDGE SCIENCE ✦ SPIES ✦ FOOTLIGHTS ✦ BOOKS
✦ CHIMES ✦ BOAT RACE ✦ PEAS PLEASE

*The Cambridge Bridge of Sighs, inspired by
the bridge in Venice over which condemned
prisoners were led to their deaths.*

◄ CAMBRIDGESHIRE FOLK ►

Octavia Hill ✦ Thomas Clarkson ✦ Sir John Berry ✦ John Maynard
Keynes ✦ Michael Ramsay ✦ Sir Christopher Cockerell ✦ Ronald Searle
✦ Sir Richard Attenborough ✦ Olivia Newton-John

Cambridge

CAMBRIDGE UNIVERSITY was established at the beginning of the 13th century by scholars fleeing from Oxford, where the students were in dispute with the townsfolk. It is THE SECOND OLDEST UNIVERSITY IN THE ENGLISH-SPEAKING WORLD, and the first Cambridge college, PETERHOUSE, was founded in 1284.

The stretch of river at Cambridge known as the 'BACKS', where the backs of the colleges run down to the river, has been described as 'the most beautiful mile in the world'. One of the buildings to be seen from the Backs is KING'S COLLEGE CHAPEL, begun by Henry VI, completed by Henry VII and considered by many people to be 'the most beautiful building in the world'. Under its matchless roof of fan vaulting

England's most famous choir sings, and those who wish to attend the traditional Christmas carol service here often have to queue outside overnight.

Cambridge Science

FRANCIS BACON and ISAAC NEWTON, pioneers of modern scientific thought, studied at Cambridge. THE CAVENDISH LABORATORY is named after the 18th-century scientist HENRY CAVENDISH, who discovered hydrogen and measured the weight of the Earth. Here, in 1897, PROFESSOR J.J. THOMPSON discovered the electron – the particle that makes up the atom, which was previously believed to be the smallest structure known. In 1952 the structure

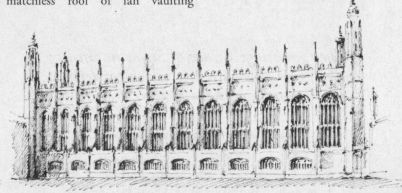

of DNA was discovered in the laboratory by JAMES WATSON and FRANCIS CRICK. This discovery has led, amongst other things, to forensic testing (pioneered at the O.J. Simpson trial) and cloning (Dolly the sheep).

Cambridge Spies

Cambridge idealism, allied to a degree of arrogance, could sometimes lead to unfortunate consequences, as in the case of the Cambridge spy ring of the 1930s, whose members were motivated by the belief that capitalism was corrupt and communism offered a better social model. PHILBY, BURGESS and MACLEAN were all recruited as spies by ANTHONY BLUNT while they were studying at Cambridge, as was a fifth man, JOHN CAIRNCROSS, whose identity was not revealed until 1990. Cairncross's activity was particularly damaging, as he leaked details of the codecracking work going on at Bletchley Park during the Second World War, which allowed the Russians to change their own codes before they were broken. He also gave away information about the atomic weapons research being pursued by the British and Americans, which the Soviets then used to set up their own nuclear programme.

Cambridge Footlights

Since it was set up in 1883 the Cambridge Footlights has been at the cutting edge of English comedy. In the 1920s and 30s the Footlights produced a wave of performers who went on to shine in the professional theatre, such as JACK HULBERT, JIMMY EDWARDS and RICHARD MURDOCH. From the 1950s came JONATHAN MILLER, PETER COOK and DAVID FROST. Two of THE GOODIES, BILL ODDIE and TIM BROOKE-TAYLOR, and three of the original MONTY PYTHON team, JOHN CLEESE, GRAHAM CHAPMAN and ERIC IDLE, learnt their trade in the Footlights, as did STEPHEN FRY, HUGH LAURIE, GRIFF RHYS

Eleanor Bron

JONES, EMMA THOMPSON and TONY SLATTERY. The first woman member was ELEANOR BRON in 1959.

Cambridge Books

The CAMBRIDGE UNIVERSITY PRESS IS THE OLDEST PRINTING AND PUBLISHING HOUSE IN THE WORLD, and stands on the site of BRITAIN'S OLDEST BOOKSHOP — books have been sold on this spot since 1581.

Cambridge Chimes

In 1793 a new clock was installed in the tower of GREAT ST MARY'S CHURCH, which stands in the centre of Cambridge between King's College Chapel and the market place, and Regius Professor of Civil Law, THE REVD DR JOSEPH JOWETT, was asked to compose a chime for it. His composition, possibly inspired by the fifth bar of the opening of Handel's aria 'I Know that My Redeemer Liveth', proved popular and was adopted in 1859 for the new Great Clock of Westminster, more widely known as Big Ben — with the result that the simple tune first heard in Cambridge is now the most famous clock chime in the world.

The Boat Race

In 1829 Cambridge University challenged Oxford University to a boat race and this took place on the River Thames at Henley. Oxford, wearing their dark blue shirts, won. The next race was run in 1836 from Westminster to Putney, and this time Cambridge, wearing light blue shirts, triumphed.

Since 1856 the race has been staged annually, except during the two world wars, over a 4½-mile (7-km) course between Putney and Mortlake. To date, Cambridge have won 79 times and Oxford 73. There was one dead heat, in 1877. According to Oxford legend the judge on the finishing line, one 'Honest' John Phelps, was asleep under a bush when the crews flashed past, and awoke to declare 'a dead heat to Oxford by four feet'.

The first woman to take part was SUE BROWN, who coxed Oxford to victory in 1981 and 1982.

Cambridge holds the course record with a time of 16 minutes and 19 seconds, recorded in 1998.

The Boat Race is one of the highlights of the English sporting calendar and some quarter of a million people normally line the riverbank to watch. Boat Race night has been known to be a rowdy occasion.

Peas Please

Anyone who thinks peas are dull should go to WITCHAM, near Ely, in July, when the pretty village hosts the WORLD PEA-SHOOTING CHAMPIONSHIPS, attracting determined competitors from all over the world. There are rounds for target and distance shooting, and a specialist round devoted to hi-tech weaponry such as steam-driven or laser-guided pea-shooters.

Well, I never knew this about
CAMBRIDGESHIRE FOLK

Octavia Hill
1838–1912

OCTAVIA HILL was born in WISBECH in 1838 into a family of reformers. Greatly influenced by both Christian Socialism and the ideals of John Ruskin, she was particularly concerned with decent social housing, and her vision was one of 'well ordered, quiet little homes behind neat little doors', rather than huge blocks of soulless, dreary tenements. Ruskin provided the finance for her first project, and the money raised in fair rents was ploughed back into maintaining and increasing the housing stock. In this way she created the template for modern housing associations.

An important feature of Octavia Hill's vision was the preservation and provision of open spaces, and in 1895 she was one of the co founders of the National Trust, donating to the Trust one of its first properties, the gardens at Toys Hill in Kent, in 1898.

Thomas Clarkson
◄── 1760–1846 ──►

The abolition of the slave trade across the world owes more to THOMAS CLARKSON than to almost anyone. He was born in WISBECH, where his clergyman father was headmaster of the grammar school. As a student at Cambridge he entered a competition to write a Latin essay on the subject of whether it was lawful to enslave anyone against their will, and during his research he came across accounts of the slave trade that horrified him. On a trip to London he pondered on what he had learnt, and at a point between Wadesmill and Ware, in Hertfordshire, he got off his horse, sat by the side of the road and resolved to do something to halt the ghastly trade. Today a memorial stands on the very spot where he made that resolution.

His essay won the competition, and he translated it into English to be read by a wider audience. The essay brought him to the attention of anti-slavery campaigner Granville Sharp, and together they set up the Society for the Abolition of the Slave Trade, which included nine prominent Quakers and William Wilberforce, the MP for Hull, who agreed to be their spokesman in the House of Commons.

Clarkson's job was to go around the slave ports and gather the evidence of cruelty and inhumanity they needed to support the case for abolition. Over a seven-year period he travelled the country inspecting ships in Deptford, Woolwich, Chatham, Sheerness, Portsmouth and Bristol. He just escaped with his life in Liverpool, after being attacked by a party of sailors sent to kill him by the ship owners whose livelihoods he was threatening. Amongst the hardware he collected were branding irons, leg shackles, handcuffs, whips and jaw locks.

After many setbacks Clarkson and his companions achieved their first goal when, in 1807, Parliament passed an 'ACT FOR THE ABOLITION OF THE SLAVE TRADE'. While this only abolished the slave trade in the British Empire, not slavery itself, it was a start and encouraged Clarkson to continue campaigning throughout Europe and America. Finally, in 1833, an attempt was made in the Slavery Abolition Act to abolish slavery itself, in that the Royal Navy was charged with closing down the trade wherever in the world they came across it.

Clarkson died at Ipswich in Suffolk in 1846 and is buried in the church at Playford, on the outskirts of the town.

Born in Cambridge

SIR JOHN BERRY 'JACK HOBBS' (1882–1963), the FIRST ENGLISH CRICKETER TO BE KNIGHTED (the first cricketer was Australian Don Bradman).

JOHN MAYNARD KEYNES (1883–1946), MOST INFLUENTIAL ENGLISH ECONOMIST OF THE 20TH CENTURY and creator of the influential Keynesian economic theory, which advocates government intervention to mitigate the ups and downs of the free market. A founder of the World Bank and the International Monetary Fund (IMF).

MICHAEL RAMSEY (1904–88), 100th Archbishop of Canterbury.

SIR CHRISTOPHER COCKERELL (1910–99), inventor of the hovercraft.

RONALD SEARLE (1920–2011), cartoonist and creator of St Trinian's.

SIR RICHARD ATTENBOROUGH (1923–2014), film actor, producer and director. In 1982 he won two Oscars with the film *Gandhi*, for Best Picture (as producer), and for Best Director.

OLIVIA NEWTON-JOHN, pop singer and star of the film adaptation of *Grease*, born 1948.

Thomas Clarkson's Monument, Wisbech

Cheshire

*Little Moreton Hall, the most perfect
black-and-white house in England.*

◄ CHESHIRE FOLK ►

Charles Dodgson + James Prescott Joule + John Speed + Sir Joseph
Whitworth + George Formby + Dixie Dean + Sir Henry Cotton + Fred
Perry + Glenda Jackson + Ian Botham + Michael Owen

County Palatine

Cheshire is one of England's two County Palatines, along with County Durham. It was established by William the Conqueror to defend the English western border against the Welsh, and was ruled by the Earls of Chester who were given wide-ranging royal powers ('palatine', or 'from the palace') and autonomy over their own affairs within Cheshire. The palatinate remained in place until 1830, and today Earl of Chester is one of the titles of the monarch's eldest son, the Prince of Wales.

Magpie County

Cheshire is the premier home of the black-and-white timbered archi-tecture so beloved of the English. Even today, the most popular choice of style for new housing is mock Tudor.

In Tudor England, there was no longer any need for fortified stone houses, and the middle classes were becoming wealthy enough to build houses for themselves. In Cheshire, and other western counties, wood, particularly oak, was plentiful and the construction material of choice. The wooden frames were in-filled with wattle, a mesh of vertical wooden stakes interwoven with thin branches, and covered in daub, a clay or mud plaster mixed with straw. For weather-proofing the timbers were painted black and the plaster white. As properties were often taxed on street frontage, the ground floor would be as narrow as possible with the upper floor overhanging, giving a top-heavy look. And because the buildings were made of wood, which bent and settled over time, genuinely old timber-framed houses often appear alarmingly crooked, which is part of their charm.

Little Moreton Hall

Perhaps the supreme example of black-and-white Tudor architec-ture, and a true English icon, is LITTLE MORETON HALL, near Congleton, begun in 1450 by the Moretons and then continued in stages over the next 150 years. The hall remained in the ownership of the Moreton family until handed over to the National Trust in 1938.

The beautiful 14th-century black-and-white timbered church at LOWER PEOVER is reputed to be THE OLDEST AISLED WOODEN CHURCH IN EUROPE. MARTON, a few miles away, claims THE OLDEST HALF-TIMBERED CHURCH IN USE IN EUROPE, dating from 1343 – and what was once

ENGLAND'S BIGGEST OAK TREE, still standing but with the trunk split into four by age.

Cranford

◄•►•►

KNUTSFORD, near Macclesfield, is Mrs Gaskell's 'Cranford'. Her most popular novel, *Cranford* is a collection of light-hearted stories about the genteel ladies who live in this 'pleasant little country town'. ELIZABETH GASKELL (1810–65) grew up in Knutsford herself, in what is now called Gaskell Avenue, close to the heath. Her fine brick house is

marked with a plaque and she is buried in the town's Brook Street Unitarian chapel. It is still possible to recognise Knutsford, or Cranford, from

her book as it has retained its tranquil, very English, Georgian air and appearance. Although Mrs Gaskell's novels were considered by some to be a bit light and frothy, they found popularity across the world and had some unlikely fans. That frivolous Russian author Dostoyevsky admitted that Mrs Gaskell's *Mary Barton* was his inspiration for *Crime and Punishment*.

Eaton Hall

In 1677 SIR THOMAS GROSVENOR of EATON HALL, Eccleston, married Mary Davies, heiress to the Ebury farm estate outside London, now Belgravia and Mayfair. This laid the fortune of the Grosvenor family, now Dukes of Westminster and, after the Crown, England's largest and richest landowners. Despite all their properties in London, Eaton Hall remains 'the jewel in the Grosvenor crown'. There has been an Eaton Hall since the 15th century, and the house has been rebuilt

several times, with perhaps the most celebrated expression being the immense Victorian neo-Gothic creation by Alfred Waterhouse. The clock tower, 178 ft (54 m) high, is all that survives of that Eaton Hall and contains THE OLDEST CARILLON OF BELLS IN ENGLAND. The rest of the house was knocked down in the 1970s and replaced with a modern, concrete structure by John Dennys, the 5th Duke's brother-in-law. This in turn was altered and encased in a new façade in 1989.

Jodrell Bank

JODRELL BANK, west of Macclesfield, was England's first proper space observatory. Begun just after the Second World War, it was set up by Dr Bernard Lovell of Manchester University to study cosmic rays. When it was built in 1947, the 218 ft (66 m) reflecting aerial was THE BIGGEST RADIO TELESCOPE IN

THE WORLD. It was at Jodrell Bank that radio noise from the Great Nebula in Andromeda was heard – the first time an extragalactic radio source had ever been detected. Jodrell Bank soon became valuable as a world source for satellite and spacecraft tracking – it was thanks to Jodrell Bank that the West knew what was really going on in the Soviet Union space programme. The original telescope was replaced in 1957 by an even bigger radio telescope, a 250 ft (76 m) steerable dish which still sits quietly on its gantry, looming over Cheshire countryside and listening to the Heavens.

Well, I never knew this
about
CHESHIRE FOLK

Charles Dodgson
◄ 1832–98 ►

'The happy spot where I was born' is how CHARLES DODGSON remembers DARESBURY, near Runcorn, where he came into the world in 1832. Now better known as LEWIS CARROLL, author of ALICE IN WONDERLAND, the most famous children's story in the English language, Dodgson spent his formative years in Daresbury, where his father was the vicar. There is a memorial window to him in the church, depicting many of the characters from his tales, including the CHESHIRE CAT, who could make its whole body disappear, save for the grin.

James Prescott Joule
◄ 1818–89 ►

JAMES PRESCOTT JOULE, THE MAN WHO GAVE HIS NAME TO THE UNIT OF ENERGY, was born in SALE. His ambition in life was to replace the steam engine with the electric motor by improving the latter's efficiency. Joule was the first to establish and measure the link between the heat created by an electrical current and mechanical energy. He also discovered

that when a gas is rapidly expanded it has a cooling effect, the principle used in modern-day refrigeration.

John Speed
◄ 1552–1629 ►

Sometimes considered the first true English historian, as opposed to just chronicler, JOHN SPEED was born in FARNDON, in west Cheshire. He spent most of his life as a tailor, but at the age of 48, when his 18 children had left home, he was finally able to devote time to his passion – making maps. He began by making the first accurate maps of the English counties, and the first town plans, along with written descriptions and the genealogy of the leading families in each county. He then wrote a history of England based on this research. John Speed's collection of maps, which formed THE FIRST ENGLISH ATLAS, proved immensely popular, and were, in their own way, as important a legacy of the Elizabethan era as the works of Shakespeare.

Sir Joseph Whitworth
◄ 1803–87 ►

STOCKPORT is the birthplace of the man who brought us precision engineering, SIR JOSEPH WHITWORTH.

He was the first to come up with a method of producing a true flat surface, and a system of measurement accurate to within one millionth of an inch. In 1841 he developed the first standardised system for screw threads, which was adopted by the railway companies and became 'BRITISH STANDARD WHITWORTH' or BSW. As anyone who owns an older British car knows, until the 1970s much of British industry used Whitworth precision tools and measurements, but since Britain's entry into the European Union, metric measurements have been adopted.

GEORGE FORMBY (1904–61), singer, comedian and ukulele player, was born in WARRINGTON. His most famous song was 'Leaning on a Lamppost'.

DIXIE DEAN (1907–80), THE ONLY PLAYER IN ENGLISH FOOTBALL TO SCORE 60 GOALS IN ONE SEASON (for Everton in 1927–28), was born in BIRKENHEAD.

SIR HENRY COTTON (1907–87), the first golfer to be knighted, was born in HOLMES CHAPEL.

FRED PERRY (1909–95), the last English tennis player to win the Wimbledon men's singles title (in 1934, 35 and 36), was born in STOCKPORT.

GLENDA JACKSON, actress and MP, was born in BIRKENHEAD in 1936. She won two Best Actress Oscars, for *Women in Love* in 1969 and *A Touch of Class* in 1973.

IAN BOTHAM, holder of the record for the highest number of Test wickets ever taken by an English cricketer (383), was born in HESWALL in 1955.

MICHAEL OWEN, the youngest footballer to play for England in the 20th century, was born in CHESTER in 1979. He scored a memorable hat-trick in a 5–1 defeat of Germany in 2001.

Cornwall

KING ARTHUR ✦ CRADLE OF WIRELESS
✦ COME TO GOOD ✦ A CORNISH ECCENTRIC
✦ JIGGING JOGGING EVERYWHERE ✦ PASTY

*Gryll's Gate in Helston, landmark on the
route of the ancient Furry Dance.*

◀ CORNWALL FOLK ▶

Richard Trevithick ✦ Humphry Davy ✦ Sir John Betjeman ✦ Daphne du
Maurier ✦ Arthur Quiller Couch ✦ Rosamund Pilcher ✦ Richard and
John Lander

[49]

Kernow

———— ◆◆◆ ————

Cornwall possesses mainland England's most southerly point (the Lizard) and most westerly point (Land's End). Surrounded on three sides by sea, Cornwall, the old kingdom of Kernow, is also England's most isolated county, and the native population are largely from Celtic stock, as in Wales and Ireland.

King Arthur

———— ◆◆◆ ————

Wherever you roam in Cornwall you are never far from KING ARTHUR.

TINTAGEL on the bleak north coast, with its dark cliff-top castle ruins, is where legend says King Arthur was born on a stormy night, after Arthur's father, King Uther Pendragon, seduced the Duke of Cornwall's wife Igema, with the help of the wizard Merlin. Even though the 12th-century castle was built 600 years too late, the setting is romantic and persuasive, and there is evidence that the site was used from the 4th century or even earlier. Below the headland, reached by clambering down the rocks to the beach, is a large cave known as Merlin's Cave, where the wizard is said to have plotted with Uther Pendragon.

Arthur may well have lived in the early 5th century, when the Romans were abandoning Britain and Anglo–Saxon mercenaries were sweeping the remaining Romano–British Celts westwards. A brave Celtic Christian warrior emerged from the west to lead the resistance against the pagan invaders, and had some success in halting their advance, with a famous victory at Mount Badon, thought to be near Bath.

There is no doubt that the legend of King Arthur is based on such a Celtic leader, and Arthur has become a symbol of hope and courage for the English in adversity. In medieval times the warrior Arthur became associated with the code of chivalry brought over from France by the Plantagenet kings (chivalry being derived from the French word 'chevalier' meaning knight), and the tale of King Arthur and the Knights of the Round Table fused the soldier with the chevalier to create the definitive British hero, claimed by Welsh and English alike.

The Cradle of Wireless

The world's first transatlantic radio signals were sent to Newfoundland from Poldhu Cove, on the Lizard, south of Helston. On a bare, windy cliff top near Mullion are the scant remains of the wireless station from where the signals were transmitted on 12 December 1901, using equipment invented by the 'father of the wireless' Guglielmo Marconi. Against all the prevailing wisdom Marconi proved that radio waves

could be sent over long distances and follow the curvature of the Earth. Radio, television and the internet all owe their existence to this remarkable achievement, and a memorial and museum on the spot tell the story.

Not far away is the GOONHILLY EARTH SATELLITE STATION, BRITAIN'S FIRST EARTH SATELLITE STATION. It was completed in 1962 and exchanged the first intercontinental picture transmissions with the US via a space satellite.

Come to Good

The quaint little thatched Meeting House, embowered in trees and set in a hollow at Come to Good, a hamlet south of Truro, was built in 1710 and is one of the oldest Quaker meeting houses in the world. Come to Good, from the Cornish 'Cwm Ty Quoit', means 'house in the wooded combe'. It is a simple white cob hut lined with plain wooden benches and a small gallery, a friendly place where meetings are still held regularly.

A Cornish Eccentric

Few people wept when the REV FREDERICK DENSHAM, Vicar

Come to Good Meeting House

of Warleggan, on Bodmin Moor, died in 1953. He was known as the rudest clergyman in Cornwall and he was so abusive to his parishioners that for ten years they refused to attend services at the pretty, 15th-century village church. Unbothered, he made himself a congregation of cardboard figures, which he propped up in the pews, and on Sundays would harangue them with fiery sermons. Thought to survive on a diet of nettles and gruel, he got rid of all his furniture in case it was stolen and, just to be doubly sure, encircled the vicarage with barbed wire.

Daphne du Maurier is thought to have based the Rev Francis Davey, the mad vicar in her novel *Jamaica Inn*, on the Rev Densham.

Helston
Dancing here, prancing there,
Jigging, jogging everywhere

The HELSTON FURRY DANCE is one of the oldest of all the English festivals, a Cornish-style May Day ritual that celebrates the end of winter and the coming of spring, and has its origins in pagan times. It is always held on 8 May, except when that is a Sunday or Monday, in which case it takes place the previous Saturday. The name 'Furry' comes from the old Cornish or Celtic word 'feur', meaning festival.

Helson prepares for its big day for weeks beforehand. Houses and public buildings are decorated with spring foliage, bluebells, gorse, sycamore, hazel and laurel; gardens are tidied up, school-children are rehearsed. Then, at 7 a.m. on the day, the Town Band strikes up and the Early Morning Dance begins, with dancers bedecked in lilies-of-the-valley pirouetting in and out of people's houses and gardens.

This is followed at 8 a.m. by the Hal-An-Tow, when English folk heroes such as Robin Hood, Friar Tuck, St Michael and St George move through the town re-enacting battles where Good triumphs over Evil, while singing the traditional Hal-An-Tow song:

With Hal-an-Tow! Jolly Rumble, O!
For we are up as soon as any day, O!
And for to fetch the Summer home,
The Summer and the May, O,
For Summer is a-come, O,
And Winter is a-gone, O

The Children's Dance starts at 10 a.m., when over 1,000 children, all dressed in white, dance in procession, and then at noon the Furry Dance itself begins. This is by invitation only. The Mayor, wearing his chain of office, leads the procession along the streets and in and out of shops and houses, banishing winter and ushering in summer. All the ladies wear long dresses with hats and gloves and the men are in full morning dress, complete with top hats.

Then, at 5 p.m., it is time for the final event, the Evening Dance, when everyone is invited to dance, residents and visitors alike, and the whole town rocks.

BOB FITZIMMONS, THE FIRST BOXER EVER TO BE WORLD MIDDLEWEIGHT, LIGHT HEAVYWEIGHT AND HEAVYWEIGHT CHAMPION, was born in Wendron Street, Helston, in 1863. His birthplace is marked by a plaque.

Helston was THE MOST SOUTHERLY POINT EVER REACHED BY THE RAILWAYS in England. The town is no longer served by trains, the nearest station being at Camborne.

Cornish Pasty

The CORNISH PASTY evolved as a convenient way of providing tin miners with a complete meal that was easy to handle while working down in the dark, narrow mine tunnels. Originally, the pasty would have meat and vegetables in one half and fruit in the other half, and would have the miner's initials raised on the casing so that it could be recognised by touch. The traditional filling is beef, onion and potato, but nowadays any filling is considered acceptable – except fish. Cornish fishermen refuse to take pasties to sea with them as they are thought to bring bad luck. The Devil, apparently, is fearful of entering Cornwall in case he ends up as a filling in a Cornish pasty.

Well, I never knew this
about
CORNISH FOLK

Richard Trevithick
◄─── 1771–1833 ───►

A tiny chapel marks the site of RICHARD TREVITHICK's birthplace in CARN BREA, near Camborne. Trevithick grew into a giant of a man, celebrated for being able to throw a sledgehammer over an engine shed. He invented THE WORLD'S FIRST PASSENGER-CARRYING STEAM-ENGINE, and on Christmas Eve 1801 his 'PUFFING BILLY' clattered through the streets of Camborne, carrying THE FIRST PASSENGERS EVER MOVED BY STEAM. The engine then puffed and wheezed up Beacon Hill, the steepest hill in Camborne, a feat beyond most horse-drawn carriages, and there is a plaque in memory of this historic feat at the bottom of the hill.

In the grand old tradition, the man who gave the world the gift of locomotion never made a penny from his inventions. The glory went to others who knew how to exploit it, and Trevithick died broke. He is

buried in a pauper's grave at Dartford in Kent.

Humphry Davy
◄─── 1778–1829 ───►

HUMPHRY DAVY, INVENTOR OF THE MINER'S SAFETY LAMP, was born in PENZANCE in 1778. A natural scientist, his speciality was experimenting with the effect of gases on humans, an interest that nearly killed him more than once, as he always used himself as a guinea pig. His research on nitrous oxide, which had recently been discovered by Joseph Priestley, led him to label it 'laughing gas' and he was the first to spot its potential as an anaesthetic.

At that time, a naked flame was the only way of illuminating mines and, in 1812, 89 miners were killed by a horrific gas explosion in a mine in Sunderland. Davy, as the acknowledged expert on the subject, was asked to design a safety lamp that could prevent this happening again. His solution was to cover the flame with a gauze that allowed air in to feed the flame, but kept out the dangerous gases.

Humphry Davy was also a founder of the Zoological Society and London Zoo.

At Paul, on the hills above Mousehole lies DOLLY PENTREATH, the last person known to have spoken only Cornish. She died in 1777 and her monument was put there, as a tribute, by Napoleon's nephew Lucien Bonaparte, who grew up in England and loved languages.

SIR JOHN BETJEMAN (1906–84), Poet Laureate, chose to be buried in Cornwall at St Enodoc's church, near his Cornish home at Trebetherick, just down from Polzeath. Cornwall was Betjeman's adopted county, and he was happier here than anywhere. St Enodoc's is tucked into the sand dunes

beside the Camel estuary, and to get there you either have to walk along the shifting sands or make a hazardous journey across the 13th hole of the golf course. It is a risk worth taking, for St Enodoc's is a magical place to be alone and reflect. You can almost hear Betjeman chuckling contentedly from his grave beside the churchyard path.

'Last night I dreamt I went to Manderley again . . .' Anyone can go to Manderley now, although only as far as the gate. Manderley is Menabilly, an old house tucked away down narrow lanes and at the end of a long drive, in wild country to the west of Fowey. Writer DAPHNE DU MAURIER (1907-89) discovered it in 1927 and used it in her 1938 novel *Rebecca* as the model for Manderley, the mysterious home of the de Winters. She actually lived in the house herself from 1943 until 1967. Du Maurier's locations are found all over Cornwall, notably Frenchman's Creek down on the Helford river and the eerie Jamaica Inn alone on Bodmin Moor. After her death, du Maurier's ashes were scattered on the cliffs near Menabilly.

One of Daphne du Maurier's friends in Fowey was the scholar and author SIR ARTHUR QUILLER COUCH (1863–1944), known as 'Q'. He was born in Bodmin and came to live in

a house called The Haven in Fowey. He is probably best remembered as the editor of the *Oxford Book of English Verse*, published in 1900. Fowey was the model for his book *The Astonishing History of Troy Town*.

Author ROSAMUND PILCHER was born at LELANT, near St Ives, in 1924. She based her best-selling novel *The Shell Seekers* in St Ives.

At the top of Truro's lovely Georgian Lemon Street there is a monument to RICHARD AND JOHN LANDER, who charted the true course of the River Niger in West Africa in 1830. They discovered that the Niger – previously thought to be a tributary of the Nile – in fact ran into the Atlantic Ocean. Richard Lander was THE FIRST PERSON TO RECEIVE THE ROYAL GEOGRAPHIC SOCIETY MEDAL.

Cumberland

BORDER TOWN ✦ GEORGIAN TOWN PLANNING
✦ CUMBERLAND DELICACIES

*Carlisle Cathedral – the only English cathedral
to have been located in two different countries.*

◄ CUMBERLAND FOLK ►

John Dalton ✦ Melvyn Bragg ✦ Eddie Stobart ✦ G. M. Trevelyan
✦ Alfred Wainwright

Carlisle

————◆◆◆◆————

The bluff on which Carlisle stands has been occupied since pre-Roman times. A border town, variously described over the years as 'the last town in England' or 'the first town in Scotland', Carlisle was fought over by the Scots and the English right up until the Jacobite rebellions of the 18th century, when Bonnie Prince Charlie, retreating into Scotland, left troops in Carlisle Castle so that he could be said to occupy at least one English town.

Carlisle Cathedral is hence the only English cathedral to have been located in two different countries. It was founded as a priory by William II and given to the Augustinian Black Canons by Henry I in 1122. However, the monks owed their allegiance to the Bishop of Glasgow, and so, in order to make Carlisle a purely English town, Henry created the see of Carlisle and made the prior a bishop. Thus Carlisle is also the only case of an Augustinian priory becoming an English cathedral.

Through the years, Carlisle Cathedral has suffered badly from the ravages of war and neglect, and there is precious little left of the original Norman nave except some strangely misshapen arches, warped by drought in the 13th century when the ground on which they were built settled unevenly. Carlisle is now England's smallest cathedral after Oxford, but the Early English chancel is glorious and the huge decorated East Window is the largest after the Crecy window at Gloucester.

Eddie Stobart's haulage company and Carr's water biscuits were both founded in Carlisle.

Whitehaven

————◆◆◆◆————

At the end of the 16th century, WHITEHAVEN was a tiny fishing village of nine thatched cottages. By the end of the 17th century it had become England's first planned town since the Middle Ages, with a population of 3,000, and was the second largest port on England's west coast after Bristol. The family behind this growth were the Lowthers (later Earls of Lonsdale), who developed Whitehaven as a port for shipbuilding and the export of Cumberland coal. Much of the planning was inspired by the way that Christopher Wren was rebuilding London after the Great Fire of 1666, and Whitehaven's elegant grid pattern layout was used as a template for the expansion of New York in America.

The SALTOM COAL PIT, south of Whitehaven, in 1729 became THE FIRST COAL PIT IN THE WORLD TO BE EXTENDED OUT BENEATH THE SEA. The ruined entrance to the old

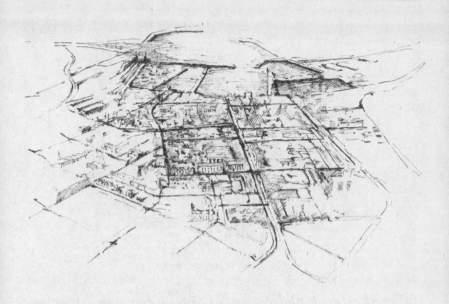

pit workings is a short walk along the coast.

In 1778, during the American War of Independence, the American privateer John Paul Jones, who was born in Scotland and had been an apprentice in Whitehaven in 1749, attacked the port in an attempt to destroy the fleet of coal ships at anchor. He was betrayed by one of his crew, who warned the town, and little damage was inflicted.

In 1782 DANIEL BROCKLEBANK set up one of the world's first shipping lines in Whitehaven, the Brocklebank Shipping Line, which eventually went on to merge with Cunard.

June 1998 saw the final closure of JEFFERSON'S WINE MERCHANTS, THE OLDEST FAMILY-OWNED WINE MERCHANT IN ENGLAND, which had traded from the same shop in Lowther Street for over two centuries. In May 2000, RUM STORY, THE WORLD'S FIRST EXHIBITION ABOUT RUM, opened in its place.

MILDRED GALE, paternal grandmother of George Washington, first president of the USA, is buried in the churchyard of St Nicholas, Whitehaven. After the death of her first husband, Lawrence Washington, by whom she had three children, in 1700 she married a sea merchant called George Gale, who had interests on both sides of the Atlantic, and settled in his home town of Whitehaven. She died in 1701.

Jefferson's Wine Merchants

Cumberland Delicacies

Whitehaven also contributes to the famous CUMBERLAND SAUSAGE, produced originally from Cumberland pigs and seasoned with the exotic spices imported into Whitehaven when it was England's third largest port. Alas, the Cumberland Pig, which had a distinct flavour, died out in 1960 and some sausage makers believed that the traditional Cumberland sausage could never taste the same again. However, today's local producers have introduced their own special varieties, and are fighting to have the Cumberland sausage protected, so that only sausages actually made in

Cumberland, from traditional recipes, can be called Cumberland sausages.

Made from pork, with a meat content of above 80 per cent, the Cumberland sausage can be over 20 inches (50 cm) long and, unlike normal sausages which are sold on a string, comes coiled up, a characteristic that perhaps comes down from the days of Elizabeth I, when German miners came to Cumberland bringing their own meaty sausages with them.

CUMBERLAND PIE is a dish of minced beef and vegetables topped with mashed potato and a further layer of breadcrumbs or cheese.

CUMBERLAND SAUCE is a cold condiment made from redcurrants

St Nicholas Church, Whitehaven, burial place of Mildred Gale

and flavoured with orange, port, ginger and vinegar. It was named after the Duke of Cumberland, son of George II, known as 'Butcher'

Cumberland to the Scots, who brought the original recipe over from Germany.

Well, I never knew this
about
CUMBERLAND FOLK

John Dalton

In 1766 an Englishman who was to have a huge influence on the development of the modern world was born at EAGLESFIELD, near Cockermouth. The son of a poor Quaker weaver, JOHN DALTON was soon recognised as supremely talented and inquisitive, and at the age of 12 he became a teacher to younger children, giving lessons in a local barn. He was still a boy when he began to realise that he saw things differently from others – for instance, the colour of a soldier's uniform and the colour of the grass both appeared to him as a shade of yellow, while what others called red he merely saw as a grey shadow. His investigations into this phenomenon led him to discover COLOUR-BLINDNESS, a disability not known about until then.

He eventually became a Professor of Mathematics at Manchester University, where he experimented with various chemicals and discovered that matter consisted of tiny particles or atoms – at that time atoms were thought to be the smallest particles that could exist. This led to the publication in 1803 of his startling and ground-breaking THEORY OF ATOMIC WEIGHTS, which formed the basis of chemistry theory and study for the next 150 years.

MELVYN BRAGG, novelist and broadcaster, was born in WIGTON in 1939.

EDDIE STOBART, owner of THE LARGEST PRIVATE HAULAGE COMPANY IN BRITAIN, was born in HESKET NEWMARKET, near Caldbeck.

John Dalton

The theory behind atoms was first presented in about 450 BC by a Greek philosopher called Democritus, who posed the question 'If you break a piece of matter in half, and then in half again, and then again, how many times would you need to break it until it was too small to break any further?' He called the smallest possible piece an atom.

G. M. TREVELYAN (1876–1962), historian, is buried in the churchyard at CHAPEL STILE.

ALFRED WAINWRIGHT (1907–91), writer and fell walker, who popularised the Lake District with his *Pictorial Guides*, had his ashes scattered on his favourite mountain, Haystacks, above Buttermere.

Derbyshire

—◆••◆—

LADY WITH THE LAMP ✦ BABINGTON PLOT
✦ WELL DRESSING

*Eyam Hall — 17th-century Hall at the heart of
Derbyshire's 'Plague Village', still in the hands of its
original builders, the Wrights.*

◀ DERBYSHIRE FOLK ▶

John Flamsteed ✦ James Brindley ✦ Herbert Spencer ✦ Barnes Wallis
✦ Dame Barbara Castle ✦ Alison Hargreaves

Florence Nightingale
1820–1910

The village of Holloway is more or less a single street that winds along the hilltops above the River Derwent, near Matlock. Buried right in the middle of England, calm and peaceful, this was the perfect place for the most celebrated woman in England to come home to, away from the noise and filth of battle, the cries of the wounded, the stench of fear and death.

Early one summer evening in 1856, she walked down the short drive from the village street and knocked on the door of LEA HURST, the grey stone house built by her father. To the astonishment of her family, England's ministering angel, FLORENCE

NIGHTINGALE, was home from the war. Talked about all over Europe, she had slipped away from the Crimea, passed through London unnoticed and arrived home before anyone knew where she was. That was the way she wanted it. No triumphant homecomings or cheering crowds. Just the sound of the Derwent carried on the western breezes to her hilltop home.

Florence Nightingale was born in Florence in 1820. She was the daughter of a wealthy family and was expected to marry well and be the perfect young lady. Florence had other ideas. She was drawn to social issues and spent much of her childhood at Lea Hurst visiting local hospitals and the sick. To the huge embarrassment and disapproval of her family she took herself off to the Continent and trained as a nurse, before becoming a superintendent at a hospital for women in London.

When the Crimean War broke out in 1854, Florence appealed in person to Queen Victoria to be allowed to take a group of British nurses to Scutari and set up a military hospital. It was unheard of for women, especially well-to-do young women, to go to the battlefront, but they made huge improvements in the standards of hygiene and sanitation, and shamed the government into sending out proper medical supplies and food. Florence made regular inspections by the light of her lamp and saved the lives of countless numbers of soldiers. All this was at a cost to her own health, and after her sudden return to Lea Hurst it took several months of bracing Derbyshire air before she was well enough to start crusading again, this time creating a training school for nurses at St Thomas's Hospital in London.

Florence Nightingale set the standards for modern nursing across the world. She overcame prejudice, ignorance and vested interests by sheer force of personality and was truly the first of the fearsome, battling Matrons – but to the men she tended she was just 'our LADY WITH THE LAMP'.

Lea Hurst is now a residential home but it can be visited by appointment. It is easy to imagine Florence sitting on her favourite balcony, gazing across the garden with its gorgeous views, and jotting down her ideas for a better health service. She died in 1910 and is buried in East Wellow, Hampshire – THE FIRST WOMAN TO BE ADMITTED TO THE ORDER OF MERIT.

The Babington Plot

A few miles from Lea Hurst down country lanes, set back from the road behind a ring of noble trees, is the Manor Farm of DETHICK,

looming over its tiny neighbouring church. In 1561 the lonely bells of this church rang out to welcome into the world the heir to this great estate, ANTHONY BABINGTON (1561–86), whose plottings, tragically, would destroy his ancient family.

The Babingtons were a wealthy Catholic family at a dangerous time, and young Anthony grew up in the remote safety of Dethick, which can hardly have changed since his time. At 16 he served as page to the captive Mary Queen of Scots and fell in love with her courage and beauty. He would frequently visit her in disguise while she was imprisoned at Wingfield House nearby, and fantasised about rescuing her and putting her on the throne.

Babington's looks and wit made him a favourite at Queen Elizabeth's court, but he grew over-confident, and was set up by Elizabeth's protector Francis Walsingham. Mary Stuart's supporters had devised a system of getting letters to her inside a special beer barrel sent from Burton on Trent every week. Walsingham's spies knew about this but allowed the correspondence to continue, so that they could discover the identity of those in league with the exiled Scottish queen. In 1586 Babington wrote to Mary outlining what became known as the Babington Plot, a plan to use money and troops from Philip of Spain to capture London, murder Elizabeth and make

Mary the Catholic queen of England and Scotland.

Babington and the ringleaders were arrested and charged with high treason, and they became THE LAST ENGLISH VICTIMS TO BE OFFICIALLY HUNG, DRAWN AND QUARTERED. This involved being dragged face down through the streets of London behind a horse, hung in Lincoln's Inn Fields for a short period and then taken down, while still alive, to have their insides ripped out. Their agonies were so horrifying that even the bloodthirsty London crowds were appalled, and Elizabeth ordered that from that day on traitors were to be dead before they were taken down from the scaffold.

Well Dressing

WELL DRESSING is the decorating of wells, springs and water sources with pictures made from flowers and other natural materials. The pictures consist of a wooden frame and a clay base on to which the materials are fixed. The outline of the picture is picked out with berries, and then the more durable elements of the plants such as mosses, tree bark, lichens and fir cones are put on, and finally the colourful flower petals. It is a highly skilled procedure, and villages vie with each other to create the most imaginative and most appealing tableau.

The well dressing ceremony, which is unique to Derbyshire, originated in pagan Celtic times, when watercourses were uncertain and sacrifices were made to appease the water gods and thank them for keeping the village supplied. At first the Church frowned upon the revival of such practices, but soon relented, and today many of the pictures have a religious theme, or reflect a local or national anniversary. Most villages hold a church service to bless the well, followed by a carnival.

The season runs from May to September and a collecting box is kept nearby for donations to chosen charities.

Well, I never knew this
about
DERBYSHIRE FOLK

JOHN FLAMSTEED (1646–1719), THE FIRST ASTRONOMER ROYAL, was born in DENBY, near Belper.

JAMES BRINDLEY (1716–72), canal engineer and builder of the first English canal of the modern era, the Bridgewater Canal, was born in TUNSTEAD, near Buxton. He designed and mapped out England's 18th-century canal system, which helped transform England into an industrial nation.

HERBERT SPENCER (1820–1903), known as the founder of modern sociology, was born in DERBY. Spencer was a great supporter of Charles Darwin and, after reading Darwin's theory of evolution in *The Origin of Species*, coined the phrase 'survival of the fittest', the concept on which he based his approach to social development.

BARNES WALLIS (1887–1979), inventor of the Bouncing Bomb, which destroyed the dams of the Ruhr valley in the Second World War, was born in RIPLEY.

ALISON HARGREAVES (1963–95), mountaineer, was born in BELPER. THE FIRST WOMAN TO CLIMB THE NORTH FACE OF THE EIGER and the FIRST CLIMBER EVER TO CLIMB SOLO THE SIX GREAT NORTH FACES OF THE ALPS IN ONE SEASON (Cima Grande di Laverado, Eiger, Grandes Jorasses, Matterhorn, Petit Dru and

Piz Badile), she died in a storm while returning from the summit of the world's second-highest mountain, K2.

DAME BARBARA CASTLE (1910–2002), politician, was born in CHESTERFIELD, a town celebrated for the gloriously warped and twisted spire of St Mary and All Saints church. As Minister for Transport in Harold Wilson's government Barbara Castle was responsible for the introduction of the breathalyser test.

Devon

FIRST COLONIALIST ✦ REVENGE
✦ AN ELIZABETHAN PIRATE ✦ FINE ENGLISH CARPETS

*Sir Francis Drake – the first Englishman
to sail around the world.*

◄ DEVON FOLK ►

Robert Falcon Scott ✦ Stephen Borough ✦ John Davis ✦ Sir Francis
Chichester ✦ Charles Kingsley ✦ Samuel Taylor Coleridge

Sir Walter Raleigh
1552–1618

S IR WALTER RALEIGH, showman, writer, poet, adventurer and explorer, was born at HAYES BARTON, a pretty, thatched farm-house that sits unobtrusively down a quiet lane near Budleigh Salterton. His wit, charm and looks made him a favourite at the court of Queen Elizabeth I, and it was entirely in keeping when he took off his expensive cloak and flung it down in front of the Queen at Greenwich, so that she wouldn't have to walk through a puddle.

After sailing to America with his half-brother Humphrey Gilbert, Raleigh decided to try and set up a colony there. In 1583 Gilbert attempted to settle a colony at St John's, in Newfoundland, but his men died or got sick on the journey and they had to return. In 1585 Raleigh sponsored the founding of what would be THE FIRST ENGLISH COLONY IN AMERICA, which he named Virginia, after the Virgin Queen Elizabeth. The settlers landed on Roanoke Island, but this was not a good spot to choose as the land was bad and the local Indians resented them. The colony did not take, and they had to be rescued by Sir Francis Drake in 1586. Raleigh sent another expedition in 1587, but this group, which was meant to try further north, landed at Roanoke once more, and were never seen again. They became known as the 'Lost Colony'.

Although Raleigh's colonies did not succeed, they planted the seeds of colonisation, and for that reason Sir Walter Raleigh can justifiably claim to be the founder of the British Empire. This in turn introduced

England's most valuable export, the English language, to the four corners of the world.

Back at home, Raleigh became Elizabeth's Captain of the Guard, but after Elizabeth died, Raleigh could not hide his suspicions that James I wanted a return to Catholicism and he was beheaded, unjustly, for 'conspiring against the King'. Before he was led to the block, Raleigh was granted a smoke of his beloved Virginia tobacco – creating the tradition of giving the condemned man a last cigarette…

Roanoke is now part of North Carolina, whose state capital is

named Raleigh, in honour of Sir Walter Raleigh.

Buckland Abbey – Home for Heroes

BUCKLAND ABBEY, a 13th-century Cistercian abbey lying in a sheltered valley on the edge of Dartmoor, near Plymouth, resounds with stirring memories of two Devon men who conquered the world for England and Queen Elizabeth.

Sir Richard Grenville 1542–91

Buckland Abbey was bought from Henry VIII in 1541 by Sir Richard Grenville, as a home for his son Roger. Four years later, Roger Grenville was drowned in Portsmouth Harbour while in command of the ill-fated *Mary Rose*, and Buckland passed to Roger's son, another Richard, and it was he who later set about making it into a home.

The younger RICHARD GRENVILLE was a cousin of Walter Raleigh, and captained the fleet that took Raleigh's first colonists to Virginia in 1585. In 1591 he was sent with 13 ships, under Admiral Howard, to capture

Buckland Abbey

a Spanish treasure fleet off the Azores.

The Spanish got wind of what was happening and sent out a fleet of 50 ships to protect the treasure. Admiral Howard got wind of this and ordered his ships to flee. Twelve of them were able to up anchor and get away, but Grenville had sick men ashore and refused to abandon them. By the time they were all boarded and ready to leave, escape was impossible.

At 3 p.m. on 31 August 1591, Grenville pointed the bows of his ship, the REVENGE, at the Spanish fleet and sailed right into them. *Revenge* was the finest ship in the Elizabethan navy and had carried Sir Francis Drake into battle against the Armada, but she was one small ship against a fleet. Wave after wave of Spanish boarders attacked, but were repulsed and hurled into the sea, and the mighty Spanish warships were driven back by constant cannon fire and ferocious spirit. For 15 hours the little English ship fought, until the masts were gone and only 20 men remained alive, with Grenville himself wounded and dying. And still he would not surrender, preferring to sink the *Revenge* himself than let the Spanish have it.

Finally he was too weak to resist, and the master gunner reluctantly allowed the Spanish to board, on the condition that the survivors were returned to England. Before the ship could be salvaged a storm blew up and took the *Revenge* to the bottom, to join 14 Spanish ships and 1000 Spanish sailors. Grenville died a prisoner on a Spanish ship, but his last fight cemented in Spanish minds the belief that English sailors were fearless – and inspired a poem by Alfred, Lord Tennyson – *The Revenge.*

Sir Francis Drake
1540–96

────◆◆◆◆────

SIR FRANCIS DRAKE was the greatest of all the Elizabethan pirate sailors. Born at CROWNDALE FARM on the River Tavy, just south of Tavistock, he grew up staunchly opposed to Catholicism, and he became an implacable foe of Spain after being double-crossed by the Spanish on a trip to Mexico. He built up a huge fortune plundering Spanish treasure ships in South and Central America, and while Queen Elizabeth I could not sanction his actions, she certainly didn't disapprove of the booty he won for her. Almost single-handedly Drake wrestled supremacy of the seas away from Spain, draining her wealth and influence. His capture of a Spanish ship carrying secret papers about Spain's East India trade was an important spur to the setting up of Britain's own powerful East India Company.

In 1577 he was secretly commissioned by Queen Elizabeth to persecute the Spanish colonies on the west coast of America, and ended up becoming THE FIRST ENGLISHMAN TO SAIL AROUND THE WORLD. He returned in 1581 with enough treasure to pay off the national debt – and purchase Buckland Abbey off Richard Grenville.

Drake was not yet finished with Spain, however. King Philip of Spain, who regarded himself as King of England through his marriage to Elizabeth's sister and predecessor Queen Mary, began preparing a battle fleet to invade England, and in 1587 Drake sailed into Cadiz harbour and sank 24 of the Spanish warships, infuriating Philip. As Drake put it, 'We have singed the King of Spain's beard.'

When the Spanish Armada did finally appear off the English coast in 1588, Drake was reported to be playing bowls on Plymouth Hoe, and the story goes that he insisted on finishing the game before he set sail to confront them – an early example of English phlegm. In fact, his ships couldn't leave the harbour as the wind was against them, but the bowls legend helped to enhance the reputation of the English sailors as fearless and unflappable – a reputation which, in future years, was to prove invaluable, as England sought to rule the waves in pursuit of her Empire.

In 1595, after a few quiet years at Buckland enjoying his second marriage, Drake went back to sea to harry Spanish possessions in the Caribbean. He became ill while sailing along the coast of Panama and died in his cabin. He was buried in a lead coffin off Porto Bello on 28 January 1596.

Buckland Abbey, which remained the Drake family's ancestral home until the 1940s, when it was presented to the National Trust, possesses a priceless treasure, Drake's Drum, which he took with him around the world. It is said that if the drum is sounded Drake will rise again to save his beloved England from her foes.

Axminster

AXMINSTER, one of England's most ancient towns, is a quiet market town today, but its name is known around the world as the home of the finest English carpets. Axminster carpets were first made in 1755 at Court House, next to the church, by cloth manufacturer THOMAS WHITTY. Inspired by watching a group of French carpet-makers at work in Fulham, he

invented and built himself an ingenious new loom, co-opted his children to be his assistants, and got to work on his first Axminster weave carpet.

For the next 80 years Axminster produced the best hand-knotted carpets in Europe, despite only having a small workshop and few staff. One visitor wrote in 1791, 'I was surprised to find such a paltry place the origin of so much magnificence.' Rather in the tradition of Italian shoemakers, whenever a new carpet was finished the church bells would ring out and the townsfolk would flock to take a look at it.

Today you can still find Axminster carpets in all the best houses, looking just as good as the day they were made. The biggest and most famous Axminster of them all was that made in 1822 for the Sultan of Turkey's legendary Topkapi Palace in Istanbul. It measured 74 ft by 52 ft (23 x 16 m) and took 30 men to carry it. Alas, the Topkapi Palace is now a museum and the carpet has vanished, its whereabouts a mystery.

In 1828 there was a disastrous fire at the workshop in Axminster, from which the company never recovered, and in 1835 they went bankrupt. Blackmores, who made ordinary carpets at Wilton, in Wiltshire, bought the rest of the Axminster stock, along with the looms, and began to make the hand-knotted carpets there.

Well, I never **knew this**
about
DEVON FOLK

Robert Falcon Scott
◂ 1868–1912 ▸

Born in DEVONPORT, ROBERT FALCON SCOTT made THE FIRST AIR BALLOON FLIGHT OVER ANTARCTICA and in 1911 set off on an overland expedition to the South Pole. He reached the Pole on 18 January 1912, only to find the Norwegian flag already planted there by Roald Amundsen, who had beaten him by two weeks. Scott and his four companions perished on the return journey, leaving behind a diary in which the last entry read: 'Had we lived I should have had a tale to tell of the hardihood, endurance and courage of my companions which would have stirred the heart of every Englishman.'

Stephen Borough
◂ 1525–84 ▸

Born in NORTHAM, near Bideford, STEPHEN BOROUGH became navigator of the *Edward Bonaventure*, THE FIRST ENGLISH SHIP TO REACH RUSSIA VIA THE NORTH CAPE above Norway and Finland. Somewhat fortuitously, the ship found its way into the White Sea, and the captain, RICHARD CHANCELLOR, became THE FIRST ENGLISHMAN TO SET FOOT IN RUSSIA. Chancellor made his way to Moscow, where he persuaded the Tsar, Ivan the Terrible, to open up trade links with England, and in 1555 THE MUSCOVY COMPANY, THE FIRST ENGLISH JOINT-STOCK TRADING COMPANY, was set up to exploit the new opportunities – Muscovy being another name for Moscow. The port of ARCHANGEL was founded for the company near where the *Edward Bonaventure* had landed, and Borough was made the company's chief pilot.

John Davis
◂ 1550–1605 ▸

Born in SANDRIDGE, near Dartmouth, JOHN DAVIS made several voyages in search of the North-West Passage to China, and the Davis Straits between Greenland and Baffin Island are named after him.

Sir Francis Chichester

Sir Francis Chichester
◄ 1901–72 ►

Born in BARNSTAPLE, SIR FRANCIS CHICHESTER WAS THE FIRST MAN TO SAIL AROUND THE WORLD SINGLE-HANDED, in 1967, and was knighted by Elizabeth II – with the very sword used by Elizabeth I to knight Sir Francis Drake on his return from becoming the first Englishman to sail around the world.

CHARLES KINGSLEY (1819–75), author of *Westward Ho!* and *The Water Babies*, was born in HOLNE, on Dartmoor.

He also explored routes around the tip of South America and in 1592 discovered the FALKLAND ISLANDS. He was killed by Japanese pirates off Sumatra.

SAMUEL TAYLOR COLERIDGE (1772–1834), poet, was born in OTTERY ST MARY.

Dorset

JURASSIC COASTLINE ✦ FIRST ENGLISH TRADE UNION
✦ DORSET'S OWN WRITER ✦ FIRST PLANNED ENGLISH
VILLAGE ✦ FIRST SMOKE ✦ THE FACE OF ENGLAND

*Sherborne Castle – built by Sir Walter Raleigh
in 1594 as his last home.*

◀ DORSET FOLK ▶

John Russell ✦ Anthony Ashley Cooper ✦ Sir James Thornhill ✦ Sarah
Fielding ✦ William Fox Talbot ✦ Verney Lovett Cameron

The Jurassic Coast

The Dorset coastline has more classic examples of geographical features than any other county coastline. These include the second largest natural harbour in the world, Poole Harbour (where the ashes of novelist H.G. Wells were scattered by his sons in 1946), the longest shingle bar in Europe, Chesil Beach, at 10 miles (16 km), the highest sea cliff on the south coast of England, Golden Cap, at 627 ft (191 m) high, an almost perfect crescent bay at Lulworth Cove and the famous rock arch of Durdle Door. Known as the Jurassic Coast, and popular with fossil hunters, the Dorset coast, along with a small section of the East Devon coast, is THE FIRST NATURAL SITE IN ENGLAND TO BE ACCORDED WORLD HERITAGE STATUS.

Tolpuddle Martyrs

TOLPUDDLE is a quiet little village to the east of Dorchester, now by-passed by the A35 and seemingly almost deserted. And yet the name of Tolpuddle reverberates around the world, for it was here, in 1834, that the trade union movement was born.

In the early 19th century, the Industrial Revolution and the gradual introduction of mechanised farming had left farm workers in a parlous position. Wages were falling, there was mass unemployment, and riots were erupting throughout the country. A farm labourer from Tolpuddle, GEORGE LOVELESS, decided to meet with the local farmers to get agreement for a guaranteed standard agricultural wage of 10 shillings. The farmers themselves pleaded poverty and, perversely, reduced the labourers' wages from 8 shillings to 6 shillings, barely subsistence level.

Loveless called a meeting of some 40 labourers at the Tolpuddle cottage of his brother-in-law, THOMAS STANDFIELD, and here they decided to form THE FRIENDLY SOCIETY OF AGRICULTURAL LABOURERS. Members would not accept any work for less than 10 shillings a week, or work for any farmer who dismissed a labourer for belonging to a union. They were non-political and utterly opposed to violence of any sort, but the local landowners, nervous of riots, were convinced this was a revolutionary organisation dedicated to their overthrow.

The downfall of the Tolpuddle labourers was their initiation ceremony, which required new members to swear an oath not to reveal the business of the society or the identities of its members. The six ringleaders, GEORGE LOVELESS, his brother JAMES LOVELESS, THOMAS STANDFIELD, his son JOHN STANDFIELD, JAMES BRINE and JAMES HAMMETT, were arrested and charged with 'administering illegal oaths', under an act brought in to deal with the Spithead Mutiny in 1797 and never repealed.

They were found guilty at Dorchester Assizes and given the maximum sentence of seven years' transportation to Australia. There was uproar. The men had done nothing wrong, and their dignity and forbearing under such injustice had made them popular heroes. Nonetheless they were shipped to Australia and it wasn't until two years later, in March 1836, that relentless public pressure,

Thomas Standfield's Cottage

including marches and demonstrations, forced the government to repeal their sentences. Only James Hammett returned to Tolpuddle, and he is buried in the village churchyard. The others all emigrated to Canada.

In 1934 the Trades Union Congress built six cottages in Tolpuddle as a memorial to the six martyrs, and every year in July a march is held in the village. There is not much left of the sycamore tree under which the martyrs met, but Thomas Standfield's cottage, birthplace of the Friendly Society, THE FIRST ENGLISH TRADE UNION, still stands.

Thomas Hardy
1840–1928

T HOMAS HARDY was born at HIGHER BOCKHAMPTON, north-east of Dorchester, in 'a long low cottage with a hipped roof of thatch' and lived there until he was 20. Higher Bockhampton becomes Melstock in his first novel, *Under the Greenwood Tree*, which is a bright and optimistic portrayal of Dorset life. Part of Hardy's importance in English literature is the invaluable insight he gives us into life in 19th-century rural England. It was a time when England was moving towards an industrial society, with all the upheavals that entailed, and it is noticeable that his novels get progressively gloomier as time passes and the traditional country life he was born into begins to disappear.

Hardy lived virtually all his life in Dorset and incorporated many Dorset towns, villages and landmarks into his novels.

Dorchester, in particular, is associated with Thomas Hardy and serves as Casterbridge in one of his more sombre stories, *The Mayor of Casterbridge*. In 1885 he built himself a home, which he called Max Gate, on the eastern edge of the town, and this is where he died in 1928. It is now open to the public.

Not only did he leave a legacy of brilliant, if harrowing, novels, but also many fine poems. For the last 30 years of his life he concentrated on poetry, and his epic poem *The Dynasts*, about the life of Napoleon, is compared by many to Milton's *Paradise Lost*.

Thomas Hardy's heart is buried in his beloved Dorset, at STINSFORD, just outside Dorchester. The nation claimed the rest of him, which lies in Poets' Corner in Westminster Abbey, alongside other great observers of English life such as Charles Dickens and Rudyard Kipling.

Buried nearby at Stinsford is the Poet Laureate CECIL DAY-LEWIS, (1904–72), who wished to be buried here because he loved Dorset and the work of Thomas Hardy. He is the father of actor Daniel Day-Lewis.

Milton Abbas

MILTON ABBAS is THE FIRST PLANNED VILLAGE IN ENGLAND. In 1771 the Earl of Dorchester built himself a mansion next to Milton Abbey and decided that the old village spoilt his view. So he knocked it down and built a new village over the hill and out of sight. This was not quite as appalling as it might seem, for the old village was dirty and tumbledown, whereas the new one was well laid out with attractive cottages, a village hall, church and inn. Today the properties in Milton Abbas are much sought after.

Sherborne

SHERBORNE CASTLE was built at the end of the 16th century by Sir Walter Raleigh in the grounds of the old 12th-century castle of the Bishop of Salisbury. The story is told that

Raleigh was sitting in the garden here enjoying a quiet smoke when a servant, having never seen tobacco before, doused him with a bucket of water, thinking that his master was on fire.

SHERBORNE ABBEY has THE HEAVIEST PEAL OF EIGHT BELLS IN THE WORLD at 7.5 tons, and the abbey's medieval fan vaulting is THE EARLIEST VAULTING IN ENGLAND TO COVER A WHOLE CHURCH CEILING.

Isle of Portland

Dorset has given a proud face to many notable English buildings, with stone carved from the quarries of the ISLE OF PORTLAND. A haunting, rocky, almost treeless peninsula, 4 miles (6.4 km) long, Portland's bleak atmosphere makes it easy to believe in the legend that in Celtic times this was the Isle of the Dead – where the insane were sent to eke out their wretched lives in caves and hollows.

The architect Inigo Jones was the first person to recognise the potential of Portland stone for building, using it for the Banqueting House in London's Whitehall. Other notable buildings constructed with Portland stone are St Paul's Cathedral, the east front of Buckingham Palace, Manchester's Central Library, and the United Nations headquarters in New York. The gravestones of British soldiers killed in the two world wars are made from Portland stone, as is Britain's national memorial, the Cenotaph.

In the mid-19th century convicts were used to quarry the stone for the great Portland breakwater, which protects the second deepest harbour, and second largest *artificial* harbour, in the world, after Rotterdam.

From a high point of 496 feet (151 m) in the north, the wedge-shaped Isle of Portland slopes down to a lighthouse at PORTLAND BILL on the southern tip. The contraception campaigner MARIE STOPES (1881–1958) used to come here to study fossils, and after her death her ashes were scattered across the cliffs. The fast currents and savage rocks off the Bill have claimed many lives, including that of the poet William Wordsworth's brother John, who went

down with his ship, the *Abergavenny*, off Portland Bill in 1805.

Portland is connected to the mainland by CHESIL BEACH, which stretches for 10 miles (16 km) to near Abbotsbury, and is THE LONGEST SEA BAR IN EUROPE. A unique feature of Chesil Beach is the precise way the pebbles are graded, increasing in size from west to east. Local fishermen, in fog or at night, can tell how far along the beach they are by the size of the pebbles. The beach encloses a lagoon known as the Fleet, part of which provides a haven for Europe's largest swannery, established in the 14th century by the monks of Abbotsbury. In stormy weather whole ships have been hurled over the bar into the lagoon, where they remain trapped for ever.

Moonfleet, J.M Falkner's classic novel about smuggling is set here.

Portland cement, the standard type of modern cement, is so called because its inventor, Joseph Aspdin, noted that the colour of the cement, when set, resembles Portland stone.

In 1961 Portland was at the centre of a spy scandal when it was discovered that two clerks at the Underwater Weapons Establishment at Portland, Harry Houghton and Ethel Gee, were supplying secrets to a Russian spy, George Lonsdale, at a secret rendezvous near the Old Vic theatre in Waterloo. He passed them on to a second-hand book dealer, Peter Kroger, and his wife Helen, who lived in a bungalow in Ruislip. The Krogers then reduced the documents to microdots, which they pasted over full stops in the books, and then sent to Russia.

Another prestige building material from Dorset is Purbeck marble, which is not a true marble but a hard, highly polished limestone that can be seen in many English churches and cathedrals, notably Lincoln, and is used for floors and pillars and occasionally for fonts.

Well, I never knew this about
DORSET FOLK

John Russell
◄ 1485–1555 ►

About a mile (1.6 km) east of Burton Bradstock lies an old grey farmhouse called BERWICK. One windy day in 1506, the owner, a young farmer called JOHN RUSSELL, rode out from Berwick to answer a cry for help from his kinsman, Thomas Trenchard, of Wolfeton House near Dorchester. Trenchard was entertaining some rather unexpected guests, Archduke Philip, ruler of the Netherlands, and his wife Joanna of Castile. They had been on their way to Madrid when bad weather had forced them to take shelter in Weymouth Bay. Sir Thomas Trenchard, as the senior man on the spot, was obliged to invite them home until the storm abated, and he was having a difficult time as he spoke no Spanish and his guests spoke no English.

Coming from a family of wine shippers, young Russell had been to

Spain and learnt the language as part of his education, and now had the opportunity to put his experience to good use. In fact, he charmed the royal visitors so much that he was later asked to accompany them to Windsor to see Henry VII. The English king was equally taken with the wit and intelligence of the young man from Dorset and bade him join the Royal Court.

Under Henry VIII, John Russell distinguished himself in war and diplomacy and was eventually made Earl of Bedford. At the Dissolution of the Monasteries, a grateful king showered him with estates, including Tavistock in Devon, large parts of Exmoor, the lands of Thorney Abbey in Cambridgeshire and several acres of London. To top it all, Russell gained Woburn Abbey, now the principal seat of his descendants, the Dukes of Bedford, and the largest privately owned park in England. Not a bad return for learning Spanish.

Anthony Ashley Cooper, 1st Earl of Shaftesbury
◄ 1621–83 ►

ANTHONY ASHLEY COOPER, 1ST EARL OF SHAFTESBURY, whose ancestral home is at Wimborne St Giles, was one of the first Whigs and was responsible for the Habeas Corpus Act of 1679, which was introduced into the English legal system as an essential safeguard against wrongful or arbitrary imprisonment by the state.

THE WHIGS were mostly Protestant aristocrats with Liberal tendencies who supported the exclusion of the Catholic James II from the English throne, championed the supremacy of Parliament over the Crown, and upheld the rights of Nonconformists. The term Whig was a derogatory name used by their political opponents the Tories, and came from the word Whiggamore, meaning a Scottish Presbyterian rebel.

HABEAS CORPUS, literally 'you may have the body', gives a detainee or his representative the right to demand that his custodian must state on which charge he is being held, and to require that he be brought before a court to determine if he is being legally held in custody. As Britain has no written constitution, habeas corpus has long been regarded as 'worth a hundred constitutional articles guaranteeing individual liberty'. In the first years of the third millennium, habeas corpus is under serious threat from the British government and European Law, for the first time since its introduction over 300 years ago.

Born in Dorset

SIR JAMES THORNHILL (1675–1734), artist who painted the interior of the dome of St Paul's and the Painted Hall at Greenwich, and the first English-born artist to receive a knighthood, was born in MELCOMBE REGIS.

SARAH FIELDING (1710–68), sister of the novelist and magistrate Henry Fielding and author of *The Governess*, the first full-length English novel written for children, was born in EAST STOUR.

WILLIAM FOX TALBOT (1800–77), photography pioneer and creator of the oldest known photographic negative (of the oriel window at Lacock Abbey in Wiltshire), was born in EVERSHOT.

VERNEY LOVETT CAMERON (1844–94), African explorer and the first European to cross Equatorial Africa from coast to coast, was born in RADIPOLE.

County Durham

Sanctuary Knocker on the door of Durham Cathedral.

◀ DURHAM FOLK ▶

Bede ✦ Elizabeth Barrett Browning ✦ William Wouldhave ✦ Ernest
Thompson Seton ✦ Dame Flora Robson ✦ Catherine Cookson
✦ Captain Richard Wallace Annand ✦ Ridley Scott ✦ Eric Idle

Durham

❦

The name Durham comes from the Old English 'dun-holm', which means 'hill-island', an apt description of the 98 ft (30 m) high sandstone rock on which Old Durham Town stands.

The story of Durham begins in 995 when monks guarding the relics of St Cuthbert, then resting at Chester-le-Street, were led to the spot by a milk-maid looking for her dun cow. They found the cow lying high up on the rock which, being surrounded on three sides by the River Wear, made a good secure site on which to establish a church to serve as Cuthbert's permanent shrine. It soon became one of England's principal places of pilgrimage for both Saxons and Normans, and in 1093 the present cathedral was begun.

tators regard Durham as the greatest Norman building in the world. It was

Cathedral

❦

DURHAM CATHEDRAL as we see it today is not that much changed from the original 11th-century conception, and with its massive round pillars, some with spiral or zigzag decoration, it is undoubtedly England's finest Romanesque or Norman cathedral – some commen-

A vault is a stone roof, found in a few churches and most cathedrals. A rib vault is one that features projecting stone strips, used either for decoration or for structural purposes. The most decorative type of rib vault is fan vaulting, as found in places such as King's College Chapel at Cambridge or Henry VII's Chapel in Westminster Abbey.

also ENGLAND'S EARLIEST VAULTED CATHEDRAL, and THE FIRST TO USE RIB VAULTS.

On the main entrance door of Durham Cathedral hangs a huge SANCTUARY KNOCKER, a relic of the days when Durham Cathedral offered sanctuary from the law. Any criminal who banged on the knocker would be admitted to the cathedral, and fed and protected from his pursuers. In return the fugitive would be obliged to don a black robe and confess his crime, and at the end of 37 days he would be sent to Durham's assigned port of Hartlepool and told to leave the country. If he disobeyed any of these conditions, the criminal would be handed over to the law. Over a period of some 50 years in the late 15th and early 16th centuries, some 330 offenders, including 280 murderers, were given sanctuary at Durham, and even King Edward IV was unable to extract an escaped prisoner accused of treason.

One of Durham Cathedral's most precious treasures is a stole given to St Cuthbert's shrine by King Athelstan in 934, and thought to be THE OLDEST EXAMPLE OF ENGLISH NEEDLEWORK IN EXISTENCE. The cathedral is also the resting-place of THE VENERABLE BEDE, who died in 735.

Durham's Bishop's Throne is THE HIGHEST BISHOP'S CHAIR IN CHRISTENDOM.

Castle

DURHAM CASTLE was begun by William the Conqueror in 1072, during his 'harrying of the North', and was the only northern castle never to fall to the Scots. Because Durham was far from London and yet in a strategically vital position on the main route from London to Scotland, William relied on the Bishops of Durham to protect and rule the North in his interests, and granted them immense powers to raise their own taxes and armies, administer their own laws and even mint their own coins. Durham Castle served as the Bishop's Palace.

In 1986 Durham Cathedral and Castle together became one of England's first World Heritage Sites.

Prince Bishops

THE COUNTY PALATINE OF DURHAM was created by William the Conqueror to defend England's northern border with Scotland. It was carved out of the old Saxon kingdom of Northumbria, Durham lying south of the Tyne and Derwent rivers and Northumberland to the north. Within Durham the Bishops ruled like princes and were known as PRINCE BISHOPS, a description applied to them until the time of the Great Reform Act in 1832.

Durham University

DURHAM UNIVERSITY was founded in 1832 by the last Prince Bishop, William Van Mildert, as ENGLAND'S THIRD UNIVERSITY, after Oxford and Cambridge. The Bishops of Durham moved their principal residence to Bishop Auckland and gave over the castle to the new university.

The university's ORIENTAL MUSEUM is ENGLAND'S ONLY MUSEUM DEVOTED WHOLLY TO ORIENTAL ART AND ARCHITECTURE.

Durham Miners' Gala

The 19th century saw Durham become a centre of the English coal-mining industry, and an important part of Durham's heritage is the annual DURHAM MINERS' GALA, when representatives of each mining village and union march behind banners and brass bands to meet at Durham race course for speeches and merriment. Established in 1871, this is England's oldest and best-known celebration of trade union pride and tradition.

THE DURHAM REGATTA, held in June, was inaugurated in 1834 and is ENGLAND'S OLDEST REGATTA.

Well, I never **knew this** *about*
DURHAM FOLK

The Venerable Bede

The ancient town of JARROW grew up around a monastery founded in 682 by a Northumbrian nobleman, Benedict Biscop, and for more than 50 years it was the home of the brilliant monk known as THE FATHER OF ENGLISH LEARNING, the VENERABLE BEDE.

Born in MONKWEARMOUTH in 673, Bede was THE FIRST PERSON TO WRITE EXTENSIVELY IN THE ENGLISH LANGUAGE. His *Ecclesiastical History of the English People* is the earliest and most important record we have of English history until 729, and tells us about the beginnings of Christianity in these islands, up to the Synod of Whitby in 664. He was also

in the south wall contains the oldest Saxon stained glass of its kind in Europe. A battered wooden seat known as Bede's Chair sits against a wall.

The church and monastery ruins, one of the most significant Christian shrines in England, occupy a rather bleak site beside a muddy creek, but it has all been jollied up as 'Bede's World', a modern interpretation centre.

the first historian to date events from the Year of our Lord, Anno Domini. On the very day he died in 735, the Venerable Bede completed an Old English translation of the Gospel of St John. He was buried at Jarrow, but 300 years later his relics were stolen by a monk, who took them to Durham, where they now lie in the cathedral's Galilee Chapel.

The church of St Paul, attached to the monastery, was dedicated in 685 and the original dedication stone, THE OLDEST DEDICATION STONE IN ENGLAND, is still in place above the chancel arch. The arch has survived, along with much of the chancel itself, from Bede's day. One of the windows

Jarrow March

Twelve hundred years after Bede, in 1936, the name of Jarrow reverberated throughout the country once again, when the men of Jarrow marched to London. Unemployment in the north-east, particularly among miners and shipbuilders, was horrendous, around 80 per cent, and 200 men set off from Jarrow to lobby Parliament for jobs and recognition of their plight. Wherever they stopped for the night, local people provided them with food and shelter. The Jarrow March took almost one month, and when they arrived in London, the MP for Jarrow, Ellen Wilkinson, handed in a petition of 12,000 signatures, which Prime Minister Stanley Baldwin ignored, refusing even to meet the marchers. Although the march did not achieve very much at the time, it was a significant landmark in the struggle for the rights of England's working men.

ELIZABETH BARRETT BROWNING (1806–61), poet, was born at COXHOE, south of Durham. One of the most quoted opening lines in the English language comes from her *Sonnets from the Portuguese* – 'How do I love thee? Let me count the ways.'

Born in South Shields

WILLIAM WOULDHAVE (1751–1821), inventor of the lifeboat.

ERNEST THOMPSON SETON (1860–1946), founder of the Boy Scouts of America.

DAME FLORA ROBSON (1902–84), character actress and theatrical *grande dame.*

CATHERINE COOKSON (1906–98) the most widely read English novelist of the later 20th century.

CAPTAIN RICHARD WALLACE ANNAND (1914–2004), of the Durham Light Infantry, the first recipient of the Victoria Cross in the Second World War.

SIR RIDLEY SCOTT, film director (*Alien, Blade Runner, Gladiator*), born 1937.

ERIC IDLE, comic actor, writer and member of the *Monty Python* team, born 1943.

Essex

FIRST TOWN ✦ BIGGEST KEEP
✦ CAPTAIN OF THE MAYFLOWER ✦ FINE WORDS
✦ TRIANGULAR TOWER ✦ FIRST IN BRICK ✦ JAM TODAY

Colchester Castle – the largest keep ever built in Europe.

◀ ESSEX FOLK ▶

Captain Lawrence Oates ✦ William Byrd ✦ Gustav Holst ✦ Sir Evelyn Ruggles-Brise ✦ Sir Alf Ramsey ✦ Dudley Moore ✦ Terry Venables ✦ Sandie Shaw ✦ Eva Hart ✦ Raymond Baxter ✦ Ian Holm ✦ Dame Maggie Smith ✦ Kathy Kirby ✦ Noel Edmonds ✦ Richard Littlejohn ✦ Jane Leeves

Colchester

COLCHESTER IS THE OLDEST RECORDED TOWN IN ENGLAND and was the capital of the kingdom of Cunobelin, Shakespeare's Cymbeline, who was the father of Caratacus, leader of the initial resistance against the Romans. Caratacus was captured and hauled off to Rome, where he was paraded in chains, but his courage and dignity earned Caesar's admiration and he was allowed to live in Rome as a free man.

Colchester, known as Camulodunum, was THE FIRST ROMAN TOWN IN BRITAIN, and ITS FIRST CAPITAL, until the town was reduced to ashes by Queen Boadicea in AD 60. It was rebuilt by the Romans, but the capital was moved to Londinium.

After the Romans left, the Saxons gave the town its modern name of Colchester, which means 'the Roman fortress on the River Colne', and in the 11th century the Normans constructed THE LARGEST KEEP EVER BUILT IN EUROPE, on top of the Roman temple of Claudius. Even though it was reduced from four storeys to two, the keep remains the largest in England, and covers one and a half times the ground space of the White Tower of London.

Harwich

CHRISTOPHER JONES (c. 1565–1622) was born in HARWICH, the son of a ship-owner, and lived at No. 21 Kings Head Street. On 23 December 1593 he was married in St Nicholas church to Sara Twitt, daughter of a neighbour. Sara died tragically young at 27, and Jones was married for a second time in St Nicholas in 1603. His second wife's family had extensive shipping interests, and Jones became part owner of a Harwich-registered cargo ship called the *Mayflower*. In 1620 the ship was commissioned to carry 102 pilgrims to start a new life in America, with Christopher Jones as captain. The *Mayflower* left Plymouth in September that year and after a 66-day voyage made landfall at Cape Cod. The pilgrims disembarked at what is now called Plymouth Rock, but spent the winter living on the *Mayflower*, which didn't set sail for England until March 1621. Christopher Jones died the following year and is buried at Rotherhithe in London.

The ancient port of Harwich, with its narrow medieval streets and passageways, has long played an important part in England's maritime heritage, serving as a haven port for English ships, a naval shipyard and as a gateway to the Continent.

In 1918 the entire German U-boat fleet surrendered to Admiral Tyrwhitt at Harwich.

On Harwich Green is THE ONLY TREAD WHEEL CRANE IN THE WORLD. It was built in 1677 in the Naval Yard and was worked by men walking on the inside of the wheels, a hazardous activity if the load took control and the wheel suddenly went into reverse.

The ELECTRIC PALACE CINEMA, in Kings Quay Street, built in 1911, is THE OLDEST UNALTERED CINEMA IN ENGLAND STILL IN USE.

Tilbury

It was at WEST TILBURY, on the River Thames, that Queen Elizabeth I addressed her troops while Sir Francis Drake was battling the Spanish Armada in the English Channel. Bareheaded, mounted on a charger, and attended by the Sword of State, the Queen uttered these inspiring words:

I know I have the body of a weak and feeble woman, but I have the heart of a King, and of a King of England too, and I think foul scorn that any Prince of Europe should dare to invade the borders of my realm.

Although the docks at Tilbury are amongst the biggest in the world now,

West Tilbury, the site of the royal camp where the stirring event took place, remains a secluded spot, set back from the river in marshland and reeking of olden times.

Coggeshall

East Anglia was the first region in England to use bricks since the Romans, and THE EARLIEST ENGLISH BRICKWORK can be found in the remains of a 12th-century abbey just south of COGGESHALL. The arches of LONG BRIDGE in Coggeshall's Bridge Street are made from the same bricks, which makes it THE OLDEST BRICK BRIDGE IN ENGLAND. The abbey's GRANGE BARN also dates from the 12th century and is THE OLDEST SURVIVING TIMBER-FRAMED BARN IN EUROPE.

Maldon

THE ONLY TRIANGULAR CHURCH TOWER IN BRITAIN dates from the 13th century and is attached to the church of ALL SAINTS at MALDON. A window in the church was given by the people of Malden, Massachusetts, to commemorate LAWRENCE WASHINGTON, who is buried in the churchyard in an unmarked grave. He was

All Saints, Maldon

the great-great-grandfather, and last English ancestor, of the first American President, George Washington.

Tiptree

Arthur Charles Wilkin was born in Tiptree, near Colchester, in 1835. In his late twenties he took over his parents' farm and began to specialise in growing fruit, which he supplied to London jam-makers. Transport difficulties eventually forced him to consider making his own jam, and when he was introduced to an Australian merchant who agreed to take as much strawberry jam as he could produce, Wilkin set to with a will. The buyer wanted jam that was free from glucose, colouring and preservatives,

and it was decided to call the product conserve, to distinguish it as being of high quality, and to use the name Britannia Preserving Company, which would give the company a good profile in Australia.

The first jam was made in his farmhouse kitchen to Wilkin's wife's recipe, using three boiling pans and a couple of traction engines brought in off the farm to provide power. Mechanisation was introduced in the 1890s, and Arthur Wilkin's 200-acre (81 ha) farm has grown into 1,000 acres (405 ha) and a factory which produces nearly 90 different conserves, preserves, chutneys, honeys and marmalades for sale all over the world. The Tiptree trademark was adopted in 1905 and the company name changed to Wilkin and Sons Ltd.

Arthur Wilkin died in 1913, but

Little Maplestead

the business is still family run, and Tiewlands, the house where Arthur Wilkin was born, has been preserved and incorporated into the works complex. There is a shop and museum and a daily 'tasting time' to make sure standards are being kept up.

The tiny, exquisite church at LITTLE MAPLESTEAD, north of Halstead, is the smallest and latest of England's four round churches.

Well, I never  *knew this about*
ESSEX FOLK

Captain Lawrence Oates
1880–1912

LAWRENCE OATES grew up in the family home of Over Hall in GESTINGTHORPE, and after his father died in 1896 Lawrence became lord of the manor. After Eton, he signed up for the Inniskilling Dragoons and fought in the South African War, where he was mentioned in dispatches, and also served in Ireland, Egypt and India. Not happy with army life in India he applied to join Robert Falcon Scott's second Antarctic expedition to be first to the South Pole, and greatly impressed Scott with his fitness and enthusiasm. Oates loved animals and so was put in charge of the expedition's ponies.

The trek to the South Pole was arduous, and when they arrived to find that the Norwegian Roald Amundsen had got there first, their spirits were dashed. On the way back their rations began to run out and Oates, suffering from terrible frostbite, found himself holding the others back. He soon realised what he must do. Waking early after a fitful night, he stumbled out into the blizzard with some of the most courageous words ever spoken: 'I am just going outside. I may be some time.'

Oates was never found, but a rough cross was set up near where the bodies of Scott and his companions were discovered, bearing the inscription 'Hereabouts died a very gallant gentleman.'

Oates's fellow officers placed a memorial tablet in the little 14th-century church at Gestingthorpe, and every week, until she died in 1937, Oates's mother walked to the church from Over Hall next door to polish the brass.

WILLIAM BYRD (1539–1623), the foremost composer of the Elizabethan age and creator of THE BAROQUE STYLE OF ORGAN AND HARPSICHORD MUSIC, is buried in the churchyard at Stondon Massey. As a Catholic 'recusant' his grave remains unmarked.

Beside the altar in the tiny church at FOSTER STREET, across the M11 from Harlow, lie Benjamin Flower and his two daughters Sarah and Eliza. SARAH FLOWER, born in 1805, wrote the hymn sung as the *Titanic* sank beneath the waves, 'Nearer My God to Thee'. She was married to WILLIAM ADAMS, who invented the UNIVERSAL FISH JOINT, still used on modern railways to connect the rails together in a way that allows trains to pass over them at high speeds.

GUSTAV HOLST (1874–1934) wrote his most celebrated work, *The Planets*, while on long weekends at his family's country home in THAXTED, during the First World

War. He also played the organ in Thaxted church and inaugurated the town's Whitsuntide festival.

SIR EVELYN RUGGLES-BRISE (1857–1935), founder of the Borstal prisons for young offenders, was born in FINCHINGFIELD.

Born in Dagenham

SIR ALF RAMSEY (1920–99), football manager with Ipswich Town and England. In 1966 he became the only England manager to win the World Cup.

DUDLEY MOORE (1935–2002), comedian, actor and musician.

TERRY VENABLES, England football team manager, born 1943.

SANDIE SHAW, pop singer, born 1947. The first UK winner of the Eurovision Song Contest, with 'Puppet on a String' in 1967, she was famous for always performing in bare feet.

Born in Ilford

EVA HART (1905–96), one of the last survivors from the *Titanic*, who became a professional singer in Australia.

RAYMOND BAXTER (1922–2006), Second World War fighter pilot and presenter of the BBC's *Tomorrow's World*.

IAN HOLM, stage and screen actor, best known for playing Bilbo Baggins in the *Lord of the Rings* film trilogy, born in 1931.

DAME MAGGIE SMITH, actress, who won two Oscars, for *The Prime of Miss Jean Brodie* in 1969 and *California Suite* in 1978, born in 1934.

KATHY KIRBY, 1960s pop singer, born in 1941.

NOEL EDMONDS, radio DJ and TV presenter and producer famed for *Multi-Coloured Swap Shop*, *Noel's House Party* and *Deal or No Deal*, born in 1948.

RICHARD LITTLEJOHN, author and newspaper columnist, born in 1954.

JANE LEEVES, actress, best known for playing physical therapist Daphne Moon in the American TV comedy series *Frasier*, born in 1961.

Gloucestershire

DARK DEEDS ✦ BIRTHPLACE OF MODERN
CONSERVATION ✦ BIGGEST NORMAN TOWER
✦ CHEESE ROLLING ✦ CHAMPAGNE
✦ MANOR HOUSES

*Tewkesbury Abbey, with the biggest
Norman tower in the world.*

◀ GLOUCESTERSHIRE FOLK ▶

Edward Jenner ✦ W.G. Grace ✦ Robert Raikes ✦ Beatrice Webb
✦ Frederick Sanger

Berkeley Castle

The little town of BERKELEY is an oasis of calm set in flat land between the River Severn and the M5. It is dominated by the castle, looming above the water meadows, impregnable and stern, proud home to the Berkeley family since the days of Henry II, and THE OLDEST CASTLE IN ENGLAND STILL INHABITED BY THE FAMILY WHO BUILT IT. The Berkeleys are one of only three English families who can trace their roots directly back to their Saxon ancestors.

Dark deeds were done at Berkeley Castle. One September night, as the mist rolled in off the Severn, the townsfolk were awoken by hideous screams that went on and on, sending birds wheeling into the sky and dogs howling with terror. Eventually the cries faded into whimpers and then a thick, brooding silence. The next morning, the horribly mutilated body of KING EDWARD II was found in his cell in the castle, done to death most foully, by two knights sent from his own Queen.

The previous year Edward II had been forced by his wife, Queen Isabella, and her lover, Roger de Mortimer, to abdicate the throne in favour of his young son Edward III. The old king was sent to end his days at Berkeley, tended to by a sympathetic Lord Berkeley. He lived too long, however, and made the guilty Queen uneasy, so she sent her men, SIR JOHN

MALTRAVERS and SIR THOMAS GURNEY, to hasten his demise. Lord Berkeley was sent away and the knights set about their task, taunting the King for his homosexuality, putting flowers in his hair and finally killing him by inserting a red-hot poker deep into his bowels.

The Abbot of Gloucester came in reverence to claim the body, and Edward III, shocked by his father's cruel death, raised a splendid tomb for him in Gloucester Cathedral. It soon became a place of pilgrimage, and the wealth the pilgrims bought with them built the glorious medieval cathedral we see today, a wondrous monument wrought from an evil act.

Slimbridge

A popular tenant of the Berkeley estate is the WILDFOWL AND WETLANDS TRUST at SLIMBRIDGE, founded in 1946 by SIR PETER SCOTT, son of the polar explorer Robert Falcon Scott. Covering 1,000 acres (405 ha) and home to 164 different species of bird, it is THE LARGEST AND MOST VARIED WILDFOWL CENTRE IN THE WORLD and THE ONLY PLACE IN ENGLAND WHERE YOU CAN SEE ALL SIX SPECIES OF FLAMINGO. Slimbridge is considered to be the birthplace of modern conservation.

Tewkesbury

The tower of TEWKESBURY ABBEY is THE LARGEST NORMAN TOWER IN THE WORLD. Buried inside the Abbey, beneath a simple brass plate on the floor of the sanctuary, is Edward, Prince of Wales, son of Henry VI, killed by the Duke of Clarence at the Battle of Tewkesbury in 1471.

The old oak door of the church at DIDBROOK, in the Cotswold Hills a few miles east of Tewkesbury, has holes in it made by Yorkist bullets, fired at Lancastrian soldiers who had fled from the Battle of Tewkesbury and sought refuge here. These marks were made by some of the earliest bullets ever fired from a handgun.

The Saxon font in the church at DEERHURST, on the River Severn near Tewkesbury, is THE OLDEST FONT IN ENGLAND.

Cheese Rolling

One to be ready!
Two to be steady!
Three to prepare!

Release the Cheese!

(The signal for the specially invited guest 'roller' to let go the cheese)

And Four to be off!

And so begins the annual CHEESE ROLLING competition at COOPER'S HILL, near Brockworth.

Slightly nutty people come from all over the world, from Japan, Australia, New Zealand, the home of dangerous sports, and even Wales, to chase an eight-pound Double Gloucester Cheese down a precipitous Gloucestershire hillside on Bank Holiday Monday at the end of May – for fun.

The ceremony, which used to take place on Midsummer's Day, dates back hundreds of years to pagan times and is thought to have its roots in fertility rites and supplications for a bountiful harvest. There are the remains of an ancient British fort at the top of the hill, which suggests that some sort of activity may have taken place here even before the Romans arrived.

There are five races, one of them for ladies, and the first person to reach the bottom of the hill in pursuit of the cheese wins . . . a cheese! The course is 600 ft (183 m) long and the average slope is 1 in 2, although in places it is 1 in 1.

In olden times there was no limit to the number of runners, but for safety reasons races are now restricted to a maximum of 15 competitors. There are no entry qualifications – it is first come, first served.

Cheese rolling can be very dangerous, and every year sees a crop of injuries, usually sprains and bruises. The cheese has been known to bounce into the crowd, and in 1997 the cheese hit a spectator and sent him flying down the hill.

The cheese has been rolled without a break every year in living memory, although the actual race has been cancelled three times recently, once for health and safety reasons, once as a result of foot-and-mouth disease, and in 2003 because of an earthquake. On these occasions the organisers rolled a solitary cheese down the hill to maintain the tradition.

Champagne

CHAMPAGNE was invented in England by a doctor, CHRISTO-PHER MERRETT, born in WINCHCOMBE in 1614. In 1662 he presented a paper to the Royal Society in which he sets out a technique for making wine sparkle by adding sugar and molasses. This had been made possible by the invention in 1630 by ADMIRAL SIR ROBERT MANSELL, of a coloured glass, incorporating iron and manganese, which could be used to make bottles strong enough to contain the fermentation process.

This 'méthode traditionelle' was adopted in 1695 by a French monk and winemaker in the Champagne

Nether Lypiatt Manor

region of France called Dom Perignon, who used it to give sparkle to his own wines.

Two English Manor Houses

Nether Lypiatt Manor

Prince and Princess Michael of Kent once lived in the exquisite, dream-like, NETHER LYPIATT MANOR, hidden away in the hills above Stroud. It was built in 1698 by 'Hanging Judge' Cox, whose son ironically hanged himself in one of the rooms, and is supposed to haunt the place. Nether Lypiatt creates a magical illusion as it appears suddenly and unexpectedly beside a tiny, single-track hill-top Cotswold lane. It has 20 acres (8 ha) of gardens and is the loveliest of English houses.

Cowley Manor

COWLEY MANOR, 5 miles (8 km) north of Cheltenham, is a stunning Palladian-style mansion, very similar in looks to Cliveden, set in 50 acres (20 ha) of informal gardens, with lakes, cascades, a big rock garden and woodland walks. It was built in the 1830s by Sir James Horlick of the milky drinks family. He is buried in the churchyard alongside, and is reputed to climb in through the large window that overlooks the graveyard and walk up and down the first-floor corridor. He is, apparently, perfectly friendly.

Also buried in the churchyard of the enchanting little 12th-century church next door is Dorset innkeeper Robert Browning, 17th-century ancestor of the poet.

Lewis Carroll's Alice in Wonderland, Alice Liddell, used to visit Cowley regularly to stay with her uncle, who was the rector there.

At the turn of the millennium Cowley Manor was bought by Jessica

Sainsbury and turned into a luxury hotel and spa. Whether Sir James Horlick still walks the corridor is not in the hotel literature.

Buried in the church at Coberley, the next-door village, is buried Dick Whittington's mother Joan. She lies beside her first husband, Sir Thomas Berkeley. Dick Whittington, Joan's son by her second husband, Sir William Whittington, was born at Pauntley, north of Gloucester, in 1358, and became Lord Mayor of London four times.

Well, I never knew this
about
GLOUCESTERSHIRE FOLK

Edward Jenner
◄ 1749–1823 ►

In sharp contradistinction to the awful murder of Edward II at Berkeley Castle, lying in the chancel of the church at Berkeley is a man who *saved* lives. Born in Berkeley, the son of the vicar, EDWARD JENNER became a doctor and naturalist, and was determined to find a cure for smallpox, the most deadly disease of his time. As a countryman, he was familiar with country lore, including the belief that milkmaids who had caught cowpox

never contracted smallpox. In May 1796 he vaccinated a farm boy, JAMES PHIPPS, in the arm, with cowpox taken from the hand of a dairymaid, SARAH NELMES. A few weeks later he inoculated the boy again, this time with smallpox, and when Phipps did not develop the disease, Jenner knew his theory was correct.

Jenner spent the rest of his life sharing his knowledge with others, and his principles of inoculation have been used to prevent diseases and infections throughout the civilised world. Although Farmer Jesty had

In 1882 he scored THE FIRST EVER CENTURY FOR ENGLAND, in 1895 he became THE FIRST MAN TO SCORE 1,000 RUNS IN MAY, and he was THE FIRST CRICKETER EVER TO DO THE DOUBLE – that is score 1,000 runs and take 100 wickets in a season. He captained England for 11 years from 1888 to 1900 and his Test cricket career lasted 28 years, making him TEST CRICKET'S LONGEST-SERVING PLAYER. He was THE FIRST PLAYER EVER TO MAKE OVER £1 MILLION FROM CRICKET.

W.G. Grace lived for a while in CLIFTON, not far from Clifton College

administered the first vaccination in Dorset 20 years earlier, Edward Jenner was the first to promote the technique to a worldwide audience, hence his title as the Father of Inoculation.

W.G. Grace
◄ 1848–1915 ►

WILLIAM GILBERT GRACE, England's greatest cricketer, was born in DOWNEND, a suburb of Bristol, and practised in Bristol as a doctor. Famous for his trademark beard, he grew to be 6 ft 6ins (1.98 m) tall and was gigantic in prowess as well as stature. He was England captain and also led Gloucestershire to four county championships. They haven't won since he retired.

where, in June 1899, a schoolboy player called A.E.L. COLLINS scored 628 not out, THE HIGHEST SCORE FOR AN INNINGS IN THE HISTORY OF CRICKET.

ROBERT RAIKES (1735–1811), the founder of Sunday Schools, was born in GLOUCESTER.

BEATRICE WEBB (1858–1943), socialist and co-founder of the Fabian Society in 1884, the London School of Economics in 1895, and the *New Statesman* magazine in 1913, was born in STANDISH, south of Gloucester.

FREDERICK SANGER, two-time winner of the Nobel Prize for Chemistry, in 1958 and 1980, was born in RENDCOMB, near Cheltenham, in 1918. He is only the fourth person to win two Nobel prizes.

Hampshire

The Bat and Ball, overlooking the birthplace of English cricket on Broadhalfpenny Down.

◄ HAMPSHIRE FOLK ►

Gilbert White ✦ Jane Austen ✦ Tommy Sopwith ✦ Sir William Petty
✦ Sir Henry Ayers ✦ Augustus John

Winchester

❖◆◆◆❖

WINCHESTER, set in a green, wooded valley on the River Itchen, was ENGLAND'S FIRST CAPITAL, established in the 9th century as home to the first English kings, and watched over by England's founding king, ALFRED THE GREAT. It remained the capital for 200 years after the Norman invasion, sharing the honour with London.

King Alfred lies here somewhere, underneath the great Norman cathedral

that broods over spacious lawns off the steep, narrow high street. Although it has no spectacular spire or high tower, the sheer size of WINCHESTER CATHEDRAL is awe-inspiring. It is THE LONGEST MEDIEVAL CATHEDRAL IN THE WORLD, 556 ft (169 m) from east to west, and covers 1½ acres (0.6 ha) within its walls.

Also within those walls, much against his will, lies King Alfred's tutor, ST SWITHUN, Bishop of Winchester. When he died in 862 he was buried, at his own request, outside 'where the rain might fall on him'. However, on 15 July 971, his body was dug up and put in a splendid new shrine inside the cathedral. This so incensed the fresh air-loving prelate that he made it rain for 40 days – hence the poem.

St Swithun's Day, if thou dost rain
For forty days it will remain.
St Swithun's day, if thou be fair
For forty days 'twill rain no mair'.

Also buried here are several Saxon kings, the Danish king Canute, and William the Conqueror's son, William II (Rufus).

In the nave is the grand tomb of WILLIAM OF WYKEHAM, who founded WINCHESTER COLLEGE in 1382, the SECOND OLDEST PUBLIC SCHOOL IN ENGLAND. Old boys are known as Wykehamists and are expected to live by the motto of their

founder, 'Manners Maketh Man'. The original schoolroom still exists and is today used as a study.

In the Cathedral Close is the PILGRIM'S HALL where those coming to visit the shrine of St Swithun were put up. IT HAS THE OLDEST HAMMER-BEAM ROOF IN ENGLAND, dating from the early 14th century.

In 1554 Mary Tudor married Philip of Spain in Winchester Cathedral, thus creating THE ONLY SPANISH KING OF ENGLAND. They spent their honeymoon in Wolvesey Castle next door.

At the top of the town is the GREAT HALL, all that remains of Winchester's castle, which was destroyed by Oliver Cromwell in 1645. The hall, built by Henry III in 1225, it is regarded as the finest medieval hall in England after Westminster Hall. Hanging on the

wall is a copy of KING ARTHUR'S ROUND TABLE, made in 1335 and repainted in Tudor times, with Arthur bearing an uncanny resemblance to Henry VIII.

A ten-minute walk along the water meadows brings you out at ST JOHN'S HOSPITAL, ENGLAND'S OLDEST SURVIVING CHARITY and site of THE OLDEST ALMSHOUSES IN ENGLAND, founded in 1136. For nearly 900 years travellers have been able to claim the WAYFARER'S DOLE here, of some bread and a drink. Visitors today still can, by knocking on the porter's door.

Winchester's 12th-century West-gate houses a museum featuring a fascinating collection of old weights and measures.

English Weights and Measurements

Up until 1965 England used the British 'Imperial' system of measurement. Since then the metric system is gradually being introduced, and today many weights, lengths and volumes are measured in metric.

The change is being made to bring England in line with the other countries of Europe, most of which had the French metric system imposed upon them by Napoleon in the 19th century. Certain well-loved English measurements are considered too precious to alter and have so far remained untouched – the mile and the pint, for instance.

The British 'Imperial' system is based on the human frame. The 5th-century philosopher Protagoras surmised that 'Man is the natural measure of all things', and units based on the human figure – the arm, thumb, foot, etc – are practical and easy to understand and visualise.

The first properly recorded unit of measurement was the Egyptian cubit, which was the length of the forearm from the elbow to the tip of the middle finger, and this was divided into such measurements as the span of the hand or the length of the fingers and thumbs.
The basic unit of the English measurement of length is the yard, which was originally taken as the distance between Henry I's nose and the tip of his outstretched arm. In the 14th century, the English foot became based on the length of the foot of St Algar, which was carved on the base of a column at the entrance to the old St Paul's Cathedral, site of one of London's busiest markets.

The Romans inherited their foot from the Egyptians and divided it into 12 unciae (inches). When they occupied Britain they brought with them the 'mille passus' or 1,000 paces, origin of the English mile. A pace was five Roman feet, and a Roman mile was therefore 5,000 feet – this was changed in the reign of Elizabeth I to 5,280 feet or eight furlongs.

A furlong, now only used in horse racing, comes from the Old English 'furh' (furrow) and 'lang' (long), and refers to the length of a long furrow in an acre of ploughed field – an acre being one furlong by one rod, or the area a team of oxen could comfortably plough in one morning. A rod was the accepted length of the ox goad or prod, as used by medieval farmers.

Although an agreement to have a national standard of weights and measures was incorporated into Magna Carta in 1215, it wasn't until 1826, during the reign of George IV, that the 'Imperial' system of weights and measures was introduced in an attempt to standardise the many different measurements that had evolved.

Weights were even more complicated, but were based on multiples of a grain of barley, except when it came to money, and then it was a grain of wheat. Money was based on weight and hence 240 pennies, which made up one pound in weight, became one pound in money terms as well.

The English pint is one-eighth of a gallon, which in 1824 was based on the volume of ten pounds of distilled water at 62°F (17°C). The word pint is thought to come from the Latin 'picta', meaning painted, referring to the painted mark on some drinking vessels indicating the correct measure.

Some old units have quietly died away. A guinea was one pound, one shilling, and was widely used as a convenient method of payment in auctions or transactions where a percentage was to be paid to a third party, such as prizes in horse-racing. The bidder would pay in guineas, the vendor would get the same number of pounds, and the third party would get the remainder as their fee. Guineas were introduced in 1663 and made of gold from Guinea (now Ghana) in Africa.

> A league was three miles, the distance a man could comfortably walk in one hour.
> *Half a league, half a league,*
> *Half a league onward...*
> *Into the valley of Death*
> *Rode the six hundred.*
>
> Alfred, Lord Tennyson, 'The Charge of the Light Brigade'

Cricket

Hampshire is the home of the English national game, cricket. Up on the wide greensward of BROADHALFPENNY DOWN at Hambledon, the game of cricket developed, matured and took shape. Cricket in various forms had been played in the south of England for over 200 years, but had never been properly regulated until, in 1750, Richard Nyren, landlord of the Bat and Ball Inn, organised the HAMBLEDON CRICKET CLUB. (The following year, Frederick, Prince of Wales, eldest son of George II, became THE FIRST PERSON TO BE KILLED BY A CRICKET BALL, when he died from an abscess caused by being hit on the head by one.)

The players were drawn from the local community and played as much for local pride as for money. They drew up rules, not just for the play but for the size of bat and ball, and their fame spread countrywide as they became the strongest team in England, defeating county sides and, in 1777, an All England XI. Their headquarters, the BAT AND BALL, still dishes out hospitality up on Broadhalfpenny Down, and there is an obelisk over the road marking where the pitch was.

In the 1780s the influence of Hambledon Cricket Club started to wane. George Finch, 9th Earl of Winchilsea, became president of the club and began to recruit many of the players for his new London team, the Marylebone Cricket Club, which he founded in 1788. The MCC slowly took over as the leading authority in cricket as the game became more and more professional.

Buried a few miles away, at WEST MEON, is the MCC's most celebrated groundsman, THOMAS LORD (1757–1832). Lord's, the present home of the MCC, and headquarters of English cricket, was purchased and laid out by Thomas Lord in 1814, and named after him.

Well, I never knew this
about
HAMPSHIRE FOLK

Gilbert White
◄ 1720–93 ►

THE WAKES, a charming 18th-century country house at SELBORNE, south of Alton, was the home of England's first ecologist, the REV GILBERT WHITE. He lived most of his life here as curate, and devoted his spare time to observing the wildlife and plants of the village and surrounding countryside. His book, *The Natural History of Selborne*, was the first book to record the natural world in such detail, and was a huge bestseller. The house is now a museum dedicated to his memory. It is still possible to climb to the top of the Hangar, the hill that overlooks the village, via the Zig Zag path cut out of the hillside by White and his brother.

Housed within The Wakes, alongside the Gilbert White Museum, are the Lawrence Oates archives (*see* Essex).

Jane Austen
◄ 1775–1817 ►

JANE AUSTEN'S last home was in CHAWTON, a very pretty red-brick and thatch village just outside Alton. Here, in a beautiful old house with a

garden full of flowers, Jane Austen spent the last seven years of her life, and here she wrote *Mansfield Park, Emma* and *Persuasion.* Even though she became ill, Jane was very happy living in Chawton with her mother and sister Cassandra. She spent her final days in Winchester and is buried in the cathedral there. The house in Chawton is now a museum in her memory.

Jane would often walk half a mile through the village to CHAWTON HOUSE, the Elizabethan manor where her brother Edward lived. It is now home to the Centre for the Study of Early English Women's Writing, which runs courses and events, and houses an impressive library with works by Mary Wollstonecraft, Fanny Burney, Mary Shelley and many others.

Tommy Sopwith
◄ 1888–1989 ►

A modest headstone outside the eastern wall of the Saxon church at Little Sombourne, near Stockbridge, marks the grave of one of England's flying pioneers, TOMMY SOPWITH. He lived at nearby Longstock House, in the Test valley, where he died aged 101. He was best known as the designer of Britain's finest First World War fighter, the SOPWITH CAMEL, but he also won a number of flying awards. In 1910 he won the Baron de Forrest award for THE LONGEST FLIGHT FROM BRITAIN TO THE CONTINENT, flying 161 miles (259 km) from Eastchurch, Sheppey, to Tirlemont, in Belgium, in three hours. In 1912 he won THE FIRST AERIAL DERBY, 81 miles (130 km) around a

circuit of London. Then, in 1913, he achieved THE BRITISH HEIGHT RECORD of 13,000 ft (3,962 m) in a tractor biplane he had designed himself. He went on to establish THE FIRST TEST PILOT SCHOOL IN THE WORLD. The Sopwith Aviation Company eventually became Hawker Siddeley.

SIR WILLIAM PETTY (1623–87), economist, philosopher and the man who first mapped Ireland, was born in ROMSEY. He designed THE WORLD'S FIRST CATAMARAN, the *Experiment*, which won the world's

first recorded open yacht race, across Dublin Bay, in 1663.

SIR HENRY AYERS (1821–97), premier of South Australia and the man after whom Ayers Rock is named, was born in PORTSEA.

AUGUSTUS JOHN (1878–1961), the portrait painter, is buried at FORDINGBRIDGE. His illegitimate daughter Amaryllis Fleming, by Ian Fleming's widowed mother Evelyn, became a noted cellist and features in the James Bond novel, *The Living Daylights*.

Herefordshire

❖❖❖❖❖

CIDER COUNTRY ✦ MEMBER FOR CIDER
✦ BIGGEST VAT ✦ WASSAILING

*Lower Brockhampton House, a picturesque 14th-century
moated manor house where time stands still.*

◀ HEREFORDSHIRE FOLK ▶

John Kyrle ✦ Albert Gamage ✦ Beryl Reid ✦ John Blashford-Snell

England's Cider Barrel

Herefordshire produces over half of England's cider. It is Cider Country, and has been ever since the first VISCOUNT SCUDAMORE planted a REDSTREAK apple pip in his garden at HOLME LACY, near Hereford, in 1639.

Viscount Scudamore brought the pip back from France, where he had been Charles I's ambassador in Paris. He had taken a keen interest in orchards and cider-making while on the Continent, and it seemed to him that cider was something that could be produced profitably when other forms of agriculture were in the doldrums. The rich red soil of Herefordshire is ideal for growing apples, and his Redstreak orchard flourished. Soon others in Herefordshire were copying his lead, until a commentator was moved to write, 'Following the noble example of my Lord Scudamore, and some other spirited gentlemen in those parts, all Herefordshire is become in a manner but one entire orchard.'

Viscount Scudamore was an ardent Royalist, and was captured and imprisoned for four years during the Civil War. On his release he retired to Holme Lacy (rebuilt at the end of the 17th century into Herefordshire's largest house, and now a hotel) and concentrated on building up his orchards. During this time he made the first sparkling cider by bottling it while it was still fermenting.

Over the next 100 years cider grew rapidly in popularity and became the national drink, until in 1763 the Prime Minister Lord Bute decided to levy a tax on it. The Cider Tax made other forms of agriculture suddenly more profitable and cider-making once more became a local industry in Herefordshire, with farmers just producing enough for their own families and workers.

Much Marcle

The next champion of Herefordshire cider was the MP for Hereford, C.W. RADCLIFFE-COOKE, of Hellens in Much Marcle – which sounds like somewhere Miss Marple might live. It is a beautiful place, especially in spring when the blossoms fill the senses and thoughts turn to a refreshing glass of Herefordshire cider. Radcliffe-Cooke suggested to his next-door neighbour, a Much Marcle farmer called HENRY WESTON, that Weston should try to market his cider commercially, and the MP even introduced WESTON'S CIDER into the bar at the House of Commons. So enthusiastic was his support for the product of his native county that he became known as the 'Member for Cider'.

Weston's Cider became so popular that Henry Weston had to plant hundreds more trees, build bigger vats and take on many more workers. Today, Weston's is still family run, and has employed many generations of local people. The cider market is today robust enough to support some 20 cider-makers of varying size in Herefordshire.

The largest of the Herefordshire cider-makers is BULMERS, which was started by Percy Bulmer, youngest son of the Rector of Credenhill, north of Hereford, in 1887, when he began producing cider from his father's orchard. Bulmers is now THE BIGGEST CIDER-MAKER IN THE WORLD and the Bulmers STRONGBOW VAT is THE LARGEST ALCOHOLIC CONTAINER IN THE WORLD, with a capacity of 15 million gallons (68 million litres).

The earliest written mention of cider found so far comes from the 15th century, in the Wycliffe 'Cider Bible' kept in THE LARGEST CHAINED LIBRARY IN THE WORLD in Hereford Cathedral. The word cider, spelt 'sidir', is used where other bibles say strong drink, in the passage about John the Baptist: 'For he shall be great in the sight of the Lord, and shall drink neither wine nor sidir . . .'

Wassailing

The cider-makers of Herefordshire still observe the ancient tradition of WASSAILING on the evening of Twelfth Night, when the farmers and their families, workers and friends gather in the orchards to celebrate the goddess Pomona and encourage a bountiful crop. Armed with sticks and a bowl of cider with bits of toast in it, they congregate around the best tree in the orchard and place a piece of toast in the branches to attract birds. They then drink some of the cider and pour the rest on the tree roots, while dancing round the trunk and beating at the base with their sticks, dislodging insects, which the birds, attracted by the toast, swoop down and eat. Wassailing songs are sung throughout. Wassail comes from the Anglo-Saxon 'was hal', meaning good health.

Well, I never knew this
about
HEREFORDSHIRE FOLK

John Kyrle

◂ 1637–1724 ▸

ROSS-ON-WYE sits perched on a rocky outcrop above the River Wye, and owes much of its handsome appearance to a generous 17th-century benefactor called JOHN KYRLE, immortalised by Alexander Pope as 'THE MAN OF ROSS'. Kyrle provided the town with its first water supply, pumped up from the river to standpipes in the street, rebuilt the lovely church spire, adding 50 ft (15.2 m) to its height, which is now 208 ft (63 m), and gave the sonorous tenor bell which rings out across the town from the bell tower. He donated the Prospect Gardens, with their far-reaching views over the river valley and into Wales, and built a causeway across the flood meadows. When he died, aged 87, he was laid in state in the church for nine days, and the whole town came out to pay their respects. His home, Kyrle House, is still standing in the Market Place, and is now occupied by a shop and the local newspaper's offices.

Kyrle House

Born in Hereford

ALBERT GAMAGE (1855–1930), founder in 1878 of Gamages store in Holborn, London.

BERYL REID (1919–96), comedy actress.

JOHN BLASHFORD-SNELL, explorer, born 1936. Made the first descent of the Blue Nile in 1968 and the first crossing by vehicle of the Darien Gap between Central and South America in 1972.

Hertfordshire

<figure>❖❖❖❖</figure>

FIRST GARDEN CITY ✦ FIRST NEW TOWN ✦ HOUSE OF
FUN ✦ PAPER TRAIL ✦ ROYAL SPIN

*Brocket Hall, Prime Ministerial retreat where the waltz
was introduced into England.*

◀ HERTFORDSHIRE FOLK ▶

Nicolas Breakspear ✦ John Eliot ✦ Sir Henry Bessemer ✦ William
Cowper ✦ Graham Greene ✦ Sir Michael Hordern ✦ Esther Rantzen

Berkhamsted

It was at BERKHAMSTED CASTLE, in December 1066, that William the Conqueror took the final surrender of the Saxons and was declared King of England. Only fragments of the castle remain, but there are impressive earthworks running along behind the main street

Letchworth

LETCHWORTH was founded in 1903 as THE WORLD'S FIRST GARDEN CITY, and is based on the vision of social reformer EBENEZER HOWARD, who wanted to relieve the crowded slums of London. The aim, supported by prominent Quakers and the Arts and Crafts movement, was to provide clean industries, low-rent housing and good services, in a healthy country environment. The town was divided up into zones, with the industrial areas kept well separated from the residential zones, and the town was ringed by an area of agricultural land, an early example of what would become known as 'green belt'. Welwyn Garden City followed shortly afterwards, and the Australian capital Canberra was designed on the same principles in 1913.

Stevenage

STEVENAGE was ENGLAND'S FIRST NEW TOWN, designated as such in 1946, and the pedestrianised town

centre, which opened in 1959, was ENGLAND'S FIRST PURPOSE-BUILT, TRAFFIC-FREE SHOPPING ZONE.

Well laid out and spacious, New Stevenage completely subsumes the village of OLD STEVENAGE from which it evolved. Old Stevenage, which dates from Norman days, grew up beside the Great North Road at its highest point between London and York. The village somehow retains much of the flavour of its 17th- and 18th-century heritage, with pleasant inns and narrow streets. The author E.M. FORSTER lived in Old Stevenage, next door to St Nicholas's Church, in a house called ROOKSNEST, which he

used as the model for the house in his novel *Howard's End*, which was made into a film in 1992.

Racing driver LEWIS HAMILTON, who in 2007 missed out, by one point, on becoming the first rookie driver ever to win the Formula One World Championship, was born in Stevenage in 1985.

Brocket Hall

B ROCKET HALL, near Hatfield, was built in 1760 by JAMES PAINE and stands in luscious grounds laid out by Capability Brown. There had been a house here since 1239, and the present Hall was built for SIR MATTHEW LAMB, whose son became the first LORD MELBOURNE.

There is something about Brocket Hall that seems to encourage bad behaviour, and the goings-on there have raised eyebrows and blood pressure since the Prince Regent used to

visit his mistress, the first Lord Melbourne's wife, there in the 1780s. Lord Melbourne didn't seem to mind – he got his rather apt position as Gentleman of the Bedchamber out of it, and a title. The Prince Regent's suite of rooms are still as he left them.

WILLIAM LAMB, the second Lord Melbourne, went on to become Queen Victoria's first Prime Minister. His wife was the spirited LADY CAROLINE LAMB, granddaughter of the first Earl Spencer. Lamb married her when she was only 17, and the first years of their marriage were full and happy. Caroline was beautiful, petite, a talented writer and a party girl. She introduced the waltz into England at Brocket Hall, and gained a certain notoriety when she emerged naked from a soup tureen and danced on the ballroom table, during her husband's birthday party. The same table is still used for banquets in the ballroom today.

As William's political career progressed, however, they spent more and more time apart. While he concentrated on Parliament, a frustrated Caroline embarked upon a brief and disastrous affair with the poet Lord Byron. Byron was 24 and, in Caroline's own words, 'mad, bad and dangerous to know'. He was also hugely feted, having just published *Child Harolde*, and their indiscreet relationship upset just about everybody. Byron tried to shake Caroline

off after just four months, but she was obsessed. At Brocket she gathered together all the local village maidens, dressed them in white and made them dance around a burning funeral pyre on which she had placed a bust of Lord Byron. Then she tore up his letters and cast them into the flames while reciting sad elegies. She turned her bedroom into a shrine to Byron, and her ghost can apparently still be heard in there, playing Chopin, late into the night.

Finally, Lord Melbourne sent Caroline to his family seat, Melbourne House in Derbyshire, to allow the scandal to die down, but after a while he relented and allowed her to return to Brocket.

One tragic day in 1824, Caroline rode out of the gates of Brocket Hall and had to wait as a funeral cortege passed by. On enquiring who it was, she was told it was Lord Byron, who had died abroad and was being taken home to Nottinghamshire. She had not known he was dead, and fell from her horse in shock. She never fully recovered.

Caroline and William Lamb parted in 1825, and she died in 1828 at the age of 43. Lamb still loved her deeply and was at her bedside.

On the death of Lord Melbourne, at Brocket in 1848, the Hall passed to his sister, who married another of Queen Victoria's Prime Ministers, LORD PALMERSTON. He also died at

Hemel Hempstead

Brocket Hall, in 1865, on the billiard table, in the arms of a chambermaid.

The most recent owner, the present LORD BROCKET, has lived up to the highest traditions of Brocket Hall, being jailed for fraud and appearing on a television show, *I'm a Celebrity, Get Me Out of Here!*, since when his showbiz career has taken off.

Brocket Hall is now leased as a luxurious hotel and country club. It played the part of the country headquarters of the Secret Service in the 2003 film *Johnny English*, starring Rowan Atkinson, and, rather appropriately, it was the scene of a wedding reception and bedroom frolics in the ITV series *Footballers' Wives.*

HEMEL HEMPSTEAD, England and Hertfordshire's third New Town, was the home of the BBC's *Pie in the Sky* detective series, starring Richard Griffiths as a detective and chef who also runs his own restaurant. The restaurant, called Pie in the Sky, is still there, in the attractive high street of the old town, overlooked by the slender 200 ft (61 m) spire of the Norman church of St Mary's.

Hemel Hempstead was also the home, until 1999, of pioneer papermakers JOHN DICKINSON & CO. Founder John Dickinson set up a mill at Apsley in 1809, after inventing a paper-cutting machine and developing a method of making paper in a continuous roll, such as used by daily newspapers. The coming of the

railways in the 1830s stimulated demand for a postal system, and John Dickinson's developed THE FIRST WRITING PAPER, STAMPS AND ENVELOPES to take advantage of the new 'Penny Post'. They also made THE FIRST PAPER NAPKINS IN EUROPE. Among the well-known stationery brands belonging to John Dickinson's are Croxley, Lion Brand, Basildon Bond, Three Candlesticks and Challenge.

John Dickinson's have now moved to Sawston, in Cambridgeshire, and the Apsley Mills have been redeveloped into a shopping and trading estate. Part of the mill, however, has been turned into a Museum of Paper, and there is an Apsley paper trail that explores the sites of BRITAIN'S FIRST MECHANISED PAPER FACTORY.

In December 2005 the Buncefield Oil Depot on the edge of Hemel Hempstead was the scene of the biggest ever explosion in peacetime Europe, when several of the storage tanks blew up. The explosion, which measured 2.4 on the Richter scale, was heard in France and Holland, and the resultant smoke could be seen from space.

Rye House Plot

On the New River at Hoddesdon stands the 16th-century gatehouse of the now vanished Rye House, centre of the infamous Rye House Plot of 1683.

After the Restoration in 1660, many Protestants were fearful that Charles II or his brother James, first in line to the throne, would bring back Catholicism. In 1681 an attempt was made to pass an Act in Parliament excluding the Catholic James from the succession, but it was unsuccessful.

At Rye House, owned by a prominent Protestant, Richard Rumbold, a plan was hatched to ambush and assassinate Charles and James on their way back to London from the races at Newmarket. However, the races were cancelled owing to a fire at Newmarket, and the royal party returned to London early, thwarting the conspirators. News of the plot leaked out and Charles arrested those suspected of being involved. Algernon Sydney and Lord William Russell were executed, and Lord Shaftesbury had to flee into exile. It is thought quite possible that the rumour of a plot was concocted by Charles himself as an excuse to cull his political opponents. Political 'spin', the scourge of the new millennium, is nothing new.

Cecil Rhodes
1853–1902

CECIL RHODES, empire-builder, statesman, millionaire, was born in BISHOP'S STORTFORD, where his father was the vicar. A sickly boy, he was sent to Natal in South Africa for the sake of his health. Before he was 25 he had made a fortune from the Kimberley diamond mine and founded De Beers Mining company. By 1891 he owned 90 per cent of the world's diamond mines.

His dream was to bring the whole of Africa under the British flag, and in 1890, marching north as the head of the British South Africa Company, he claimed the territory that came to be known as Rhodesia (later divided into Northern and Southern Rhodesia, now independent countries Zambia and Zimbabwe). In the same year he became Prime Minister of the Cape Colony of South Africa.

In 1896 he resigned the premiership as a result of a number of setbacks. Chief among these was his entanglement with the scheming Russian adventuress Princess Radziwill. She was busy building her own, mainly financial, empire and seduced the bachelor Rhodes for her own ends, forging his signature on letters, committing fraud and making deals in his name. She was eventually imprisoned.

Cecil Rhodes died in Cape Town in 1902. His last words were 'So little done, so much to do.' He is buried at the top of a flat mountain in Zimbabwe's Matapos national park at a place he called View of the World. It is a sacred place of the Ndebele, but they held Rhodes in such esteem that permission was given to allow his burial there, and at his funeral the Ndebele conferred Hayate, a silent tribute. Cecil Rhodes is the only European ever to be given this honour.

The bulk of his fortune was left to Oxford University to endow the Rhodes Scholarship for Americans, Germans and colonials. The requirements for Rhodes scholars are:

1. literary and scholastic attainments
2. fondness for, and success in, sports
3. truth, courage, devotion to duty, sympathy for, and protection of, the weak, kindliness, unselfishness and fellowship
4. moral force of character and instincts to lead, and to take an interest in one's fellow beings

Also 'they should esteem the performance of public duties as their highest aim'.

Perhaps the most famous Rhodes scholar is former President Bill Clinton. Rhodes' birthplace in Bishop's Stortford is now the Rhodes Museum.

Well, I never knew this
about
HERTFORDSHIRE FOLK

Nicholas Breakspear
◄ 1100–59 ►

NICHOLAS BREAKSPEAR, THE ONLY ENGLISHMAN EVER TO BECOME POPE, was born in ABBOTS LANGLEY, just north of Watford. Abandoned when his father went off to become a monk at St Albans Abbey, Breakspear went to Europe and himself rose through the ranks of the clergy, finally being elected as Pope Adrian IV in 1154.

John Eliot
◄ 1604–90 ►

The colourful east window in the little 14th-century church at WIDFORD, east of Hertford, is a tribute to JOHN ELIOT, 'Apostle to the Indians', who was born here in 1604. A Puritan, he emigrated to America in 1631 and settled in Boston. Relations between the settlers and the native Red Indians were poor, and Eliot reckoned that the way to improve things was to preach the Gospel to the Indians in their own tongue. He went out into their camps and lived amongst them, learning their words and ways, so that eventually he was able to translate the Book of Psalms into the native language. His BOOK OF PSALMS was THE FIRST BOOK EVER PRINTED IN AMERICA. Eliot then got to work on the Bible, and in 1663 his translation of the Bible into the Algonquin Indian language became THE FIRST BIBLE EVER PRINTED IN AMERICA.

Eliot spent the rest of his days establishing Indian settlements and ministering to the newly arriving slaves. He is THE FIRST MAN KNOWN TO HAVE RAISED HIS VOICE IN PROTEST AGAINST THE SLAVE TRADE.

SIR HENRY BESSEMER (1813–98) inventor of the Bessemer process, which radically lowered the cost of producing steel, was born in CHARLTON, near Hitchin.

Born in Berkhamsted

WILLIAM COWPER (1731–1800), author of *The Diverting History of John Gilpin* and collaborator with John Newton on the *Olney Hymns*.

GRAHAM GREENE (1904–91), novelist. Amongst his works are *Brighton Rock, The End of the Affair* and *The Quiet American*. He also wrote the screenplay for *The Third Man*, Carol Reed's classic *film noir*.

SIR MICHAEL HORDERN (1911–95), stage and film actor.

ESTHER RANTZEN, TV presenter, born 1940. Best known for BBC consumer programme *That's Life* and for setting up Childline.

Huntingdonshire

CROMWELL COUNTRY ✦ PRESIDENTIAL ANCESTORS
✦ A UNIQUE COMMUNITY

Little Gidding, where Charles I and T.S. Eliot found peace.

Capability Brown ✦ Catherine of Aragon ✦ Rula Lenska

Ramsey Abbey

Huntingdon is renowned as the birthplace of that most famous of Cromwells, Oliver the Lord Protector, but the Cromwells were a leading Huntingdonshire family for long before that. It began with Thomas Cromwell, Henry VIII's chief agent and advisor during the Dissolution of the Monasteries, who used his position to distribute lands and estates to his relatives in Huntingdonshire. RAMSEY ABBEY, in the north of the county, one of the richest of the English abbeys, third after St Albans and Glastonbury, he gave to his nephew Richard Williams, along with the manor of Hinchingbrooke, outside Huntingdon. This was on condition that Richard changed his name to Cromwell, which he did, and hence these estates became the property of the Cromwell family.

Only the ruins of the 15th-century gatehouse remained from the original abbey at Ramsey, and Richard's son Sir Henry Cromwell built a fine new house from the ruins over the site of the Lady Chapel. Oliver Cromwell's spendthrift uncle Oliver moved to Ramsey after he was forced to sell Hinchingbrooke in 1627, as a result of entertaining James I too lavishly, and he died there not long afterwards, a pauper. Oliver's cousin William died there too, from the plague in 1666, infected by a piece of cloth he had ordered to be sent from London to make a new coat with. Over 400 people in the area died as well. The Abbey house is now a school.

The Howlands of Fenstanton

Fenstanton, a pleasant, watery village with a curious 18th-century

Ramsey Abbey School

lock-up on the green, is the birthplace of JOHN HOWLAND, one of the Pilgrim Fathers, and buried in the parish church are his parents, Henry and Margaret, ancestors of an impressive list of US Presidents.

HUMPHREY BOGART, the Bishop of Massachusetts PHILLIPS BROOKS, who wrote the Christmas carol 'Oh Little Town of Bethlehem', the poet

American descendants of John Howland include the film actor

HENRY LONGFELLOW, and US Presidents FRANKLIN D. ROOSEVELT, GEORGE BUSH and GEORGE W. BUSH.

Not long after John sailed on the *Mayflower*, in 1620, his two brothers Henry and Arthur also emigrated to America. HENRY HOWLAND JNR'S descendants include Presidents RICHARD NIXON and GERALD FORD. ARTHUR HOWLAND'S descendants include SIR WINSTON CHURCHILL.

Nicholas Ferrar
1593–1637

L ITTLE GIDDING is nothing more than a tiny chapel hidden in woods to the west of the Great North Road, but the sense of deep peace and seclusion felt here is strangely potent, more than almost anywhere else in England. Here, in 1625, came NICHOLAS FERRAR and his family, refugees from the plague in London, and here they founded the only Church of England religious community to be created between the Dissolution of the Monasteries and the Oxford Movement Revival of the 19th century.

Nicholas Ferrar was born to a London merchant who counted amongst his friends Sir Francis Drake and Sir Walter Raleigh. Nicholas grew up to be a director of the Virginia Company, sponsor of the first American colonies, and when the company failed, he turned to the more spiritual calling that had always attracted him. He was ordained a deacon and set out to find a quiet place where he could form his own religious community. The half-derelict manor house and chapel of Little Gidding, deserted since the Black Death in the 14th century, were perfect.

The community he formed consisted of his mother and brother and their extended families, about 30 people in all. They restored the house and chapel, which was being used as a hay barn, held regular services, taught and assisted the local poor, and lived their lives to the rhythms of Cranmer's *Book of Common Prayer*.

They also wrote and bound essays and stories, and the greatest works to come out of Little Gidding were the 'Harmonies', a blending of the four Gospels in chronological order, which Ferrar composed by getting his nieces to cut out the passages as he directed, and then pasting them on to a manuscript in order. When a curious Charles I came to visit, he was so taken with the 'Harmonies' that he asked Ferrar to create one for his son, the future Charles II – the gorgeously produced book is now in the British Museum.

In the run-up to the Civil War the King came back to Little Gidding to find refuge on his way to Nottingham, even though Nicholas Ferrar had long since died and was buried in his tablet tomb outside the chapel. During the Commonwealth the chapel and the manor were ransacked by the Puritans, and the community was broken up, leaving just the chapel, with its exquisite Jacobean stalls, as a reminder of a unique and special Anglican community.

In the spring of 1936, when the hedgerows were-white with Queen Anne's Lace and mayflower, the poet T.S. ELIOT paid a visit to Little Gidding. He was so overwhelmed by the beauty and solitude he found there that he was moved to write the final part of his poetical reflections, the *Four Quartets*, which he called 'Little Gidding'.

Well, I never knew this
about
HUNTINGDONSHIRE FOLK

Capability Brown
——— 1716–83 ———

Buried in the churchyard at Fenstanton is England's greatest landscape gardener, LAUNCELOT 'CAPABILITY' BROWN. Born in Northumberland, Brown learnt his trade under William Kent, who was working on his 'new English style' at Stowe, in Buckinghamshire, and eventually married Kent's daughter.

He left Stowe to set up his own business and quickly became highly sought after. His nickname came from his habit of saying, on being shown around a new property, 'This site has great capabilities.' His aim was to 'perfect nature', with smooth undulating lawns leading the eye away from the house towards clumps of trees, hills and lakes, creating a very English view. Some accused him of vandalising the more formal gardens of

Ireland, he declined, saying, 'I have not finished England yet!'

At the end of his life he was given a lovely 17th-century manor house in Fenstanton by the Earl of Northampton, as a thank you for his work on the Earl's gardens at Castle Ashby. He became High Sheriff of Huntingdonshire and died in Fenstanton in 1783.

CATHERINE OF ARAGON, Henry VIII's first wife, was sent under house arrest to KIMBOLTON CASTLE in 1534, for refusing to recognise her divorce from the King. Already suffering from her cruel treatment, she was further weakened by the damp fenland air and died at Kimbolton in 1536. Her body was taken to Peterborough Cathedral for burial, although she is said to haunt the castle, which has been partly rebuilt and now houses a school.

previous generations, as based on the French style found at Versailles, but his 'English' designs proved very popular and he eventually laid out some 170 gardens, including those of almost all the best-known English country houses, Bowood, Petworth, Althorp, Burghley, Longleat, Stowe and Blenheim, the latter being considered his masterpiece.

When asked to go and work in

RULA LENSKA, actress, was born in ST NEOTS in 1947.

Kent

*Christ Church Gate which leads to the Mother Church
of the worldwide Anglican Community.*

◄ KENT FOLK ►

Sir John Spilman ✦ William Stevens ✦ King Stephen ✦ Augustus Pugin
✦ Kenneth Clark ✦ Richard Trevithick ✦ Mick Jagger ✦ Keith Richards

Kingdom of the Cantii

Kent is England's oldest county, first recorded by the Romans in 55 BC as the Celtic kingdom of the Cantii – the Celtic root 'canto' means edge. It was also the first of the Anglo-Saxon kingdoms.

Canterbury

CANTERBURY, the Roman city of Durovernum, has long been the very heart of English Christianity, possibly since the days of the Romans.

ST MARTIN'S CHURCH, set on a hill just outside the city walls, is THE OLDEST CHURCH IN ENGLAND IN CONTINUOUS USE. It was mentioned by the Venerable Bede, who wrote, 'There was on the east side of the city a church dedicated in honour of St Martin; built of old while the Romans were still inhabiting Britain.' It is not clear if the church was used for Christian worship by the Romans, or whether it was a pagan temple that was later converted into a church. What is not in doubt is that St Martin's was where Ethelbert of Kent, the first Saxon king to be converted to Christianity, was baptised by Augustine, first Archbishop of Canterbury, in AD 597.

In 598 Augustine founded a monastery nearby, now THE OLDEST MONASTIC SITE IN ENGLAND, and in 600 he established the KING'S SCHOOL AT CANTERBURY, THE FIRST AND OLDEST ENGLISH SCHOOL.

Work began on the cathedral at Canterbury in 1070. The crypt of this building survives more or less intact and is THE LARGEST NORMAN CRYPT IN THE WORLD. The murder of Thomas à Becket in the cathedral in 1170 attracted pilgrims to Canterbury from all over the world, making it England's pre-eminent shrine, and the wealth the visitors brought helped to finance the glorious structure we see today. The pilgrims also inspired the first great work in the English language, Geoffrey Chaucer's *Canterbury Tales*.

Since the Reformation, Canterbury Cathedral has been the Mother Church of the worldwide Anglican community, which consists of 70 million Anglicans in 160 different countries. The head of the Anglican Church is the Archbishop of Canterbury, who is also Primate of All England.

EDWARD THE BLACK PRINCE, eldest son of Edward III and father of Richard II, is buried in Canterbury Cathedral. He died one year before his father and was thus the first English Prince of Wales not to become king.

Also buried in the cathedral are Henry IV and his Queen, Joan of Navarre. Henry, the only monarch to be buried at Canterbury, wished to lie near to the shrine of Thomas à Becket.

Maidstone

MAIDSTONE, the administrative centre of Kent, lies in the middle of the county on the River

Medway, which runs from north to south and divides Kent into east and west. From east of the Medway come the 'Men of Kent', while west of the river they are 'Kentish Men'.

Born in Maidstone was the political journalist and philosopher WILLIAM HAZLITT (1778–1830), who has been described as the first English art critic, the first English theatre critic and the greatest English expert on the writings of William Shakespeare.

Anthony Woodville

In the middle of the 15th century, Anthony Woodville, Earl Rivers, lived at Mote Park in Maidstone, now a cricket ground. Brother-in-law to

---

Sayings of William Hazlitt

A hair in the head is worth two in the brush.

I like a friend the better for having faults one can talk about.

The love of liberty is the love of others, the love of power is the love of ourselves.

The most learned are often the most narrow-minded.

Edward IV, Woodville was made guardian to Prince Edward, the Prince of Wales, and when King Edward IV died in 1483, Woodville accompanied the new King Edward V from Ludlow, where they had been living, to London for his coronation. On the way they were ambushed by men sent from Edward's uncle, the Duke of Gloucester. Woodville was beheaded, and Edward was taken off to the Tower of London, where he was joined by his brother Richard. Neither of them was ever seen again, and the Duke of Gloucester ascended the throne as Richard III.

Anthony Woodville's translation from the French of *The Sayings of the Philosophers*, printed by William Caxton in 1476, was THE FIRST BOOK EVER PRINTED IN ENGLAND.

DR BEECHING (1913–85), Chairman of British Rail and architect of the infamous railway closures known as the Beeching Axe, was born in Maidstone.

Percy Pilcher
1867–99

It could so easily have been the quiet village of EYNSFORD, in the Darent valley of Kent, that achieved immortality by hosting man's first powered flight, rather than Kitty Hawk in North Carolina.

The River Darent cuts through the North Downs, and the hills around Eynsford are perfect for gliding. In 1896, in a big shed by the road to Upper Austin Lodge (now a golf course), aviation pioneer PERCY PILCHER built a glider constructed mainly from bamboo and weighing less than 50 pounds (23 kg), which he called the Hawk. He spent many hours gliding the Hawk off a hilltop named the Knob, experimenting with and refining techniques for flying through the air. Unaided he could glide for 100 yards, and with the aid of a pulley he could soar for over a quarter of a mile (0.4 km).

The next step was to build a plane with an engine and so achieve powered flight. For this Percy designed a four horsepower engine and a propellor, but the real problem was to create a new wing that could provide enough lift for the combined weight of engine, pilot and plane. Increasing the wing area also increased the weight, requiring more lift and hence a bigger wing, and so on. A friend of Percy's, Octave Chanute, was making some progress with two small, light wings stacked one on top of the other, making a biplane, but Percy went one better and came up with a triplane, with three sets of wings.

On paper, the triplane worked perfectly. Now all Percy needed was finance, so in 1899 he took the Hawk to a show at Stanford Hall in Leicestershire, to give a gliding demonstration in the hope of attracting sponsorship. It was raining heavily, but Percy did not want to disappoint the crowd, so he went ahead with the flight despite the conditions. He reached a height of 30 ft (9 m), but then the tail collapsed, the ropes perhaps affected by the wet, and he plummeted to the ground, dying from his injuries two days later.

In 2003 an aviation historian called Phillip Jarrett tracked down the designs of Percy Pilcher's triplane and had a replica constructed. Remarkably, it achieved a controlled flight of one minute and 26 seconds – considerably longer than the

Wright brothers managed on their celebrated first flight in 1903. This seems to suggest that, had it not been for the rain, Percy Pilcher might have become the first man to achieve powered flight – and Eynsford might now be in the history books instead of Kitty Hawk.

Ale

THE OLDEST BREWERY IN ENGLAND is the SHEPHERD'S NEAME BREWERY in FAVERSHAM, which opened in 1698. Faversham already had a tradition of brewing going back to the 12th century when King Stephen founded a Benedictine abbey in the town – monasteries, as places of hospitality for pilgrims and travellers, were great brewers and the pure spring water of Faversham combined with the local barley crop produced exceptional ale.

Ale, being the product of malted grains, is the liquid equivalent of bread and has been the staple diet of the English since Roman days. In the days when water was quite likely to be polluted, and food was scarce, ale was a cheap and satisfying source of nutrition.

In the 15th century hops were added to ale to make beer, after the Flemish and Dutch custom, and hops have since become a traditional Kent

crop and a familiar sight, along with oast houses and their distinctive conical roofs, which were built to house the oasts or kilns for drying the hops.

The term 'warm beer' refers to the fact that traditional English beers are served at room temperature, unlike the Continental 'lager' beers, which are served chilled.

Cockles and Winkles

THE WORLD S FIRST REGULAR STEAM PASSENGER RAILWAY, which opened on 3 May 1830, ran from Canterbury to Whitstable and was known as THE COCKLE AND WINKLE LINE. Its purpose was to connect Canterbury to the coast, because the original outlet, the River Stour, had silted up.

A significant innovation on the Cockle and Winkle Line was THE FIRST TUNNEL EVER BUILT FOR A PASSENGER RAILWAY. There was no need for a tunnel, but the members of the Canterbury Committee responsible for the railway were not about to spend all that money and not have a tunnel to show for it. Civic pride demanded it. 'What, no tunnel?' the Chairman had expostulated when shown the original plans. 'We must have a tunnel!'

And so George Stephenson was summoned, the railway was diverted, and an 800-yard tunnel was driven under Tyler's Hill. At the Whitstable end the tunnel had to be very narrow, and this restricted the width of the carriages that could be used, which proved a major obstacle to the further development of the line in later years.

The Cockle and Winkle line was closed for passengers in 1930 and for freight in 1952. The tunnel entrances can still be seen by walking along the route of the disused railway.

Well, I never knew this
about
KENT FOLK

Sir John Spilman
◄ c. 1535 1626 ►

SIR JOHN SPILMAN started THE FIRST COMMERCIALLY SUCCESSFUL PAPER MILL IN ENGLAND, at Dartford in 1586. He somehow managed to secure a monopoly for the production of highly sought-after, good-quality white paper, while other paper mills were allowed to make only cheap brown paper, and so completely did Spilman capture the market that white paper only became widely available after his death in 1626.

Sir John Spilman, who is buried in Dartford's Holy Trinity Church, is also thought to have been responsible for introducing the lime tree to England.

A poet called Thomas Churchyard wrote a long-winded poem about Spilman's mill, the first description of paper-making ever to appear in print.

There it is stamped and washed as
    white as snow
Then flung on frame and hanged to
    dry, I trow
Thus paper straight it is to write
    upon
As it were rubbed and smoothed with
    slicking stone

William Stevens
◄ 1732–1807 ►

Nobody is buried in the churchyard at OTHAM, just outside Maidstone. Nobody is, in fact, WILLIAM STEVENS, a writer and philanthropist who made a fortune from the hosiery trade, never married and gave away most of his money to charities. He took the pen-name 'Nobody', saying of himself, 'as a member of society he is nobody, neither father, husband, uncle or brother'.

In 1800 he founded a charitable dining club called The Society of Nobody's Friends, with 50 members, half churchmen, half laymen, who met three times a year. The club still exists and includes distinguished peers, judges, bishops and writers who get together, without publicity, to discuss the topics of the day and toast the Immortal Health of Nobody. When a member dies, a new one is elected to keep the membership at 50, and the new member must make a speech at his first dinner. The membership is kept secret, but you must be a Somebody to be Nobody's friend.

KING STEPHEN and his wife MATILDA were buried in Faversham Abbey, but when their tomb in the abbey church was excavated in 1964 there were no remains to be found. It is thought that the bones were thrown into Faversham Creek at the Dissolution of the Monasteries.

AUGUSTUS PUGIN (1812–52), the architect, who designed the interior of the Houses of Parliament, and the clock faces of 'Big Ben', is buried in St Augustine's Church in RAMSGATE. Next door is The Grange, a house he designed and built himself, now owned by the national Trust.

KENNETH CLARK, Baron Clark of Saltwood (1903–83), historian and presenter of the BBC television series *Civilisation*, is buried in the churchyard at Saltwood, beside his home SALTWOOD CASTLE. This had been the childhood home of journalist BILL DEEDES (1913–2007), the only Englishman ever to be both a Cabinet Minister and the editor of a major newspaper (the *Daily Telegraph*), and the recipient of Denis Thatcher's fictional 'Dear Bill' letters. Saltwood Castle is where the four knights who murdered Thomas à Becket, in Canterbury Cathedral in 1170, met to plot their evil deed.

RICHARD TREVITHICK, one of the greatest inventors of all time and builder of the world's first railway steam engine (*see* Cornwall), is buried in Dartford, in an unmarked pauper's grave.

Two Rolling Stones, MICK JAGGER and KEITH RICHARDS, were both born in Dartford in 1943.

Lancashire

◆◆◆

House of Lancaster ✦ Scousers ✦ Mersey Beat
✦ Liver Building ✦ Two Cathedrals
✦ Gladstone and Hitler ✦ Hotpot
✦ Greatest Steeplechase

The Beatles, the most iconic English band in history.

◀ LANCASHIRE FOLK ▶

John Ruskin ✦ Donald Campbell ✦ Arthur Ransome ✦ Richard Tattersall
✦ Sir John Barrow ✦ Sir Richard Owen ✦ Sir Henry Tate ✦ Eric Sykes
✦ Bernard Cribbins ✦ Warren Clarke ✦ Louise Brown ✦ Richmal
Crompton ✦ John Kay ✦ Sir Robert Peel

House of Lancaster

THE HOUSE OF LANCASTER descends from Edward III's oldest surviving son John of Gaunt (his name comes from his birthplace, the Dutch city of Ghent). Monarchs of the House of Lancaster were John of Gaunt's son Henry Bolingbroke who, as Henry IV, was the first King of England to have English as his mother tongue, his son Henry V and Henry VI. The emblem of the House of Lancaster was a red rose.

John of Gaunt's younger brother was Edmund of Langley, the first Duke of York, whose emblem was a white rose, and it was descendants of these two brothers who fought for supremacy during the Wars of the Roses. The war was brought to an end when the Lancastrian Henry VII defeated the Yorkist Richard III at Bosworth Field in 1485. Henry then married Elizabeth of York, daughter of Edward IV, and joined the red and white roses to make the Tudor Rose.

The House of Lancaster survives as the Duchy of Lancaster, a personal property of the reigning monarch.

The office of the Chancellor of the Duchy of Lancaster is a useful tool by which the Prime Minister can bestow Cabinet rank on a Minister he wants in the Cabinet, but who has no specific portfolio.

The rivalry between Yorkshire and Lancashire continues today, although on a (slightly) less violent basis. The Wars of the Roses are still fought every year at the WORLD BLACK PUDDING THROWING CHAMPIONSHIPS held in Manchester, when Lancashire folk hurl black puddings at a stack of Yorkshire puddings to see who can dislodge the most. The shoot-out is apparently based on an occasion during the conflict when both sides ran out of ammunition and began pelting each other with food. Black pudding is made from cooked pig's blood, pork fat, oatmeal and onions.

Liverpool

WHEN the River Dee silted up and cut Chester off from the sea, LIVERPOOL grew from a small fishing village into one of the busiest ports of the world. At the end of the 19th century, over 40 per cent of the world's trade was carried on Liverpool-registered ships, and even today, after half a century of decline, Liverpool is still the biggest English port after London.

A magnet for immigrants, especially from Ireland during the Great Famine, Liverpool is one of the most cosmopolitan of English cities, and Liverpudlians have a character all their own. They are sometimes referred to

as 'Scousers', after a local dish, a type
of stew called 'scouse'.

Liverpool Music

Music is perhaps Liverpool's most
celebrated modern export. In
the 1960s bands like GERRY AND THE
PACEMAKERS, BILLY J. KRAMER AND
THE DAKOTAS and THE SEARCHERS
created the MERSEYBEAT SOUND,
while the Beatles changed the pop
music world for ever. THE BEATLES
learnt their trade at the self-styled
'most famous club in the world', THE
CAVERN CLUB, at No. 10 Mathew
Street. The original club closed in
1973, but has since been rebuilt on
the same site, using bricks from the
old club, and re-opened in 1984.

In front of the Cavern Club is the
LIVERPOOL WALL OF FAME, which
pays tribute to Liverpool acts that
have reached No. 1 in the English
charts. The wall was unveiled in 2001
by the jazz singer LITA ROZA, 80, who
was THE FIRST LIVERPUDLIAN AND
THE FIRST WOMAN TO REACH NO. 1,
with 'How Much is that Doggie in
the Window?' in 1953.

Other acts on the wall include
ATOMIC KITTEN, CILLA BLACK, DEAD
OR ALIVE, FRANKIE GOES TO HOLLY-
WOOD and MEL 'C' or 'Sporty Spice',
who holds the record FOR MOST UK
NO. 1 SINGLES AS A FEMALE CO-WRITER

(along with Madonna) and is THE
ONLY FEMALE TO REACH NO. 1 AS A
SOLO ARTIST AND AS PART OF A
QUINTET, A QUARTET AND A DUO.

Liverpool Landmarks

Liverpool can boast quite a few
English landmarks, perhaps the
most recognisable of which is the
ROYAL LIVER BUILDING on the water-
front. Completed in 1911, the Liver
Building sports THE LARGEST CLOCK
FACES IN ENGLAND. The clock was
started at the exact moment that King
George V was crowned in Westminster Abbey, 1.40 p.m. on 22 June 1911.
The twin clock towers are each topped
by a Liver Bird, one female, watching
out over the sea, and one male,
watching out over the city. The Liver
Bird, probably based on a cormorant,

Roman Catholic Cathedral

has been a symbol of Liverpool since the 14th century, and used to carry in its beak a sprig of laver, an edible seaweed found along the coast from which Liverpool takes its name.

Liverpool Cathedrals

Liverpool's two great cathedrals are outstanding. The Roman Catholic cathedral, known affectionately as the 'Wigwam', was built in the 1960s and has 2,000 TONS OF STAINED GLASS, THE LARGEST DISPLAY IN ENGLAND.

The stupendous Anglican cathedral was designed by Giles Gilbert Scott when he was 22 years old. The first stone was laid in 1904, and although Scott worked on the building until he died in 1960, he never saw its completion. With work interrupted by two world wars, it took 74 years to build, finally opening in 1978. Liverpool Cathedral is not only ENGLAND'S BIGGEST CATHEDRAL, but THE LARGEST CATHEDRAL IN THE WHOLE OF CHRISTENDOM after St Peter's in Rome. It has THE LARGEST CATHEDRAL ORGAN IN EUROPE, THE LARGEST GOTHIC ARCHES IN THE WORLD, and THE LARGEST BELL TOWER AND HEAVIEST PEAL OF BELLS ON THE PLANET. Liverpool Cathedral is breathtaking, big and beautiful, perhaps the greatest English building of the 20th century.

Just north of the cathedral is Rodney Street, a fine Georgian street, where Prime Minister WILLIAM EWART GLADSTONE was born in 1809, at No. 62.

From 1910 until 1914, Adolf Hitler's half-brother ALOIS HITLER lived near the cathedral, in Upper Stanhope Street, with his first wife Bridget. Their son William Hitler was born there in 1911. Ironically the house was destroyed by a German air raid in 1942.

Lancashire Hotpot

LANCASHIRE HOTPOT is an economical dish of meat, sometimes beef, more usually lamb, mixed with kidneys and vegetables, covered with a layer of sliced potatoes, all cooked slowly in a large pottery hotpot. It was generally prepared for the workers when they returned from the cotton mills, but occasionally taken to the mill for consumption at the workplace. Oysters were often included when inexpensive and easily obtainable.

The Grand National

THE GRAND NATIONAL, run over 4½ miles (7 km) at AINTREE, north of Liverpool, is the world's most famous steeplechase, and a highlight of the English sporting calendar. It was first run at Aintree as the Liverpool Grand Steeplechase in 1839, and the first winner, aptly enough, was a horse called Lottery.

The Aintree fences are made up of spruce from the Lake District, and include some of the most feared jumps in the world. The broadest is THE CHAIR, which is also the tallest fence, at 5ft 3ins (1.6 m). There was once a seat for the distance judge alongside, hence the name.

BECHER'S BROOK, the most dangerous fence on the course, got its name from Captain Martin Becher, a top jockey who was unseated there during the inaugural race, and had to take refuge in the brook while the rest of the field passed over – his only comment afterwards was 'Water tastes disgusting without the benefit of whisky.' The phrase 'a Becher's Brook' has become a metaphor for a daunting challenge.

All at Sea

In 1904 the Grand National was won by a horse thought to have been lost at sea. In 1903 MOIFFA was being shipped to Liverpool from New Zealand when the ship on which he was travelling was wrecked in the Irish Sea, and the horse was feared drowned. The next day, a fisherman heard strange noises coming from a tiny uninhabited rock off the south coast of Ireland, and upon investigating found the exhausted Moiffa washed up on the beach – the horse had swum over 50 miles (80 km) to safety. Moiffa was reunited with his trainer and went on to Grand National glory the following year.

Unluckiest Loser

In 1956 the Queen Mother's horse DEVON LOCH, ridden by Dick Francis, was way out in the lead and just 50 yards from the finish when he suddenly leaped an invisible fence and collapsed, with his four legs splayed out and the jockey still seated on his back. Although Devon Loch got up and completed the race, he was overtaken and beaten by ESB. No one knows why Devon Loch collapsed, but his jockey Dick Francis was so mystified that he

Grand National Facts

The largest number of finishers was 23 in 1984, and the smallest number just two in 1928.

The youngest jockey ever to win the Grand National was 17-year-old Bruce Hobbs in 1938, on the smallest horse ever to win, Battleship; the oldest was 48-year-old Dick Saunders, on Grittar in 1982.

The most successful horse in Grand National history is RED RUM, the only horse to win three times, in 1973, 1974 and 1977.

Red Rum

The most successful jockey is George Stevens, with five wins in the 1860s and 70s.

The only horse to win the Grand National and the Cheltenham Gold Cup in the same year was GOLDEN MILLER in 1934.

retired to write his own bestselling mystery thrillers about horse racing – had he won the Grand National that day there would probably have been no Dick Francis novels.

Champion

Nineteen eighty-one saw the most courageous and unlikely Grand

National triumph of all when BOB CHAMPION, who had been diagnosed with terminal cancer only two years earlier, rode ALDANITI, who had almost had to retire with a leg injury, to victory. Second was Spartan Missile, ridden by 54-year-old grandfather and amateur jockey John Thorne. The story inspired a film, *Champions*, starring John Hurt, in 1983.

Aintree was once also a motor racing circuit, host to one European and five British Grands Prix. It was at Aintree that STIRLING MOSS won his first Grand Prix, in 1955.

Well, I never knew this
about
LANCASHIRE FOLK

John Ruskin
◄ 1819–1900 ►

'Remember, the most beautiful things in the world are the most useless: peacocks and lilies, for instance' – John Ruskin

JOHN RUSKIN was a prominent art critic and social philosopher whose essays and writings had a huge influence on the thinking and institutions of the 19th century. He was born in London, the son of a rich wine importer, founder of the company that became Allied Domecq, and hence had the time and money to spend on his personal crusades. His last 30 years were spent at BRANTWOOD HOUSE beside Coniston Water, in the Furness district of Lancashire.

His three great passions were the paintings of Turner, Decorated Gothic architecture and the Pre-Raphaelites, the latter until his wife Effie annulled their unconsummated marriage so that she could run off and marry the pre-Raphaelite artist Sir John Millais.

While a Professor at Oxford, Ruskin became great friends with Hardwicke Rawnsley, and in 1875 he introduced Rawnsley to another of his friends, the social reformer Octavia Hill. Rawnsley and Hill, encouraged by Ruskin, formed the National Trust in 1896.

Ruskin's writings about society, in which he argued that labourers should be seen as men, who needed enjoyment in their work, rather than soulless tools, were admired by reformers such as William Morris, the author Leo Tolstoy and Mahatma Gandhi. He put forward radical proposals on such diverse issues as a National Health Service, a minimum wage, old age pensions, public libraries and art galleries, and global warming, and early members of the Labour party claimed that John Ruskin was their greatest influence.

Ruskin is buried in the churchyard of St Andrew's in Coniston, and Brantwood is now kept as a museum in his memory.

Donald Campbell
◄── 1921–67 ──►

In 2007 an extension was added to the Ruskin Museum to house the remains of Donald Campbell's BLUEBIRD, the boat in which he died while trying to break his own world water speed record on Coniston Water in 1967.

Son of the world record holder Sir Malcolm Campbell, DONALD CAMPBELL set seven world water speed records between 1955 and 1964, when he reached 276 mph (445 kph) on Lake Dumbleyung in Perth, Australia. In that same year he had already set the land speed record of 403 mph (649 kph) at Lake Eyre, in Australia, becoming THE ONLY PERSON EVER TO HOLD BOTH THE WATER AND LAND SPEED RECORDS AT THE SAME TIME.

In 1967 on Coniston Water, where his father had set a world record of 141 mph (228 kph) in 1939, Donald attempted to be the first person to go over 300 mph (483 kph) on water, and had achieved 297 mph (478 kph) on his first run when, on his second run, at 303 mph (487.5 kph), his boat flipped over and broke up.

The wreck of *Bluebird* was recovered in March 2001 and in May that year Donald Campbell's body was found. He was given a funeral in September 2001 and finally laid to rest in St Andrew's churchyard in Coniston, not far from John Ruskin.

ARTHUR RANSOME (1884–1967), author of the *Swallows and Amazons* children's books, is buried in the churchyard at RUSLAND. Ransome settled in the Lake District in 1929 and set his stories around Coniston Water and Lake Windermere. His second wife Evgenia, who is buried beside him, was Leon Trotsky's secretary. They met when Ransome was covering the Russian Revolution in 1917 as a journalist.

Born in Lancashire

RICHARD TATTERSALL (1724–95), founder of Europe's leading racehorse auction house, was born in HURTSWOOD, near Burnley.

SIR JOHN BARROW (1764–1848), travel author, First Sea Lord during the Napoleonic Wars and founder of the Royal Geographical Society in 1830, was born in ULVERSTON.

SIR RICHARD OWEN (1804–92), naturalist, known as the 'father of modern palaeontology', was born in LANCASTER. Founded the Natural History Museum and invented the word 'dinosaur' – from the Greek 'deinos' (monstrous) and 'sauros' (lizard).

SIR HENRY TATE (1819–99), sugar merchant and founder of the Tate Gallery, was born in CHORLEY.

Actors ERIC SYKES (1923–2012), BERNARD CRIBBINS (1928) and WARREN CLARKE (1947–2014) were all born in OLDHAM, as was LOUISE BROWN, THE WORLD'S FIRST TEST-TUBE BABY in 1978.

Born in Bury

RICHMAL CROMPTON (1890–1969), author of the *Just William* stories.

JOHN KAY (1704–80), inventor of the 'flying shuttle', which began the mechanisation of the weaving process.

SIR ROBERT PEEL (1788–1850) who, as Home Secretary, oversaw the formation of THE WORLD'S FIRST ORGANISED POLICE FORCE, the Metropolitan Police Force – known as 'Peelers' or 'Bobbies'.

Leicestershire

❖❖❖

Unspeakable ✦ An English Sport ✦ Red Cheese

The Fox – part of England's heritage.

◄ **LEICESTERSHIRE FOLK** ►

Robert Bakewell ✦ Jenny Pitman ✦ C.P. Snow ✦ Joc Orton ✦ Graham
Chapman ✦ Stephen Frears ✦ Sue Townsend ✦ Gary Lineker

Hunting

'The Unspeakable in Pursuit of the Uneatable'

OSCAR WILDE

Leicestershire is hunting country, home to some of the most famous English hunts, including the QUORN and the BELVOIR, both based around Melton Mowbray. Fox-hunting originated in England in the 14th century, when Edward I was known to own a pack of hounds, although the earliest recorded mention of a fox-hunt comes from 1534, when a Norfolk farmer attempted to chase a fox with his hounds as a means of pest control.

Fox-hunting really began to develop in the late 17th century, when

it became necessary to control the growing fox population in order to protect sheep and poultry farms, and in 1660 the first formal hunt was established at Blisdale, in Yorkshire.

In the 19th century, the leisured aristocracy and gentry took up fox-hunting as a country pastime. Jumping fences, which had been erected as a result of various enclosure acts, became an essential part of the sport. Chasing across difficult country is highly skilled and is the origin of the sports of steeple-chasing, point-to-point racing and National Hunt racing.

Various ceremonial elements were introduced in the 18th and 19th centuries. At the meet, before the hunt moved off, a 'stirrup cup' of port or sherry was offered, as given by Scottish Highlanders to their departing guests.

After a successful hunt new members were 'blooded' by having the blood of the fox smeared across their faces.

The most important member of the hunt is the Master of Foxhounds or MFH, who runs the hunt, organises the finances and has the last say over all matters while out in the field. The Huntsman is responsible for directing the hounds during the hunt and blows the horn to communicate with the hounds, the hunt followers, and the 'whippers-in', whose job is to keep the pack together and prevent hounds from straying. The role of the hunting 'whippers-in' is the origin of the 'Whips', who are responsible for discipline in political parties. The professional hunt members wear scarlet coats so that they can be easily seen during the hunt, while the hunt followers traditionally wear black.

The Quorn is the second oldest English hunt and was formed in 1696 by Thomas Boothby of Tooley Park. It takes its name from the village of Quorn, where the hounds were kennelled from 1753 until 1904. The hunt is now based at Kirby Bellars, near Melton Mowbray.

The Belvoir was founded in 1750 and is based at Belvoir Castle, home of the Dukes of Rutland. The hounds are kennelled nearby at Woolsthorpe-by-Belvoir.

Hunting with hounds was banned in 2005.

Red Leicester

RED LEICESTER cheese is a mellow, slightly flaky, russet-coloured cheese that gets its rich colour from the inclusion of Annatto,

Belvoir Castle

a natural dye extracted from a South American bush. It is traditionally made in a large cartwheel shape.

Red Leicester cheese was first made on Sparkenhoe Farm at Upton, near Hinckley, in 1745 by George Chapman. The Chapmans stopped making it in 1875 as there was no money to be made from cheese at that time, and in 1956 Red Leicester actually made in Leicestershire ceased production, the last being produced by dairy farmer Mr Shepherd, of Bagworth. However, in 2005 the Leicestershire Handmade Cheese Company began making genuine Red Leicester at Sparkenhoe Farm once again.

Well, I never knew this
about
LEICESTERSHIRE FOLK

Robert Bakewell
◄—— 1725–95 ——►

ROBERT BAKEWELL was born into a farming family at DISHLEY, near Loughborough, and grew up during the Industrial Revolution, when workers began moving off the land into the new towns. People were no longer able to grow their own food and the inefficient smallholdings left behind were unable to supply the growing demand for milk and meat. Bakewell travelled around Europe studying other farming methods and returned to Dishley to put into practice what he had learnt.

Until then, sheep had been bred mainly for wool and cattle mainly for leather, and the animals were thin and under-nourished. Bakewell intro-duced irrigation, and set aside some of his land for growing grass and crops to feed his animals during the winter months, so they could fatten up to provide good meat. He also improved the condition of his cattle by building winter stalls that were raised above ditches, so that manure fell into them and could be gathered for fertiliser, and the cattle did not have to lie down in their own waste.

He also began to separate male and female animals, allowing them to breed only at certain times and putting together those with the most desirable characteristics. The resulting sheep were known as New Leicesters, and they were big, with good-quality fleece and plenty of fatty mutton, which was popular at that time.

Bakewell noticed that Longhorn

cattle seemed to eat less but put on more meat than other breeds, so he inbred them to enhance these qualities. Soon he began to hire out his prize rams and bulls to other farmers and quickly became a wealthy man.

For a while, Robert Bakewell's farm was the most famous farm in the world. He was visited by farmers and producers from all over the world who wanted to learn his breeding techniques. His methods enabled a small number of efficient farms to provide enough food for the populous towns, and the same methods are still practised everywhere by farmers today.

Leicester City football club are known as the Foxes, because – in addition to the county's fox-hunting associations – on the map the county of Leicestershire resembles, appropriately enough, a fox's head.

JENNY PITMAN, first woman to train a Grand National winner (Corbiere, 1983), was born in HOBY, near Melton Mowbray, in 1946.

Born in Leicester

C.P. SNOW (1905–80), physicist and novelist, who coined the phrase 'corridors of power'.

JOE ORTON (1933–67), playwright, whose black comedies included *Entertaining Mr Sloane, Loot* and *What the Butler Saw.*

GRAHAM CHAPMAN (1941–89), Monty Python actor and writer.

STEPHEN FREARS, film director (*My Beautiful Launderette*, 1985, *The Queen*, 2006), born 1941. In 1987 directed *Prick Up Your Ears* about fellow Leicesterarian Joe Orton.

SUE TOWNSEND (1946–2014), author. Her *Adrian Mole* series was set in Leicester.

GARY LINEKER, England footballer, born 1960. Never sent off throughout his career, which began at Leicester City. Now TV presenter.

Pop group SHOWADDYWADDY were formed in Leicester in 1973. In 1976 they reached No. 1 with 'Under the Moon of Love'.

Lincolnshire

Lincoln's High Bridge, England's oldest bridge with houses.

◀ LINCOLNSHIRE FOLK ▶

John and Charles Wesley ✦ John Foxe ✦ Captain John Smith ✦ Frances
Brooke ✦ Herbert Ingram ✦ George Boole ✦ Joan Plowright
✦ Tony Jacklin

Lincoln Cathedral

*'the most precious piece of
architecture in England . . .'*

John Ruskin

Few sights in England can take the breath away like the first glimpse of Lincoln Cathedral, its honey-coloured towers and long nave crowning the hilltop 200 ft (61 m) above the River Witham. The stupendous central tower, 271 ft (83 m) high, is THE HIGHEST CATHEDRAL TOWER IN EUROPE. How even more spectacular it must have looked when topped with THE HIGHEST SPIRE IN THE WORLD, 525 ft (160 m) tall, making Lincoln THE FIRST STRUCTURE EVER TO BE BUILT HIGHER THAN THE GREAT PYRAMID. For over 200 years, from when the spire was constructed at the end of the 13th

Lincoln Cathedral West Front

century until it blew down in 1548, Lincoln Cathedral remained THE WORLD'S TALLEST BUILDING.

The first cathedral at Lincoln was begun by Remigius, England's first Norman bishop, on the orders of William the Conqueror in 1072. Remigius moved his see to Lincoln from Dorchester in Oxfordshire and it grew to be the largest diocese in medieval England, with more monasteries than the rest of England put together. All but a portion of the great west front of Remigius's cathedral was destroyed by an earthquake in 1185, and the new Bishop of Lincoln, Hugh of Avalon, began work on the magnificent Early English cathedral we see today. Bishop Hugh was one of the witnesses at the signing of Magna Carta in 1215, and the finest of the four surviving original copies belongs to Lincoln Cathedral and is kept in the castle.

The Angel Choir at Lincoln, so called from the many angel carvings around the arches, is considered to be the pinnacle of English Gothic architecture. It was created as a fitting shrine for Bishop Hugh, and became a place of pilgrimage almost equal to that of Thomas à Becket at Canterbury. High up on a pillar squats the scampish 'LINCOLN IMP', fashioned as a bit of fun by a medieval sculptor, and now a symbol of the city.

Lincoln is the second largest medieval English cathedral after York Minster. The 13th-century Chapter House, THE EARLIEST POLYGONAL CHAPTER HOUSE IN ENGLAND, contains a wooden chair where

Edward I sat when he held a Parliament here in 1301. In 2005 the Chapter House stood in for the one at Westminster Abbey during the filming of the controversial The *Da Vinci Code*, as the authorities of the Abbey would not allow filming there.

Lincoln City

Lincoln was originally the Roman settlement of Lindum Colonia and retains two remarkable features from its Roman days. One is the NEWPORT ARCH, near the cathedral, THE OLDEST COMPLETE ARCH IN ENGLAND and THE ONLY ROMAN GATEWAY IN ENGLAND STILL IN USE BY TRAFFIC. The other is the FOSSDYKE NAVIGATION, built in the 3rd century to link the River Witham to the Trent, 11 miles (18 km) long and ENGLAND'S OLDEST CANAL.

After the Romans left, Lincoln became part of the Saxon province of Mercia and a small stone church was built within the Roman walls – the source of Lincoln's claim to being England's oldest recorded Saxon town. It then became an important town under the Danelaw, and in Norman times was the third largest city in England. Lincoln's wealth came from wool and Lincoln cloth, especially the dyed 'Lincoln green', as worn by Robin Hood and his band of merry men.

Jew's House

Running down from the cathedral is Steep Hill, on which can be found the 12th-century Norman House, one of the oldest English domestic buildings still in use, and the equally ancient Jew's House, dating from the days when Lincoln was home to one of the most important Jewish communities in England.

Carrying the High Street across the River Witham is ENGLAND'S OLDEST BRIDGE WITH HOUSES ON IT, known as the HIGH BRIDGE or Glory Hole. The bridge was built in 1160 and the houses were added in 1540.

THE WORLD'S FIRST TANK was designed and developed in Lincoln, by William Foster & Co. Ltd. It first saw action at the Battle of Flers, in France in 1916. Tanks were developed in great secrecy under the auspices of the Navy Department, and experiments were carried out using huge empty water tanks normally associated with ship design, hence the project was codenamed 'tank' – and the name stuck.

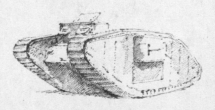

Gilbert of Sempringham

SEMPRINGHAM, north of Bourne, was once a famous place, for here stood a mighty priory, first home of THE ONLY PURELY ENGLISH MONASTIC ORDER, THE GILBERTINE ORDER.

Their founder, Gilbert, was born in Sempringham in 1083, the son of a Norman knight. Unable to become a soldier because of a deformity, instead he became a priest, built a priory at his birthplace, and there founded the Gilbertine Order. It was a 'double order', open to both monks and nuns, and had two of everything so that the sexes could live separately within the same monastery – two dining-rooms, two dormitories and two cloisters.

The Gilbertine Order spread across England, inspired by the piety and saintliness of its founder Gilbert. He lived to be over 100, and by the time of his death there were 11 Gilbertine houses boasting 700 brothers and 1500 sisters. He was buried beneath the altar of his church, and his grave became a place of pilgrimage, visited even by 'bad' King John. Gilbert was canonised in 1202.

Of the priory of Sempringham, once the size of a cathedral, there is nothing left. It was pulled down at the Dissolution of the Monasteries

and now only the solitary Norman church of St Andrew's, to which the priory was attached, remains, perched on a hillock amongst the potato fields, at the end of a cart track.

A Princess of Wales

IN 1283 an infant child was brought to Sempringham, to be hidden away there for the rest of her life, lest she grew up to inspire rebellion against the might of the Plantagenet Kings of England. She was GWENLLIAN, daughter and heir of the last ruling Prince of Wales, Llywelyn ap Gruffudd. Llywelyn was killed in a skirmish with Edward I's men at Cilmery on the Welsh border in December 1282, and Edward wanted to ensure that Llywelyn's line would die with Gwenllian. Gwenllian was not just heir to the Welsh principality. Her maternal grandmother was Henry III's sister Eleanor, giving Gwenllian a distant claim to the English throne, and Edward was taking no chances. Thus Gwenllian was committed to the care of the nuns of Sempringham, and here she died quietly in 1337 at the age of 54. She still lies beneath the soil at Sempringham, no one knows exactly where, and the Princess Gwenllian Society have erected a memorial on the site, marking the lonely burial place of THE LAST WELSH-BORN PRINCESS OF WALES.

St Andrew's Church

Well, I never knew this
about
LINCOLNSHIRE FOLK

John and Charles Wesley

Set upon a low hill, with views across the rich farmland of North Lincolnshire, is the small, isolated market town of EPWORTH where, in 1696, Samuel and Susannah Wesley moved into the small thatch and plaster rectory where they would live for the next 38 years.

On 17 June 1703, their 15th child, John, was born in the Rectory. Four years later their last child Charles was born on 18 December 1707. Two boys

John Wesley

whose influence would spread across the world, through preaching and music. But one of them almost didn't survive.

One night in 1709, one of the children awoke to find her bed on fire, and great beams of burning wood falling from the ceiling. She roused the household and Samuel managed to shepherd the children, his sick wife and their nurse out into the garden, from where they watched the conflagration. Suddenly, to their horror, a tiny figure appeared at the bedroom window, silhouetted against the flames, waving and crying pitifully. In the confusion, five-year-old John had been left behind. The stairs were ablaze, the wooden building was all but consumed by fire and there seemed no hope when, all at once, two burly young men broke from the crowd of

onlookers and ran towards the house. One of them climbed on the shoulders of the other, reached up and pulled the terrified infant through the window like, as John himself later put it, 'a brand plucked from the burning'.

And so JOHN WESLEY, founder of the worldwide Methodist church, was rescued from the fire, an event that would come to serve for Methodists everywhere as a powerful illustration of salvation from the flames of Hell.

Within months the Rectory was rebuilt into the fine Georgian house we see there today, which is now a museum in the Wesley's memory.

When John and Charles went to study at Oxford they formed the Oxford Holy Club, in 1729, where they and others would worship together and organise visits to the sick and those in prison. They ordered their lives and studies in such a regular and methodical fashion that the other students began to refer to them as those 'Methodists'. The Holy Club was Charles's idea, so he is considered to be the first Methodist, while John, the older brother, became the first leader of the Methodists.

In 1735 they both travelled as missionaries to the new colony of Georgia in America, an experience that opened their eyes to the harsher side of life, disease, squalor and poverty, and on their return to England they began to travel round the country preaching against unfairness, slavery and poor

Epworth Rectory

working conditions. Thousands would come and listen to them talk and thousands more would sing the hymns that Charles wrote – he composed over 6,000 hymns during his life. The evangelical revival inspired by the Wesleys helped to subdue in England the seeds of revolution that were beginning to tear apart many countries on the Continent.

Charles died in 1788 and is buried in the churchyard of the parish church at Marylebone. John, more dedicated to Methodism, is buried in the chapel he built just outside the City of London, which is now the mother church of the Methodist faith.

John Wesley's cry was 'The world is my parish!' and today there are some 70 million Methodists worldwide –

the legacy of the boy snatched from the flames of a burning Lincolnshire rectory is great indeed.

The list of prominent Methodists includes five American Presidents to date, James Polk, Ulysses S. Grant, Rutherford Hayes, William McKinley and George W. Bush, as well as Vice-President Dick Cheney, Hillary Rodham Clinton, Bishop Muzorewa, former President of Zimbabwe and Chiang Kai-Shek, former President of Taiwan.

Born in Lincolnshire

JOHN FOXE (1517–87), author of *The Book of Martyrs*, an account of the persecution of English Protestants, was born in BOSTON.

CAPTAIN JOHN SMITH (1580–1631), founder of Jamestown, first permanent English settlement in America, first 'Governor' of Virginia, who coined the name 'New England', was born in WILLOUGHBY, near Alford.

FRANCES BROOKE (1724–89), author of the first novel in Canadian literature, *The History of Emily Montague*, was born in SLEAFORD.

HERBERT INGRAM (1811–60), founder of the first pictorial journal, the *Illustrated London News*, first published in 1842, was born in BOSTON.

GEORGE BOOLE (1815–64), philosopher and mathematician who invented Boolean algebra, upon which modern computer calculations are based, was born in LINCOLN.

JOAN PLOWRIGHT, actress and third wife of Sir Laurence Olivier, was born in BRIGG in 1929.

TONY JACKLIN, the only English golfer to be Open Champion and US Open Champion at the same time (1969–70), was born in SCUNTHORPE in 1944.

FISH FINGERS were first produced in England at GRIMSBY in 1955.

Middlesex

❖◆◆◆❖

WORLD'S OLDEST FILM STUDIOS ✦ EALING COMEDIES ✦ THE LONGITUDE PROBLEM ✦ EARLY CARTOONIST ✦ G AND T

Alexandra Palace, the birthplace of BBC television.

◄ MIDDLESEX FOLK ►

Matthew Arnold ✦ Evelyn Waugh ✦ Sir Alan Ayckbourn ✦ John Constable ✦ Arthur and Sylvia Llewelyn Davies ✦ Lord Joseph Lister ✦ Sir Charles Wyndham ✦ Francis James Barraud ✦ Marie Lloyd ✦ Nigel Balchin

Ealing Studios

EALING STUDIOS are THE OLDEST FILM STUDIOS IN THE WORLD. They were established in 1902 by Will Barker, who made silent movies there until, with the introduction of the 'talkies' in the 1920s, the studios were taken over by Associated Talking Pictures and rebuilt as the studios there today.

It was after the Second World War, in the late 1940s and early 50s, that Ealing Studios had their heyday, producing the classic 'EALING COMEDIES' for which they are famous. Since it was almost impossible to get hold of Hollywood films during the war, Ealing Studios had been forced to develop their own English brand of film-making, and the Ealing comedies built on this heritage, portraying England as a charming, rather quaint place, full of dogged characters battling to keep the country unsullied.

The films are consistently anti-authority and, rather like the novel *1984*, which George Orwell was working on at that time, feature the struggles of the little man up against a faceless bureaucracy or corporate bullying. The films are feel-good fantasies that give expression to the ordinary Englishman's dreams of rebellion, where pluck and ingenuity can win out over tyranny, rather as England herself had won out over the might of Germany.

These characteristics come to the fore in films such as *Kind Hearts and Coronets, Passport to Pimlico* and *The Lavender Hill Mob,* all of which were released in 1949 and made stars of actors such as Alec Guinness and Margaret Rutherford.

A coarser but equally funny example of this very English humour surfaced ten years later in the *Carry On* films, of which 30 were made at various locations between 1958 and 1978.

John Harrison
1693–1776

B uried in the churchyard of St
John's Church, HAMPSTEAD, is
the horologist JOHN HARRISON,
whose marine chronometer solved the
'longitude problem' – how to calculate
the distance east or west a ship had
sailed – which had baffled such lumi-
naries as Galileo, Sir Isaac Newton
and Edmond Halley.

Longitude is the angular distance
from any meridian (in this case the
Prime Meridian at Greenwich), and is
vital in calculating a ship's position at
sea. Until Harrison's clock, sailors had
to rely on guesswork, and many had
lost their lives as a result of mistaking
where they were. Perhaps the most
famous example occurred in 1707,
when the fleet of Admiral Sir
Clowdisley Shovell miscalculated its
position and was wrecked off the Scilly
Isles, with the loss of over 2,000 lives.

The principle behind the calculation
of longitude is simple. For every 15
degrees travelled eastward the local time
moves forward by one hour; for every
15 degrees travelled west it goes back
by one hour. If you know the local
time, and also the time at a fixed point
(in this case Greenwich), then you can
calculate your longitude. In those days,
while it was easy enough to calculate
the local time by using the sun and

stars, the only way to tell the time at
Greenwich was with a clock, and the
only clocks that existed then were
pendulum clocks, which were rendered
useless by the motion of the sea.

In 1714 Parliament set up
ENGLAND'S FIRST SCIENCE FUNDING
BODY, THE BOARD OF LONGITUDE,
which offered a prize of £20,000 to
whoever could invent a means of
calculating longitude to within 30
miles (48 km), after a voyage of six
weeks to the West Indies.

John Harrison, a humble joiner
with a passion for making clocks, was
determined to win the prize and, at
the fourth attempt, he designed a
timepiece that looked like a large
watch, with a new balance mechanism
unaffected by the sea. It lost just five
seconds in six weeks at sea and
Harrison claimed the prize, but the
Astronomer Royal, Nevil Maskelyne,

miffed that his own experiments with lunar charts had failed, persuaded the bureaucrats on the Board not to award the money to the upstart Harrison. Harrison spent the rest of his life petitioning Parliament for his money, which he was finally awarded just before he died, on the personal intervention of George III. H4, an exact replica of Harrison's prize-winning design, was carried by Captain Cook on his two final voyages of discovery. Cook called it 'our faithful guide through all the vicissitudes of climate'. John Harrison's ingenuity revolutionised sea travel, and for a while gave the English a huge advantage in the race to explore the globe.

William Hogarth
1697–1764

WILLIAM HOGARTH is the only major English artist to have a roundabout named after him, a dubious honour that would no doubt have tickled him, as one of England's great satirists. The roundabout, a busy junction on the M4 at Chiswick, lies close to Hogarth's House, where the artist lived during the summer months for the last 15 years of his life, with his wife Jane, daughter of SIR JAMES THORNHILL, THE FIRST ENGLISH-BORN ARTIST TO RECEIVE A KNIGHT-HOOD.

Hogarth's House

Gin and Tonic

One of Hogarth's most evocative pictures is *Gin Lane*, which portrays the debauchery and degradation of a 17th-century London awash with cheap gin.

Gin was invented in Holland in the mid-17th century by Dr Franciscus Sylvius, as a cure for stomach disorders. It is distilled from grain spirits flavoured with juniper oil, and the name comes from 'genever', the Old Dutch word for juniper. English soldiers serving in Holland developed a taste for gin, which they called 'Dutch courage'.

Gin production was then promoted in England by William of Orange, who slapped a tax on French brandy, and since it was already cheap to make, being a by-product of ordinary grain, gin rapidly became the tipple of choice for the poor, leading to the rampant drunkenness and disorder depicted in Hogarth's picture. The government tried to curb this by bringing in the Gin Act of 1736, which led to rioting in the streets and drove gin distilling underground.

The development of the more refined London Dry Gin in the late 19th century made gin more respectable, and it became an essential ingredient in the newfangled cocktails.

'Pink Gin', with angostura bitters, a tonic formulated from herbs in the West Indies, was popular amongst naval officers, while gin and tonic was developed for the British army in India. The quinine in tonic water was believed to help fight off malaria, and the addition of gin made the tonic more palatable.

London Dry Gin is considered best in a gin and tonic, while Plymouth Gin, distilled in Plymouth since 1793, is preferred when making a Dry Martini Cocktail.

William Hogarth started life as a copper engraver, but soon turned to painting as a more lucrative occupation, and became known for his narrative pictures that told moral tales, in an early form of the comic strip. The eight pictures in his celebrated *The Rake's Progress* tell of the dissolute life of wealthy Thomas Rakewell, who throws away his inheritance on drinking, whoring and gambling, and ends up in Bedlam, a reflection of the decline Hogarth saw all around him. He loved to poke fun at self-serving politicians and at affectation, and he was especially good at capturing real life, as he had an almost photographic memory and could remember scenes that he could later recreate in the most precise detail. It was this realism, both in the subject and the artwork, that he is remembered for.

Well, I never knew this
about
MIDDLESEX FOLK

Born in Middlesex

MATTHEW ARNOLD (1822–88), poet and renowned literary critic, was born in LALEHAM. His father was Thomas Arnold, headmaster of Rugby School, famously portrayed in *Tom Brown's Schooldays*. Both father and son are buried in the family plot in the churchyard of All Saints, Laleham.

EVELYN WAUGH (1903–66), novelist (*Decline and Fall, A Handful of Dust, Scoop, Brideshead Revisited*), was born in FORTUNE GREEN.

SIR ALAN AYCKBOURN, the writer of 71 full-length plays, and the most successful and prolific English playwright since William Shakespeare, was born in HAMPSTEAD in 1939.

Buried in Middlesex

JOHN CONSTABLE (1776–1837), pre-eminent English landscape painter, is buried in the churchyard of St John's, Hampstead.

ARTHUR AND SYLVIA LLEWELYN DAVIES, parents of the boys who inspired J.M. Barrie's 'lost boys' in *Peter Pan*, are buried in the churchyard of St John's, Hampstead. Peter Pan himself, PETER LLEWELYN DAVIES (1897–1960) lies in Hampstead Cemetery in Fortune Green.

Also buried in Hampstead Cemetery are:

LORD JOSEPH LISTER (1827–1912), the pioneer of anti-septic surgery, after whom Listerine is named.

SIR CHARLES WYNDHAM (1837–1919), actor-manager and founder of Wyndham's theatre. Trained as a doctor, but by inclination an actor, Wyndham travelled to America to find work and served as an army surgeon under Ulysses S. Grant in the American Civil War. In 1863 he managed to obtain employment as an actor at Grover's Theatre in Washington, where the leading man was John Wilkes Booth, who two years later would murder President Abraham Lincoln. Wyndham later recalled: 'I saw nothing there that would foreshadow such an act as his except where the subject of politics was introduced. Then, even in those days of heated discussion, his excitement was remarkable, and his friends who wished to be on pleasant terms with him, gradually learned to avoid the discussion of politics.'

FRANCIS JAMES BARRAUD (1856–1924), who painted 'Nipper' the dog on the His Master's Voice record label.

MARIE LLOYD (1870–1922), the 'Queen of the Music Hall'.

NIGEL BALCHIN (1908–70), who thought up the name for Britain's bestselling chocolate bar, the Kit Kat, and who also conceived the Aero chocolate bar.

Norfolk

❖◄◆►❖

THE FIRST ENGLISH HOLIDAY CAMP
✦ EARLY ENGLISH BRICKWORK ✦ PASTON LETTERS
✦ FIRST STEEPLECHASE ✦ NORFOLK TERRIER

*King's Lynn Custom House,
a Norfolk landmark for 300 years.*

◄ NORFOLK FOLK ►

Margery Kempe ✦ Thomas Paine ✦ George Vancouver ✦ Horatio Nelson
✦ Parson Woodforde ✦ Sir James Dyson

[185]

Caister

THE FIRST HOLIDAY CAMP IN ENGLAND was established in CAISTER, on the bracing Norfolk coast north of Great Yarmouth. In 1906 former grocer JOHN FLETCHER DODD paid a visit to Caister to relax and ingest the sea air. He was so taken with the place that he bought himself a house on the front in Ormesby Road and settled in to enjoy his new domain. Fletcher Dodd, however, was an active socialist and founder member of the Independent Labour Party, and it was not in his nature to wallow in pleasure while others were working hard, so he pitched a few tents in the garden and invited some working-class families from London's East End to come and stay for a week.

The idea was a huge success, and soon people were coming from all over the country, including whole families – parents, children, even grandparents. The camp spread across the road to the edge of the beach, and Fletcher Dodd began building wooden huts for extra accommodation. The camp was run on strict socialist lines with no alcohol, no gambling, no swearing and lights out by 11 p.m., and everyone had to pitch in with the cooking and cleaning. The cost of one week, full board, was kept at no more than a week's wages, and the meals were good and wholesome.

Leading socialist worthies such as George Bernard Shaw, Herbert Morrison and Keir Hardie all came along to taste the delights, although Fletcher Dodd welcomed people of all political persuasions.

Within ten years the camp had beach huts, a shop, bicycles for hire, sports facilities and a dining hall for 200, which was used in the evenings for entertainment, as well as opportunities for bus trips, picnics and rambles.

The camp continued to expand until it covered 100 acres (40 ha), and it was finally sold by the Dodd family some years after the Second World War. It is now part of Haven Holidays – and the rules have been relaxed somewhat.

Caister Castle

To the west of Caister is the shell of CAISTER CASTLE, built in 1432 by SIR JOHN FALSTOLF, leader of the English archers at the Battle of Agincourt, and model for William Shakespeare's Sir John Falstaff. It is one of England's earliest brick buildings and the only English example of a 'Wasserburg'-style moated castle, as more commonly found in Flanders and the Rhineland.

Caister Castle was left to the Pastons, much to the annoyance of Falstolf's relatives, and was besieged for over a year, captured and then eventually returned to the Pastons. The story is told in the celebrated *Paston Letters.*

The Paston Letters
1422–1509

THE PASTON LETTERS consist of over 1,000 letters written between various members of the Paston family during the 15th century, and give a unique and intimate insight into the social and domestic life of an English family in medieval times – the earliest known archive of private correspondence in English

The Pastons were a remarkable family that rose from humble peasants to landowning aristocrats in two generations, in the aftermath of the Black Death and during the turmoil of the Wars of the Roses.

The story begins with the Black Death of 1348, which wiped out nearly half the rural population of England. One young man who survived was Clement Paston, a yeoman farmer in the village of Paston, on the north-east coast of Norfolk. Taking advantage of the confusion, Clement built up a substantial landholding by quietly annexing the lands of those who had died, and using this to raise money for the education of his son William as a lawyer.

This decision showed great foresight, for with the breakdown of the feudal system caused by the Black Death, society began to rely much more on the rule of law rather than the brute force of those with private armies. William rose to become a respectable judge and made a good marriage to an heiress, Agnes Berry, who brought with her more land and the beautiful manor of Oxnead, in the countryside north of Norwich.

William's oldest son John also became a lawyer and made an advantageous marriage to Margaret Mauteby, bringing yet more lands and property into the family. In London, John befriended his fellow Norfolk landowner Sir John Falstolf and became his lawyer, somehow ending up as the major beneficiary of the elderly knight's will and inheriting all of Falstolf's estates, including the magnificent castle at Caister.

This upset Falstolf's relatives, who immediately contested the will, beginning a long-running wrangle, centred on the 'jewel in the crown', Caister Castle, and it is this dispute that forms the background to the Paston Letters. They were written between the two sons of John Paston Senior, who took over the castle when their father died, and their mother, Margaret, who was living at Oxnead – confusingly, both the sons were also named John, Elder and Younger.

Not long after John Paston Senior died in 1466, Thomas Mowbray, the Duke of Norfolk, a distant kinsman of Falstolf who had always expected to inherit Caister, decided to take advantage of the lawlessness existing while the Wars of the Roses were being waged and seize Caister by force. He laid siege to the castle with 3,000 men, but it took over a year and another 3,000 men before the Pastons finally surrendered.

For the next 11 years the Pastons dragged the Duke of Norfolk through the courts to get Caister back, a course of action unthinkable before the changes wrought by the Black Death, when a powerful lord could help himself to any property he desired. The upstart Pastons even fought against the Duke on Henry VI's side at the Battle of Barnet in 1471, and when Norfolk died in 1476, John the Elder moved quickly to establish his claim to Caister with the King, who granted the castle to his supporters the Pastons and threw out the Duke's widow.

This victory propelled the Pastons into the ranks of the great courtiers and landowners – just three generations after they had been yeomen farmers. They ruled at Caister for 200 years and even became Earls of Yarmouth, until the castle had to be sold in the 17th century to pay the debts of a dissolute descendant, and eventually fell into ruin.

First Steeplechase

The first recorded steeplechase in England was run in Norfolk at EAST WINCH, near King's Lynn, and was won, appropriately enough, by a horse called Useful. The course continued in use until 1905, when the racecourse at Fakenham was opened.

Norfolk Terrier

The Norfolk terrier is the smallest breed of working terrier and is distinguished from the Norwich terrier by having drop ears as opposed to pricked ears. Both terriers were developed for hunting rats and other vermin by crossing Irish terriers with Cairn terriers.

Well, I never **knew this**
about
NORFOLK FOLK

Margery Kempe
— c. 1364–c. 1440 —

MARGERY KEMPE was born in the flourishing port of LYNN, now King's Lynn, daughter of the mayor. After bearing 14 children for her husband, John Kempe, she received a heavenly vision urging her to set off on a pilgrimage to the Holy Land. So she struck a bargain with John, that if he would cease to trouble her with his attentions and allow her to go off on her travels, she would settle all his debts. He agreed with alacrity and off she went. While on her pilgrimage she began to suffer from frequent bouts of loud wailing and weeping during her devotions, which did not endear her to the other pilgrims, nor indeed to the people of Lynn on her return.

She made many further pilgrimages and travelled widely throughout Europe, before finally settling down in her home town in 1436 at the age of 72 and embarking on her memoirs, which she dictated to a local priest. Lynn, isolated as it was from the French-speaking court in London, had become the first English town to abandon Latin and French and adopt English as its main language. And so Margery Kempe's life story was written down in English – THE FIRST AUTOBIOGRAPHY EVER WRITTEN IN THE ENGLISH LANGUAGE.

Thomas Paine
— 1737–1809 —

THOMAS PAINE, political philosopher and radical, was born in Thetford. Credited with coming up with the name United States of America, he is known as 'Father of the American Revolution' by virtue of his pamphlet *Common Sense*, which advocated independence from the monarchy for the American colonists, and acted as inspiration for George Washington, John Adam and Thomas Jefferson. His most famous works are *The Rights of Man*, written in support of the ideals behind the French Revolution, and *The Age of Reason*, which argues against organised religion. He also championed radical ideas such as a progressive income tax, minimum wage and old-age pensions. He was buried in New Rochelle, New York, near the farm where he lived out his final years. A few years after his death, however, the author of *Rural Rides*, William Cobbett, dug up Paine's bones and shipped them back to England, intending to give them a heroic burial in Paine's birthplace, Thetford. However, this never happened and the bones were eventually lost, their whereabouts unknown to this day.

George Vancouver
━━◄ 1757–98 ►━━

GEORGE VANCOUVER, was born in King's Lynn, the son of the Collector of Customs. As a boy of 13 he went off round the world

with Captain Cook, witnessing his death on Hawaii in 1779, and gaining a taste for exploration and adventure. When he revisited New Zealand he was amused to rename a bay that Cook had called 'Nobody Knows What', as 'Somebody Knows What'.

Vancouver's lasting legacy was the charting of the west coast of America, from Mexico to Alaska, during the longest mapping expedition in history. His charts were so accurate that they have been used until very recently, when electronic mapping was introduced. While on this voyage Vancouver won the island of Nootka

George Vancouver

from the Spanish – after which it was renamed Vancouver Island. Worn out from his harsh life at sea, Captain George Vancouver retired to Petersham, in Surrey, to write his memoirs, and died there at the young age of 40. He is buried in Petersham churchyard.

Horatio Nelson
—◄ 1758–1805 ►—

England's greatest naval hero, VISCOUNT HORATIO NELSON, was born in BURNHAM THORPE a year after the execution of Admiral Byng, an event that had a remarkable effect on the navy that Nelson would eventually join. Byng had fallen foul of the Articles of War that required naval officers to 'do their utmost' and proved that officers could no longer hide behind their orders. They were expected to use their initiative and to stand or fall by their decisions made on the spot – it didn't matter so much if you failed, but it was fatal if you didn't 'do your utmost'.

An example of Nelson using his initiative was during the Battle of Copenhagen in 1801, when he disobeyed the order to retreat by putting his telescope up to his blind eye and remarking, 'I really do not see the signal.' He then went on to break the Danes' defensive line and win the battle.

Under Nelson, and officers like him, the Royal Navy gained a reputation for courage and aggression that became a huge psychological advantage over the enemy, who knew that the English would not, indeed could not, surrender – at the Battle of Trafalgar, for instance, Nelson's fleet went into battle expecting to win or die trying, while their opponents were already half expecting to lose.

PARSON WOODFORDE (1740–1803), author of *The Diary of a Country Parson*, is buried in WESTON LONGVILLE, where he was Rector for 30 years. His diary is an invaluable first-hand account of everyday life for the folk of an 18th-century English village.

SIR JAMES DYSON, inventor of the 'ballbarrow' and the world's first bagless vacuum cleaner, was born in CROMER in 1947.

Northamptonshire

✦•••✦

CHURCH ARCHITECTURE ✦ SAXON ✦ NORMAN ✦ EARLY ENGLISH ✦ DECORATED ✦ PERPENDICULAR

*All Saints, Earls Barton – unique
10th-century Saxon architecture.*

◄ NORTHAMPTONSHIRE FOLK ►

George Gascoigne ✦ John Dryden ✦ Charles Montagu ✦ William Smith
✦ Sir Alfred East ✦ H.E. Bates ✦ Edmund Rubbra ✦ William Alwyn
✦ Malcolm Arnold

English Church Architecture

Northamptonshire is full of delightful honey-coloured towns and villages built from the local soft golden stone, and can boast churches showing supreme examples of every style of medieval English architecture, from 7th-century Saxon to 15th-century English Perpendicular.

Saxon

There are very few stone churches surviving from the Saxon period in England, mainly because the Saxons built very few in stone, preferring to use wood as they had done in the forests of Northern Germany from whence they came. ALL SAINTS, BRIXWORTH, north of Northampton, is the largest and oldest stone Saxon church in England, one of seven 7th-

century English churches still standing, and outranked in antiquity only by St Martin's in Canterbury and St Peter's at Bradwell, in Essex.

If Brixworth is brute Saxon strength, then ALL SAINTS, EARLS BARTON shows us the more artistic side of Saxon architecture. The 10th-century tower, half-timbered in stone, is the most ornate piece of Saxon work in England. Decorative masonry strip-work climbs the walls of the tower from bottom to top, breaking out in hoops and lozenges at different stages, the whole pattern derivative of timber framework, and dazzling in its effect. On the top portion of the Saxon tower is a delicate arcade of five-lights, found nowhere else in English architecture.

Norman

Northampton, the county town, possesses two fine examples of Norman architecture in the Church of the Holy Sepulchre and St Peter's.

There are four round churches in England modelled on the Holy Sepulchre in Jerusalem, and Northampton's CHURCH OF THE HOLY SEPULCHRE is said to be the most like the original. Built in 1100 for the first Earl of Northampton, Simon de Senlis, who had just returned from the Crusades, the church is Northampton's oldest surviving building. The original circular nave is called the Round and consists of an arcade supported by eight massive

traffic island a little way out of the city centre, shows an extraordinary Norman exterior, with a short, heavily buttressed tower and extended nave, laced with a continuous row of small Norman arches, quite unlike any other church in England. The interior is almost completely Norman, wide and long with no chancel arch, but with the most beautiful carved round tower arch and incredibly detailed carvings of foliage, winged creatures and human forms on the pier capitals. Built in 1140 on the site of an 8th-century Saxon church, St Peter's is one of the great Norman treasures of England, but was almost lost to damp and traffic pollution until, in 1998, the Churches Conservation Trust stepped in and set about preserving what is a masterpiece.

round pillars with sturdy square bases and craved capitals – the rounded arches above the pillars were replaced by pointed ones when the church was extended eastwards in the 14th century. An ambulatory or aisle runs around the arcade, and set in the middle is the altar.

After years of neglect, the church has been sympathetically restored and is now in frequent use for services, concerts and presentations.

ST PETER'S, NORTHAMPTON, which sits redundant and isolated on a

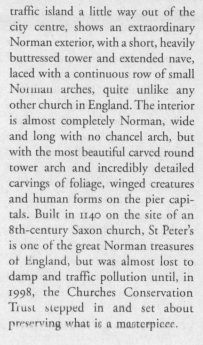

Early English

The glorious tower and broach steeple of St Mary's, Raunds, soaring 183 ft (56 m) above the Nene valley east of Northampton, is 13th-century Early English Gothic style at its finest. The square tower is rich in arches, which only accentuates the simplicity of the octagonal spire above. The body of the church shows all styles of Gothic with pointed arches in the arcades and windows. St Mary's is also noted for its 15th-century wall paintings portraying the Seven Deadly Sins, the Three Living and Three Dead Kings and St Christopher.

While accepted wisdom tells us that the pointed arch was imported from the Continent, it seems equally likely that English church builders got the idea from observing the intersection of round arches, as seen on the decorative blind arcading found in many Norman churches.

Decorated

Sir Nikolaus Pevsner describes the slender, 15th-century spire of St Peter and St Paul, King's Sutton as 'one of the finest, if not the finest spire, in a county of spires'. The tower on which it rests shows a gallery of flamboyant (Decorated) carving, which becomes more exuberant towards the top and particularly around the base of the spire. Lying in the far south of the county, the soaring spire of King's Sutton, 198 ft (60 m) high, is often

the first glimpse the traveller has of Northamptonshire, a fitting welcome.

Perpendicular

Perpendicular is a uniquely English style, the crowning achievement of medieval English church architecture, and seen nowhere else in Europe. A supreme example is ST PETER'S, LOWICK, which can be found towering over its tiny, one-street village hidden away in a valley east of Kettering. A feast of pale golden pinnacles and weather vanes and battlements, the exquisite 15th-century octagon tower of St Peter's is a masterpiece of grace and balance, while huge, delicately traced windows allow sunshine to flood into the interior, creating an impression of movement and space that is breathtaking.

St Peter's was begun by a wealthy friend of Richard II, Henry Greene, of nearby Drayton House, and added to over the years by the Greene family, which explains how such a small village as Lowick comes to possess such a magnificent church.

By the end of the 15th century English church architecture had reached its height, and had met all the challenges thrown up by the desire to create churches as works of art.

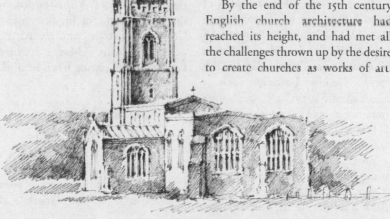

Money and effort and imagination began to be directed into domestic architecture, and although there were periods of prolific church building after this, such as during the late Stuart era with Sir Christopher Wren in London, and again under the Victorians, subsequent designs were usually revivals of these medieval styles.

Well, I never knew this
about
NORTHAMPTONSHIRE FOLK

George Gascoigne
◄ C. 1539–77 ►

BARNACK, from where the stone came that built Peterborough and Ely cathedrals, has over the years found itself in Huntingdonshire and in Cambridgeshire, owing to boundary changes. It was originally, however, a Northamptonshire village, certainly so in the days when GEORGE GASCOIGNE, one of the founders of English literature, was laid to rest in the church of St John the Baptist, with its high Saxon chancel arch, Saxon tower and one of the earliest English spires. George Gascoigne was a kinsman of Martin Frobisher, something of a man about town and a favourite of Elizabeth I. A lawyer working out of Gray's Inn, he was also a prodigious writer who explored many innovative forms of writing, and a play he wrote for his colleagues at the Inn called *The Supposes* was THE FIRST PROSE DRAMA EVER PRODUCED IN ENGLISH. He is also credited with writing the first masque and the first essay on poetry in English. *The Spoyle of Antwerp*, his vivid eye-witness account of the sacking of Antwerp by the Spaniards, the brutality of which inspired Rubens' masterpiece *The Massacre of the Innocents*, earned Gascoigne the title of THE FIRST ENGLISH WAR CORRESPONDENT. He is buried in the family vaults of his best friend George Whetstone, who owned the nearby Walcot Manor where Gascoigne was staying when he died.

Charles Montagu, 1st Earl of Halifax
◄ 1661–1715 ►

CHARLES MONTAGU was born in HORTON, just south of

Northampton. He entered Parliament in 1691, where he was an early campaigner for 'legal aid', particularly for those accused of high treason. He was eventually appointed to the Treasury, where he oversaw the introduction of proper silver coins. Until then coins were cut crudely straight from the metal, and could easily be 'clipped', so that the face value of the coin did not necessarily match the true value of the silver in it. To pay for the new coinage Montagu introduced the infamous WINDOW TAX, whereby each household was taxed according to the number of windows their house possessed. As a result, many people bricked up a number of their windows, to reduce their liability. As Lord of the Treasury he proposed the idea of the National Debt, and in 1694 he introduced the bill establishing the Bank of England.

John Dryden
◄ 1631–1700 ►

Poet Laureate JOHN DRYDEN, regarded as the best English poet of the late 17th century, after the death of Milton, was born in ALDWINCLE, south of Oundle. He often stayed with his uncle who lived at Canons Ashby, a delightful small manor house near Northampton, constructed from a 12th-century Augustinian priory by the Drydens. Although the property

now belongs to the National Trust, the Dryden family still have an apartment in the house.

William Smith
◄ 1769–1839 ►

Not only is St Peter's Church in Northampton an important national monument, by virtue of its unsurpassed Norman architecture, but it is also the burial place of the 'FATHER OF ENGLISH GEOLOGY', WILLIAM SMITH. By profession a surveyor,

John Dryden

> Only man clogs his happiness with care,
> Destroying what is
> with thoughts of what may be . . .
>
> Happy the man . . . who can call today his own
> He who . . . can say . . .
> Tomorrow do thy worst, for I have lived today
>
> None but the brave deserves the fair
>
> *Quotes from the work of John Dryden*

Smith began studying and recording the various rock strata he came across while surveying and excavating a canal being constructed near Bath by the engineer John Rennie.

In 1799 he wrote down his observations, and the resulting document, the 'Table of the Strata near Bath', resulted in the establishment of geology as a science. At the same time he began colouring in the geological features on a map of Bath and the surrounding area, thus creating THE OLDEST GEOLOGICAL MAP IN EXISTENCE. In 1801 he did the same with a small map of England, and from this created the first ever geological map of England, which was published in 1815, and laid the foundations for geological surveys and discoveries across the world.

He died in Northampton while staying at Northampton's Hazelrigg Mansion, en route to a conference in Birmingham.

Born in Northamptonshire

SIR ALFRED EAST (1844–1913), landscape artist, was born in KETTERING. Now regarded as one of the finest of the Victorian landscape painters, he was also one of the first English artists to paint the landscape of Japan.

HERBERT ERNEST (H.E.) BATES (1905–1974), described by Graham Greene as 'Britain's successor to Chekov', and author of the English classic *The Darling Buds of May*, was born in RUSHDEN, home of John White Shoes. His early works evoke the atmosphere of the Northamptonshire shoe towns and countryside in which he grew up.

Three 20th-century composers were born in Northampton:

EDMUND RUBBRA (1901–86), best remembered for his 11 symphonies.

WILLIAM ALWYN (1905–85), composer of five symphonies and scores for over 200 films, including *The History of Mr Polly* and *The Fallen Idol.*

MALCOLM ARNOLD (1921–2006), composer of nine symphonies, two operas, a musical and scores for 132 films, including *Whistle Down the Wind* and *Bridge on the River Kwai,* for which, in 1957, he became THE FIRST ENGLISH COMPOSER TO WIN AN OSCAR.

Northumberland

NORTHERN SAINT ✦ HOLY ISLAND
✦ THE MAN WHO INVENTED THE 20TH CENTURY
✦ NORTHUMBERLAND GREYS ✦ TEA

Lindisfarne Priory, a cradle of English Christianity.

◄ NORTHUMBERLAND FOLK ►

Admiral Lord Collingwood ✦ Emily Wilding Davison ✦ Mary Astell
✦ Sir George Airey ✦ Jackie Milburn ✦ Jack and Bobby Charlton

St Cuthbert
635–87

Lying off the coast of Northumberland is LINDISFARNE, or Holy Island, one of England's most sacred places and spiritual home of Northern England's patron saint, ST CUTHBERT.

Born in 635, Cuthbert became a shepherd boy in the Northumbrian hills and at the age of 16, while tending his sheep, he had a vision of stars falling from the sky, which he interpreted as angels descending from Heaven to carry away the soul of St Aidan, first Bishop of Lindisfarne, who that night had died.

Cuthbert joined the monks of Melrose Abbey and in 664, when the Synod of Whitby settled in favour of Roman Christianity, he was sent to Lindisfarne to help the monks there with the transition from the Celtic traditions. Here he gained a reputation for healing and miracles, and brought great fame to Lindisfarne as a place of sanctuary and retreat.

Craving solitude himself, Cuthbert retired to a rocky islet off Lindisfarne, now called St Cuthbert's Isle, where he built himself a tiny chapel and fashioned rosaries out of 'St Cuthbert's Beads', tiny fossils found on the shore.

Cuthbert eventually became Bishop of Lindisfarne, where he remained until, feeling his days were coming to a close, he took himself off to lonely Farne Island, where he died in March 687.

Cuthbert was buried on Lindisfarne, where his grave became a place of pilgrimage. Not long after his death the monks there produced a glorious manuscript, illustrated by the new Bishop, Eadfrith, which became known as the Lindisfarne Gospels.

In 793 Lindisfarne suffered the first Viking raid on the coast of England. The monastery was looted and burned, but St Cuthbert's shrine was fortunately overlooked.

Nearly 100 years later, in 875, Lindisfarne was again threatened by Danish invaders, and this time the monks fled the island along with Cuthbert's coffin, in which they had placed the head of St Oswald, Christian King of Northumbria, and the Gospels. For the next seven years they wandered through the north of England, seeking somewhere safe to rest their precious burden.

On one occasion, when they were crossing the Irish Sea, the Gospels were washed overboard and the monks despaired, until St Cuthbert appeared to them in a vision and guided them to a spot on the Scottish coast near Whithorn, where they found the manuscript washed ashore and undamaged, except for some minor staining from the sea. The

Gospels are now in the British Museum, where they were analysed and found to be indeed marked with seawater stains.

St Cuthbert's coffin eventually came to rest at Durham, where his shrine is today. Before being placed in his new tomb in Durham Cathedral in 1104, Cuthbert's remains were examined and his body found to be perfectly preserved, as was the head of St Oswald, which was hence adopted as St Cuthbert's symbol.

Lindisfarne remains a beautiful, haunting and sacred place, isolated and cut off by the high tide, windswept and crowned at the southern end by a castle built on top of a conical mound 100 ft (30 m) high. The castle was transformed into a private home by Sir Edwin Lutyens in 1903, and is now owned by the National Trust.

Sir Charles Parsons
1854–1931
The Man who Invented the 20th Century

Kirkwhelpington is a sturdy stone village on the edge of the Northumberland Moors west of Morpeth. Standing on a hillock above the Wansbeck is a long, narrow 13th-century church, and in the churchyard is the stone burial plot of the Englishman who gave power to the world, SIR CHARLES PARSONS.

The third son of the Earl of Rosse, he came from a remarkable family of pioneers and inventors already renowned in the worlds of science, astronomy, photography and engineering, and it was therefore not considered too unusual when, after studying mathematics at Cambridge, he took up an apprenticeship at the Newcastle

engineering works of William Armstrong. During this time he applied himself to designing a steam turbine engine.

The steam turbine, which converts the kinetic energy of steam directly into rotation, is many times more efficient than the up and down movement of a steam piston engine. Parsons' prototype was capable of 18,000 rpm compared with the maximum 500 rpm of the average piston engine, and is considered to be the single most important invention in the history of the generation of electricity.

In 1888 Parsons installed his turbine engines in the Forth Banks power station in Newcastle, the first public power station to use turbine generators anywhere in the world. By the time of his death in 1931 all the major power stations in the world had adopted Parsons' steam turbine generators.

Parsons also designed

steam turbines to propel ships. He established the Parsons Marine Steam Turbine Company at Wallsend and in 1895 launched *Turbinia*, THE WORLD'S FIRST STEAM TURBINE DRIVEN BOAT. In order to demonstrate its phenomenal speed Parsons took *Turbinia* to the Spithead Review celebrating Queen Victoria's Diamond Jubilee in 1897, and there, in front of leaders from all the world's great naval powers, he proceeded to race around the biggest fleet of warships ever assembled, at over 30 knots. The Royal Navy patrol ships sent to challenge *Turbinia* were unable to catch her, and *Turbinia* proved herself to be the fastest ship in the world. Within ten years all warships were equipped with steam turbines. In 1906 THE WORLD'S FIRST TURBINE-POWERED BATTLESHIP, HMS *Dreadnought*, was launched at Portsmouth.

The year before, the Allen Line ships

> The Order of Merit was founded by Edward VII in 1902 to recognise exceptional service to the Crown or the advancement of arts, learning, law and literature, and is the only Order specifically awarded to artists, scientists and intellectuals. It is also one of the few Orders awarded free from political recommendation, along with the Order of the Garter, the Order of the Thistle and the Royal Victorian Order.

Victorian and *Virginian* had become THE FIRST TURBINE-DRIVEN PASSENGER LINERS TO CROSS THE ATLANTIC, and in 1907 the Cunard liners *Mauretania* and *Lusitania* began regular Atlantic service. *Lusitania* gained the coveted Blue Riband for the fastest Atlantic crossing a month after her maiden voyage, while *Mauretania*, built at the Swan Hunter yard on Tyneside, held the Blue Riband for longer than any other liner, over 20 years. Modified Parsons turbine engines powered the liners *Queen Elizabeth* and *Queen Mary* as well as the battleships HMS *George V* and HMS *Hood*.

Sir Charles Parsons was the first engineer to be admitted to the Order of Merit.

The Greys

'The lamps are going out all over Europe; we shall not see them lit again in our lifetime.'

These famously haunting words were spoken on the eve of the First World War by the Foreign Secretary, VISCOUNT GREY OF FALLODON, President of the League of Nations, and the longest-serving Foreign Secretary of the 20th century.

The Greys are one of the great Northumberland families. FALLODON HALL, on the coast north of Alnwick, used to have its own private railway station where the Greys had the right to flag down trains on the main line to Edinburgh.

The 1st Earl Grey was a general who introduced marching in step to the British army, a procedure last used by the Roman legions. The 2nd Earl Grey was the Prime Minister

who introduced that milestone in the history of English democracy, the Great Reform Act of 1832. He also introduced Earl Grey tea to England.

Tea
The National Drink

——◆◆◆◆——

TEA was introduced into England in the 1650s, brought in from China by the East India Company and marketed as a tonic that was bene-ficial to health. First sold by Thomas Garraway at his coffee-house in London's Exchange Alley, it was made fashionable by Charles II's wife Catherine of Braganza, daughter of the King of Portugal, the first European country to trade in tea.

Along with tea from China came delicate china cups from which to drink it. These were very fragile and expensive, and the sudden demand for home-produced tea things sparked the rise of the English pottery industry, based at Stoke-on-Trent. Early in the 19th century Josiah Spode invented 'bone' china, which proved perfect for tea, being translucent and refined, yet less fragile than porcelain and able to withstand high temperatures.

Once the English had learned to sweeten tea with sugar, it became popular with all classes and during the 18th century even replaced ale as England's favourite drink.

Boston Tea Party
Throughout the 18th century tea was very heavily taxed, and this led to a great deal of tea smuggling, which hit the profits of the East India Company, who had a monopoly of the tea trade. In order to recoup the losses they were making in England, the Company began exporting to the American colonies. Not only was this tea taxed but the Company was given the sole distribution rights in America. In 1773

three East India Company ships laden with tea arrived in Boston Harbour, but the townsfolk refused to allow the tea ashore or pay the duty, and eventually boarded the ships and threw the tea overboard, in one of the first incidents leading up to the American War of Independence. It is because of the Boston Tea Party that tea is not as popular in the United States as it is in England – patriotic Americans turned to coffee instead.

At the start of the 19th century tea plantations were established in India, using seeds from China, by officials of the East India Company who wanted to grow tea for themselves, and today tea is India's biggest industry after tourism.

Afternoon Tea

Afternoon tea was the brainchild of ANNA, DUCHESS OF BEDFORD, who in 1840 decided she needed something to keep her going between lunch and the evening meal. Amongst the upper classes dinner was often not served until eight o'clock or later, a custom imported from the Raj in India, where it was sensible not to eat until the heat of the day had cooled. The Duchess ordered her butler to bring her some bread and butter and a cup of tea at 5 p.m., and this proved so refreshing that she began inviting her friends to join her for tea – and a new social occasion was born. The idea soon caught on with the working classes too, who made 'tea' into the main meal of the day.

Tea Clippers

While the East India Company had the monopoly of the tea trade, it wasn't necessary to transport the tea from China to England very quickly, but once the monopoly was broken in the mid-19th century speed became of the essence. The competition to build the fastest tea clipper was fierce, and races between the graceful vessels caught the public imagination. Only one of those tea clippers survives, the CUTTY SARK, which is now berthed at Greenwich.

THE FIRST TEA SHOP was opened in 1864 by the lady manager of the AERATED BREAD COMPANY at London Bridge, who started to sell cups of tea to her customers, and soon there was a chain of ABC tea shops all over London.

In the early 20th century TEA DANCES became popular, while today a great treat is to take tea in a posh hotel such as the Ritz or Browns. Britain is still the world's largest market for exported tea.

Well, I never knew this
about
NORTHUMBERLAND FOLK

Admiral Lord Collingwood
◄ 1748–1810 ►

CUTHBERT COLLINGWOOD was born and educated in Newcastle and joined the Royal Navy in 1761, aged just 12. He distinguished himself in the Caribbean during the American War of Independence and here met Lord Nelson, with whom he became firm friends. He was Nelson's second-in-command at the Battle of Trafalgar in 1805, and his ship the *Royal Sovereign* fired the first shots, almost sinking the Spanish flagship, the *Santa Ana*, before any other English ship had even entered the fray. When Nelson was mortally wounded, Collingwood took control and saw the English fleet through to victory without the loss of a single ship. England's mastery of the seas was assured, a domination that was to last for over 100 years.

Collingwood's smart family home in Morpeth still stands on the town's oldest street, Oldgate, and is now a priest's home. 'Whenever I think how I am to be happy again, my thoughts carry me back to Morpeth,' he once said, but he never returned there after Trafalgar and died at sea off Minorca in 1810. He is buried beside Lord Nelson in St Paul's Cathedral.

Collingwood's House in Morpeth

Emily Wilding Davison
◄ 1872–1913 ►

Buried in the churchyard at Morpeth, under a headstone bearing the phrase 'Deeds, not Words', is EMILY WILDING DAVISON, a passionate suffragette who lived her life by Benjamin Franklin's adage 'Rebellion against tyrants is obedience to God'. She wrote this down on pieces of paper, which she then wrapped around rocks and threw at David Lloyd-George. She was frequently arrested, tried to fling herself off the roof of Holloway prison and went on hunger strike. On one occasion, when she blockaded her cell

door, a warder fed a hose pipe through the window bars and filled the cell with ice-cold water. The door was broken down just before she drowned, but she managed to successfully sue the prison authorities.

On 4 June 1913, at the Epsom Derby, carrying a banner of the Women's Social and Political Union, she stepped out in front the King's horse, Anmer, and tried to grab the reins, but was trampled under foot and died from her injuries a few days later. Her handbag was found to contain a return ticket to Epsom and a diary full of forthcoming events, which seems to indicate that she was not intending to commit suicide. Although her death had no immediate effect, she became an enduring symbol of the fight for women's rights, and her brave but foolish gesture undoubtedly brought votes for the women of England much closer – it may indeed have done more for the extension of English democracy than her fellow Northumbrian Earl Grey's Great Reform Act.

Born in Northumberland

MARY ASTELL (1666–1731), author of *A Serious Proposal to the Ladies for the Advancement of Their True and Greatest Interest*, regarded as the first English feminist, was born in NEWCASTLE.

SIR GEORGE AIREY (1801–92), Astronomer Royal responsible for establishing Greenwich as the Prime Meridian, was born in ALNWICK.

Footballers JACKIE MILBURN (1924–88) and the World Cup winning CHARLTON brothers JACK (b.1935) and BOBBY (b. 1937) were all born in ASHINGTON.

Nottinghamshire

Robin Hood ✦ Major Oak

Robin Hood, a very English hero.

Nottingham

N ottingham and Sherwood Forest will for ever be associated with the best-loved and most famous English folk hero of them all, ROBIN HOOD. Wielding an English longbow, battling a Norman king and defending downtrodden English folk from tyrannical French aristocrats such as Guy de Gisburne, his story mirrors the struggles against arbitrary authority that were the background to medieval England, and led to Magna Carta.

Like King Arthur, Robin Hood was probably an amalgam of several real characters. One suggested candidate is Robert FitzOdo (1160–1247), Earl of Huntingdon, born at Loxley in Warwickshire (Robin Hood is sometimes referred to as Robin of Loxley), and buried in the churchyard there. He was outlawed at the end of the 12th century and his lands were transferred to Ranulf, Earl of Chester, an event that is mentioned in William Langland's *Piers Plowman*, written in 1377, which includes the earliest known literary reference to Robin Hood.

There is another Loxley (spelt Locksley), in Barnsdale Forest in Yorkshire, which could be the birthplace of Robin Hood, and indeed the early ballads talk about Robin of Barnsdale. This might favour the idea that Robin Hood was Robert Hood (1290–1347), who was outlawed by the court in Wakefield for supporting the Earl of Lancaster against Edward II at the Battle of Boroughbridge.

A further suggestion is that he was Robert, Earl of Huntingdon, the great grandson of King David of Scotland and a kinsman of Robert the Bruce, who was dispossessed of his lands by King John.

While Barnsdale Forest has some claims to be Robin Hood's stamping ground, most stories place him in Sherwood Forest, which in his day covered over 100,000 acres (40,000 ha) of the heart of England, and although it has shrunk to just 450 acres (182 ha) today there are still many places associated with Robin Hood and his Merry Men that can be visited.

Edwinstowe

A good place to start is St Mary's Church in the pretty village of EDWINSTOWE, set in the heart of Sherwood Country Park beside the River Maun.

Edwinstowe is named after the Saxon King Edwin of Northumbria, whose kingdom at that time stretched from the River Trent to Edinburgh (Edwin's borough). Having been converted to Christianity by his wife Princess Ethelburga of Kent, Edwin marched south in 633 to fight the pagan King Penda of Mercia, and was killed during the ensuing Battle of Hatfield, at a small settlement in Sherwood Forest now called Cuckney. His body was secretly buried in a forest clearing to conceal it from Penda, and when Edwin's followers returned to take Edwin to his final resting-place at Whitby Abbey, a wooden chapel was raised over where he had lain – 'Edwin's Holy Place', or Edwinstowe.

In 1175 a stone church was built to replace the wooden chapel, one of many churches put up by Henry II as penance for the murder of Thomas à Becket. It was here, at 'the church in the forest', that Robin Hood and

Maid Marian were said to have been married.

Buried in the churchyard to the west of the tower is a distinguished incumbent of St Mary's, the REV DR EBENEZER COBHAM BREWER (1810–97), who compiled *Brewer's Dictionary of Phrase and Fable.*

Major Oak

Not a mile from the church at Edwinstowe is Robin Hood's main hideout, the MAJOR OAK, named after the antiquary Major Hayman Rooke, who wrote about the tree in 1790. It is one of the oldest and biggest oak trees in England, and stands in its own clearing with smaller oaks and silver birches keeping a respectful distance. In the hollow trunk, 30 ft (9 m) round, Robin Hood and his men would hide and plot their next ambush.

The oak tree has long been a symbol of English strength and resilience – with Charles II having hidden in an oak tree and English sailors having 'hearts of oak' – and for Robin Hood to make an oak his fortress is somehow fitting.

Further south near Newstead Abbey is the village of BLIDWORTH, where Maid Marian is said to have lived before her marriage to Robin and from where she was escorted to Edwinstowe by Will Scarlet – who may lie in the churchyard. A little way to the west in lovely

Fountaindale is Friar Tuck's Well, near a moated area where the Friar had his home, and where he and Robin disputed the right of way, with Robin ending up in the water. A footbridge used to carry the public path across the moat and it may have been on this bridge that Robin and Little John fought.

Further south again is PAPPLEWICK, where Robin Hood stabled his horse, near the main route through the forest, the King's Great Way, in a cave guarded by yet another oak tree. The minstrel Alan a Dale married his 'fair lady Ellen' in the original 12th-century church at Papplewick and may be buried under the present church.

St James's church at Papplewick, built in the late 12th century, was another of Henry II's 'penance' churches like that at Edwinstowe. It was restored in 1795 by the Hon. Frederick Montagu, Squire of Papplewick Hall, up on the hill. Inside, at the east end, is his 'squire's pew' retaining its private fireplace – Montagu would rattle the coals with his fire iron if he thought the sermon was going on too long.

Well, I never **knew this**
about

NOTTINGHAMSHIRE FOLK

Thomas Cranmer

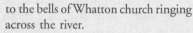

◄ 1489–1556 ►

THOMAS CRANMER, THE FIRST PROTESTANT ARCHBISHOP OF CANTERBURY, was born in ASLOCKTON, a small village in the Vale of Belvoir east of Nottingham. Although the old manor house where he came into the world has gone, there is a moated hillock in a field near the site known locally as 'Cranmer's Mound'. Here, as a boy, he would sit and admire the view, while listening

to the bells of Whatton church ringing across the river.

Cranmer studied at Cambridge and took Holy Orders in 1523. He came to the attention of Henry VIII when he suggested that the King should ignore the Pope and allow English churchmen to decide on the legality of his marriage to Catherine of Aragon, taking their guidance from the Scriptures. On becoming Archbishop he declared Henry's marriage to Catherine illegal and publicly married Henry to Anne Boleyn.

Cranmer was a leading figure in the English Reformation, and a founder of the Church of England. He urged the Dissolution of the Monasteries, believing that the money would be better spent on religious teaching and education, and strongly supported the translation of the Bible into English, so that more people could read the Scriptures and learn for themselves. In 1545 he wrote the first Litany in the English language, which is still used today, while his greatest work was the BOOK OF COMMON PRAYER, published in 1549, which many people think contains some of the most beautiful written English ever composed. Used day after day by millions of English churchgoers during the later 16th century, Cranmer's *Book of Common Prayer* spread a shared English language across the country, undoubtedly contributed to the brilliance of Shakespeare, and gave to English writers and poets the richest and most adaptable language in the world as their tool.

Cranmer's leading role in the Reformation and his annulment of Henry VIII's marriage to Queen Mary's mother Catherine of Aragon earned the hatred of the Bloody Queen (Mary, Mary, quite contrary) and he was burned at the stake in Oxford in 1556.

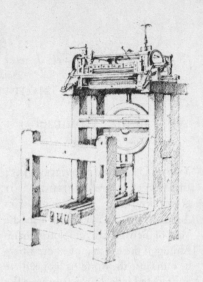

The Reverend William Lee
◄ 1563–1614 ►

An early pioneer of the Industrial Revolution, THE REV WILLIAM LEE, was born in CALVERTON, a large straggling village at the foot of the hills between Nottingham and Southwell. In 1589 he patented THE STOCKING-FRAME, the first piece of apparatus ever made that could produce looped or knotted fabric, and which could make 12 stockings, woollen or silk, for every one knitted by hand. It was an astonishing inven-

tion that pre-dated the machinery of the factory age by nearly 200 years, and was the prototype for every machine in use in the world today.

The story goes that Lee was driven to create his frame so that his sweetheart might spend less time knitting and devote more time to him. Unfortunately, Elizabeth I refused to recognise the stocking-frame, afraid that it might cause unemployment amongst the hand-knitters, which indeed it did, and Lee had to go to France for patronage. The frames made there were eventually returned to Nottinghamshire and led to the growth of the county as a centre for the hosiery trade. Like so many brilliant men, Lee was no businessman and died a pauper in Paris, where he lies in an unknown grave, having made nothing from his invention that would one day create untold wealth for England and millions of Englishmen.

D.H. Lawrence
──◄ 1885–1930 ►──

Nottinghamshire village life colours and infuses the novels of controversial writer D.H. LAWRENCE, who was born the son of a coalminer in EASTWOOD, where his birthplace, 8A Victoria Street, is now a museum in his memory. Lawrence's semi-autobiographical *Sons and Lovers*, published in 1913 and set in a coalmining village, is regarded as the first English novel to originate from, and focus on, the English working class.

Not far from his home is Haggs Farm, where Lawrence's first love Jessie Matthews lived. She appears as Miriam in *Sons and Lovers*, as does her farm – 'Miriam's farm, where I got my first incentive to write'.

The sexually explicit nature of his work, particularly *Lady Chatterley's Lover*, shocked the censors of the day and led to a celebrated trial that rewrote the obscenity laws as applied to English literature. Although published in Italy in 1928, *Lady Chatterley's Lover* was banned in Britain for its obscene content until 1960, when Penguin sought permission to publish it, along with Lawrence's other works, to celebrate the 30th anniversary of his death. After a six-day hearing at the Old Bailey objections to the publication were overruled, and within a year the book had sold over two million copies.

Born in Nottinghamshire

WILLIAM BREWSTER (1567–1644), leader of the Pilgrim Fathers, was born in SCROOBY. His descendants include Katherine Hepburn, Bing Crosby, Richard Gere, Chevy Chase and the 12th US President, Zachary Taylor.

NICHOLAS HAWKSMOOR (1661–1736), architect, known for Easton Neston in Northamptonshire, the west towers of Westminster Abbey and six London churches, was born in EAST DRAYTON.

ERASMUS DARWIN (1731–1802), inventor, founder of the Lunar Society and grandfather of Charles Darwin, was born in ELSTON.

ERIC COATES (1886–1957), composer of the signature tune for *Desert Island Discs*, was born in HUCKNALL.

Oxfordshire

❧❧❦❧❧

ENGLAND'S SMALLEST CATHEDRAL ✦ OXFORD CULTURE
✦ OXFORD MARTYRS ✦ AN EARLY ENGLISH CAPITAL
✦ AN EARLY ENGLISH FAMILY
✦ ENGLAND'S OLDEST STATE SCHOOL
✦ PROVISIONS ✦ NATIONAL GALLERY OF WORDS

Home of the Oldest English University

◄ OXFORDSHIRE FOLK ►

Lady Celia Fiennes ✦ Sir Ranulph Twisleton Wykeham Fiennes ✦ Flora
Thompson ✦ Dorothy L. Sayers ✦ P.D. James ✦ Lennox Berkeley
✦ Jacqueline du Pré ✦ Stephen Hawking ✦ Hugh Laurie

Oxford Cathedral

B uilt on the site of an 8th-century Saxon church of St Frideswide, the present OXFORD CATHEDRAL, which is 12th-century Norman, is THE SMALLEST OF ALL ENGLISH CATHEDRALS. It is also unique in being THE ONLY CHURCH IN THE WORLD THAT IS BOTH A CATHE-DRAL AND A COLLEGE CHAPEL. In 1524, a few years before the Dissolu-tion of the Monasteries, Cardinal Wolsey took over what was then the Priory church of St Frideswide, intending to demolish it and use the

land for a new 'Cardinal's College'. Fortunately he died before this could happen, and the old church survived as the chapel for the new college. In 1546 Henry VIII gave it to the first Bishop of Oxford as his cathedral, while at the same time it continued to serve as the chapel of the college of Christ Church.

Oxford Culture

O xford has ENGLAND'S FIRST BOTANICAL GARDENS, which were opened in 1621 – the first in the world were created by the Venetian nobleman Daniele Barbaro, in Padua in Italy in 1545.

Opened in 1683, Oxford's ASHMOLEAN MUSEUM WAS THE FIRST OFFICIAL PUBLIC MUSEUM IN THE WORLD – indeed the word 'museum' had to be created to describe it. The original contents came from the private collection of plants and curiosities gathered from around the world by the gardening Tradescants, father and son, and stored in their private museum in South Lambeth, the Ark. The collection was willed to the antiquarian Elias Ashmole, who donated it to Oxford, along with his own books and artefacts.

Oxford was also the scene of THE FIRST ENGLISH IQ TEST. It was conducted in 1908 by Sir Cyril Burt, using various groups of schoolchildren, and utilising the scale developed by French psychologist Alfred Binet.

Oxford also gives us the OXFORD BOOK OF ENGLISH VERSE, which first appeared in 1900, edited by Arthur Quiller-Couch, and OXFAM (Oxford Committee for Famine Relief), England's leading aid agency, founded in 1942 by a group of Oxford people, to send food to German-occupied countries such as Greece, which were suffering from British trade embargoes.

In 1954 Oxford hosted the first successful attempt to run A MILE IN UNDER FOUR MINUTES. The feat, which had been thought impossible, was achieved by 25-year-old ROGER BANNISTER, who covered the mile in 3 minutes 59.4 seconds at Oxford's Iffley Road sports ground.

Hugh Latimer, Bishop of Worcester, and Nicholas Ridley, Bishop of London, refused to recant their Protestant faith and in 1555 were condemned to a fiery death. As the flames took hold Latimer cried out, 'Be of good comfort, Master Ridley, and play the man. We shall this day light such a candle by God's grace in England as I trust shall never be put out.'

The following year Thomas Cranmer, Archbishop of Canterbury, was burnt at the stake on the same spot, despite recanting at the last minute. When he got to the stake, Cranmer thrust his right hand into the flames first – the hand with which he had signed his recantation. His death, and the manner of it, are said to have advanced the cause of the Reformation more than any other martyrdom.

Oxford Martyrs

On Broad Street, in the centre of Oxford, stands Sir George Gilbert Scott's Martyrs' Memorial, marking the spot where the Oxford martyrs Latimer, Ridley and Cranmer were burnt at the stake during the reign of Bloody Queen Mary. In 1553 Mary began the task of restoring England to the Catholic faith, and to this goal she had nearly 300 Protestant dissenters burnt and executed.

Dorchester

The beautiful Oxfordshire town of DORCHESTER was once a capital of England, and its unostentatious but ravishing little abbey, once a cathedral. It stands beside the River Thame, near where it meets the River Thames, on the spot where Christianity was confirmed as the principal religion of England. Here, in the 7th century, St Birinius

baptised the Saxon King Cynegils of
Wessex, in front of King Oswald of
Northumbria, uniting them against
the last pagan king, Penda of Mercia.
Dorchester remained a cathedral
until King Alfred transferred part of
the see to Winchester in the 9th
century. The present abbey church
dates from Norman times and
possesses a rare Jesse window, with
the Tree of Jesse illustrated not only
in the stained glass but also on the
stone mullions. The Tree burgeons
upwards from a reclining Jesse, the
delicate boughs exquisitely carved
with Biblical figures, mirrored in the
window lights and complemented by
the faint memory of vivid ancient
wall paintings. A glorious composition to find in a lovely, almost
forgotten town.

Upriver from Dorchester, the
correct name for the Thames is the
Isis. However, the river is now only
known by this name as it runs through
the city of Oxford.

Alice, Duchess of Suffolk

Lost in a fold at the foot of the
Chilterns is the pretty, wooded
village of EWELME, where a gently
flowing brook leads the quiet main
street past mellow cottages, water-
cress beds, manor house and church.

Lying beneath a sumptuous monument in the church at Ewelme is the
last of one of England's first great

families, ALICE CHAUCER, DUCHESS OF SUFFOLK.

Alice was the granddaughter of Geoffrey Chaucer, author of the first great work written in the English language, the *Canterbury Tales*. Chaucer's sister-in-law, Katherine Swynford, was mistress and then third wife of the mighty John of Gaunt, Duke of Lancaster, third surviving son of Edward III. Geoffrey's oldest son, Thomas Chaucer, fought at Agincourt, rose high in the favour of Henry V and married an heiress, Matilda Burghersh, who brought him the manor of Ewelme. Their only child was Alice, married as a child to John Phelip, who was killed at Harfleur, then to the Earl of Salisbury, who died at the siege of Orleans, and finally to William de la Pole, Earl of Suffolk.

In 1444 Suffolk was responsible for negotiating the marriage of Henry VI to Margaret of Anjou, and he and Alice travelled to France to bring the new Queen to England, where she stayed as a guest in their palace at Ewelme.

As Lord High Chamberlain and the power behind the throne of the young King Henry, Suffolk was blamed for the loss of English lands in France, notably by his arch-enemy the Duke of York, who wanted to install his own son Edward (later Edward IV) on the throne. At York's prompting, Suffolk was banished to the Continent, but he never reached his exile. His ship was waylaid off the coast of Kent, probably by agents of York, and Suffolk was hustled into a small boat where he was beheaded with six strokes from a rusty sword, and his body dumped on the beach near Dover.

Alice lived on at Ewelme, where she left a wonderful heritage, a group of medieval buildings without parallel in an English village. They owe their superb state of preservation to the fact that they are built of brick, a new and costly material at that time, and also because Ewelme has been left largely undisturbed over the years, being far from any main roads and well concealed in its own valley.

The schoolhouse, put up by Alice in the 1430s, is still used as a school and is THE OLDEST SCHOOL IN THE STATE SYSTEM STILL HOUSED IN ITS ORIGINAL BUILDING. Most other schools established at that time, notably Eton, founded in 1440 under the Earl of Suffolk's supervision for Henry VI, became private schools.

Ewelme School

Next door are the superb cloistered almshouses, designed for 13 poor men and fashioned around a square, flower-filled courtyard. They are still run as almshouses by the Ewelme Trust.

A steep, covered stairway leads to St Mary's Church, which shows signs of William de la Pole's Suffolk influence with space, light, a high roof and flint walls. The interior retains its screen and high, pinnacled oak font cover, and is rich with monuments and carving because, according to the villagers, Cromwell's rampaging soldiers couldn't find the village. In St John's Chapel are the simple tombs of Thomas and Mildred Chaucer, their portraits picked out in bronze on top.

But the chief treasure is the dazzling, stone-carved Gothic monument of the last of the Chaucers, Alice, Duchess of Suffolk. On the lid of the tomb, lying beneath a grand stone canopy and watched over by

monks and princes, the alabaster figure of Alice rests, her pillow attended by angels. She wears the order of the garter on her arm, one of the few women so honoured, and apparently Queen Victoria came here to learn how the garter should be worn by a lady.

Inside the cabinet is an emaciated figure covered by a shroud, gazing up at an amazing hidden frescoed roof, which can only be seen by lying down on the floor next to the tomb.

Outside in the churchyard a much less ostentatious gravestone marks the burial place of JEROME K. JEROME (1859–1927), author of *Three Men in a Boat.*

Of Alice's grand home, where Henry VIII honeymooned with Catherine Howard, and Queen Elizabeth stayed, little remains, just a few bits of wall embedded in the Georgian manor house which stands on the site.

The Provisions of Oxford

O XFORD is a name that has long reverberated through the story of the English, as home to THE FIRST ENGLISH UNIVERSITY. When Henry II discovered in 1167 that his rebellious Archbishop Thomas à Becket had taken refuge in France, he petulantly ordered all the English students who were studying over there to return home. Many came to Oxford, renowned as a place of scholarly debate since the time of Alfred the Great, and set up halls of learning similar to those they had known on the Continent. The first college, University College, was founded by William of Durham, in 1249.

Nine years later, in 1258, Oxford experienced the first stirrings of English democracy when Simon de Montfort and a group of disgruntled nobles, upset by Henry III's expensive foreign commitments, met in Oxford and drew up THE PROVISIONS OF OXFORD. These reaffirmed and refined the principles of Magna Carta, and formally stripped the King of his absolute power by setting up a number of committees and councils to oversee church matters and taxation. A 'Council of Fifteen' was formed which Henry had to consult over the handling of the 'common business of the realm and of the king'. These bodies would meet several times a year at a Great Council or Parliament.

Henry's subsequent disregard for the Provisions led to war between the King and the barons, and in 1265 Simon de Montfort looked to widen his support by summoning the barons, the knights of the shires and some burgesses, or 'commoners', to meet at Westminster for England's, and the modern world's, first truly representative Parliament.

The Provisions of Oxford was THE FIRST DOCUMENT OF ITS KIND TO BE WRITTEN IN ENGLISH AS WELL AS IN FRENCH AND LATIN, so that it could be understood by everyone – which is the aim of another of Oxford's contributions to English . . .

The Oxford English Dictionary

————————

A 'National Gallery of the race of English words' is how editor Frederick Furnival described his vision for the OXFORD ENGLISH DICTIONARY in 1861. He reckoned it would take four years to compile – in fact the first edition was not completed until 1928.

The OED is THE LARGEST RECORD OF ENGLISH WORDS, containing over 600,000 words and 2.5 million quotations – William Shakespeare is the most quoted writer, with *Hamlet* the most quoted of his works, while George Eliot is the most quoted female. The OED is continually being updated, although an obscure book written in 1634 is still the most quoted source of neologisms or new words – physician Sir Thomas Browne's *Religio Medici*, described as 'a sort of private diary of the soul' and full of imaginative vocabulary and imagery.

The most common word in the English language is 'the'. The most common noun is 'time', the most common verb is 'be' and the most common adjective is 'good'.

Because the English language was taken to the New World by the Pilgrim Fathers, and to Africa and the East by the British Empire, it is the most widely spoken second language in the world, and is now the language of the computer age – over 80 per cent of information stored electronically is written in English.

It also helps that English originates from and continues to borrow from so many different sources – mostly Latin, Saxon, Viking, French – and does not have too many fixed rules, making it the richest and most adaptable resource for literature and invention.

Well, I never knew this
about
OXFORDSHIRE FOLK

Ride a cock horse to Banbury Cross
To see a fine lady on a white horse

The lady in question was LADY CELIA FIENNES, who rode on a white horse from her home at Broughton Castle to Banbury Cross, as part of the May Morning celebrations in medieval times. The original Banbury Cross was torn down by Cromwell's Puritans and replaced by the Victorians.

The Fiennes still live at the picturesque moated manor house known as BROUGHTON CASTLE, built in 1300 and enlarged in the 16th century. A present member of the family, SIR RANULPH TWISLETON WYKEHAM FIENNES, belongs to that quintessentially English breed of character, the eccentric English explorer. He completed THE FIRST EVER UNSUPPORTED CROSSING OF THE ANTARCTIC ON FOOT, in 1993.

BANBURY was the model for 'Candleford' in Flora Thompson's trilogy, *Lark Rise to Candleford*. FLORA THOMPSON (1876–1947) was born and lived not far away at Juniper Hill, which is Lark Rise,

and her novel is an account of life in the villages of North Oxfordshire at the turn of the 19th century.

Born in Oxford

Oxford is the home of one of television's most celebrated detectives, Colin Dexter's Inspector Morse. It also the birthplace of two popular crime story writers, DOROTHY L. SAYERS (1893–1957), creator of amateur sleuth Lord Peter Wimsey, and P. D. JAMES (1920–2014), creator of Commander Adam Dalgliesh.

LENNOX BERKELEY (1903–89), composer.

JACQUELINE DU PRÉ (1945–87), cellist.

STEPHEN HAWKING, theoretical physicist and author of *A Brief History of Time*, born in 1942.

HUGH LAURIE, comedy actor, born in 1959.

Rutland

AMAZING ✦ THE POX

Normanton Church, a much loved landmark
of England's smallest county.

◄ RUTLAND FOLK ►

Sir Gilbert Heathcote ✦ Canon Hardwicke Rawnsley ✦ Ernest
Hornung ✦ Sir Malcolm Campbell ✦ William Pratt ✦ John Schlesinger
✦ Rick Stein ✦ Stephen Fry

Wing Maze

The pleasant village of WING sits on the brow of a hill with a view over Rutland Water to the north. There are plenty of interesting old houses and an old hall, and on the edge of the village is the superbly preserved WING MAZE, one of eight surviving English turf labyrinths.

Described in 1846 as 'an ancient maze, in which the rustics run at the parish feast', the Wing Maze measures 46 ft (14 m) across and is made up of paths that wind round to a centre in a series of decreasing circles, between low banks made of turf. The maze is a medieval English reproduction of the Cretan labyrinth constructed by Daedalus, father of Icarus who flew too close to the sun, and was devised by the Church as a form of penance. Wrongdoers were placed in the centre and had to make their way out on their knees, stopping at certain points to say prayers and meditate.

Liddington

Carved out of the wing of a medieval palace of the Bishops of Lincoln, the picturesque LYDDINGTON BEDE HOUSE was

converted by Sir Thomas Cecil into an almshouse for 12 poor 'bedesmen' over 30 years old, and two women over 45, all 'free of lunacy, leprosy or the French pox'.

Well, I never knew this
about
RUTLAND FOLK

Sir Gilbert Heathcote
◄ 1652–1733 ►

SIR GILBERT HEATHCOTE, the builder of Normanton Hall, of which only the clock tower and stable block survive, on the edge of Rutland Water, was one of England's most successful merchants and an early pioneer of free trade, who took on and defeated the richest monopoly of them all, the East India Company. In 1693, Heathcote bought a ship called the *Redbridge*, filled her with cargo and prepared her to sail for Alicante. The East India Company, which ruthlessly protected its monopoly of Far East trade, immediately ordered the arrest of the *Redbridge*, while it was still anchored in the Thames, and the confiscation of her cargo. While the Company could get away with this on the High Seas away from the eyes of Westminster, such high-handed behaviour at the heart of London caused outrage, and when Heathcote stood up in Parliament to denounce the action,

the arrest was declared illegal and a resolution passed declaring that no one could be restricted from trading unless specifically prohibited by law.

Heathcote went on to become a founding director of the Bank of England and twice its Governor. He was also elected Lord Mayor of London, and during the Lord Mayor's procession he was unceremoniously thrown from his horse, when it was startled by a drunken gypsy girl. As a result it was decided that in future the Lord Mayor should make the journey by coach so as to 'maintain his civic dignity'.

Sir Gilbert Heathcote was buried in the church at NORMANTON, which was rebuilt in the early 19th century to resemble St John's, Smith Square, in London. When England's largest man-made lake, Rutland Water, was created in the 1970s, the church was below the high water line and at risk of drowning. In order to save it the floor was raised by 10 ft (3 m) and the lower half of the building was filled with rubble, while a stone embankment was constructed around the church, along with a causeway for access. The Heathcote coffins and memorials, including one to Sir Gilbert by Rysbrack, were removed to the church in Edith Weston.

Normanton's church today appears to be sailing on the water and forms a memorable and picturesque tourist attraction. Sir Gilbert Heathcote, the ultimate entrepreneur, would be proud.

Duke of Rutland

The first Earl of Rutland was Edward Plantagenet, grandson of Edward III and son of the Duke of York. The Earldom remained a title of the House of York until it eventually passed to Thomas Manners, son of Richard Plantagenet's granddaughter Anne St Leger, in 1525, and the title has stayed in the Manners family to the present day. In 1703 the 9th Earl was made Duke of Rutland and Marquess of Granby. John Manners, Marquess of Granby and son of the 3rd Duke, was a celebrated soldier whose name is commemorated by numerous English pubs.

The Duke of Rutland's main homes are Belvoir Castle in Leicestershire and Haddon Hall in Derbyshire.

Uppingham

Noted alumni of Rutland's most famous school, Uppingham College, are known as Uppinghamians and include:

CANON HARDWICKE RAWNSLEY (1851–1920), co-founder of the National Trust.

ERNEST HORNUNG (1866–1921), author and creator of A.J. Raffles, 'gentleman thief'.

SIR MALCOLM CAMPBELL (1885–1948) and his son DONALD (1921–67), world speed record holders on land and water.

WILLIAM PRATT (1887–1969), better known as *Frankenstein* actor BORIS KARLOFF.

JOHN SCHLESINGER (1926–2003), film director.

RICK STEIN, TV chef and restaurateur, born 1947.

STEPHEN FRY, actor, writer and TV presenter, born 1957.

Shropshire

❖❖❖

BIRTH OF EVOLUTION ✦ AN APE OR A BISHOP
✦ EMPIRE BUILDER

Charles Darwin, the Father of Evolution.

◄ SHROPSHIRE FOLK ►

William Penny Brookes ✦ Wilfred Owen ✦ Thomas Minton
✦ Edith Pargeter

Charles Darwin

CHARLES DARWIN, one of the most influential and controversial Englishmen of all time, who challenged and changed the accepted wisdom of much of the world, was born at THE MOUNT, in Shrewsbury, in 1809. He was the fifth of six children and second son of Dr Robert Darwin, who had built The Mount in 1797.

Dr Robert was a keen gardener and planted many varieties of trees and shrubs in the extensive garden he laid out around the house. No doubt Charles's interest in botany and plants was nurtured by walking around the garden and studying his father's 'perennial garden diary'.

In 1831 Charles embarked upon one of mankind's most far-reaching voyages of exploration, spending five years sailing around the world on HMS *Beagle* as an unpaid naturalist. What he saw of the animals and plant life in such places as the Great Barrier Reef and the Galapagos Islands led him to develop his THEORY OF EVOLUTION.

Charles Darwin's birthplace, The Mount, used for many years as a Local Valuation Office, is to be developed as a museum in his memory. Much of the garden has been built over, but standing in what remains are trees and shrubs grown from seeds brought back from that extraordinary voyage by Shrewsbury's most famous son.

In 1897 a statue of Charles Darwin was erected outside what in his day was the school and is now the public library. A short time before, the steeple of nearby St Mary's church collapsed – a sign, some people thought, of God's disapproval of Darwin's theory, which

challenged the Bible's account of Creation.

Darwin had an impressive pedigree. His maternal grandfather was the pottery maker Josiah Wedgwood, while his paternal grandfather was ERASMUS DARWIN, inventor and member of that powerhouse of the Industrial Revolution, the Lunar Society. Erasmus had come up with his own theory of evolution 60 years before his grandson in a book called *Zoonomia, or the Laws of Organic Life*, published in 1794. Earlier still he had devised a family coat of arms consisting of three scallops with the motto 'E Conchis Omnia' or 'everything from shells'.

Darwin's Theory of Evolution

Darwin put forward the argument that all species have evolved from a limited number of original species by adapting to their environment over time, resulting in the 'natural selection' of those organisms best suited to survive and reproduce in their particular environment, or what the philosopher Herbert Spencer called 'the survival of the fittest'. This ran counter to the biblical explanation that God created the world and all the creatures in it just as they are. It also challenged the accepted science on the age of the earth, since evolution would have taken millions of years to achieve.

Many people were offended by the idea that man might be developed from apes, an argument that came to a head during the legendary debate between the Bishop of Oxford, Samuel Wilberforce (Soapy Sam), son of the anti-slavery campaigner William Wilberforce, and 'Darwin's Bulldog', the pro-evolution zoologist Thomas Huxley. When Wilberforce asked Huxley, 'Is it through your grandfather or your grandmother that you claim descent from a monkey?', Huxley replied with words to the effect that he would rather be descended from an ape than a Bishop.

Darwin himself was deeply upset by the controversy caused by his theory, and by the stridency of supporters such as Huxley, for he never believed that evolution was incompatible with a belief in God. Weakened by his long voyage on the *Beagle* he retired to Downe House in Kent, where he pottered happily with his wife and children for the remaining 40 years of his life. He is buried in Westminster Abbey.

Clive of India
1725–74

D escribed by William Pitt the Younger as 'a Heaven-sent General', ROBERT CLIVE, the Englishman who won India for the British Empire, was born in 1725 at Styche Hall in the village of MORETON SAY, near the busy market town of Market Drayton, one of 13 children of a lawyer. Brought up largely by childless relatives in Manchester and greatly spoilt, he was something of a tearaway, climbing the tower of Market Drayton church and frightening passers-by by pretending

to be a gargoyle and setting up a protection racket in the town to extort money from the town's shopkeepers. He was expelled from three schools.

Finally, much to the relief of Market Drayton, Clive's father sent him to India, as a clerk with the East India Company in Madras. Suffering from what we now know as manic depression, he quickly got bored and homesick and felt that life was not worth living. When he tried to kill himself, however, his pistol failed to go off twice and he concluded, 'I am reserved for something.'

In 1746 Madras was captured by the French, and Clive escaped to obtain a commission in the East India Company's army and find his true calling. He established his reputation in 1751 by taking the city of Arcot with just 200 men, and then defending it from a siege by over 10,000 attackers. In 1756 he was sent to retake Calcutta from the new Nabob of Bengal, Suraj Dowlah, who had imprisoned 146 members of the East India Company staff in stifling temperatures in a cell measuring 14 ft by 18 ft (4 x 5.5 m), later known as the Black Hole of Calcutta. Only 23 people came out alive. In 1757 Clive's 3,000 troops defeated the 50,000-strong army of the Nabob, complete with French artillery, at the Battle of Plassey, a remarkable victory which gained control over Bengal for the British and effectively drove the

French out of India for ever. Clive then installed a new Nabob, Mir Jaffier, and was himself appointed as the first Governor of Bengal.

Over the next ten years Clive established British rule over vast areas of India, but his great wealth and influence caused envy back in England and Clive was accused many times of corruption, despite Parliament conceding that he had rendered 'great and meritorious service to his country'. On 22 November 1774, his depression finally took its toll and Clive of India was found dead, most likely by his own hand, at his house in London's Berkeley Square.

Well over 200 years later, in 2006, Clive of India's pet tortoise ADWAITYA, brought from the Seychelles by an English seaman in the 1760s as a gift to Clive, finally died of old age at Calcutta Zoo, aged 255.

Well, I never knew this
about
SHROPSHIRE FOLK

William Penny Brookes
── 1809–95 ──

Father of the Modern Olympics

If you go down to the beautiful, and usually quite quiet old town of MUCH WENLOCK in July, you're sure of a big surprise. It was here, in 1850, that local doctor WILLIAM PENNY BROOKES, a prime mover in the introduction of physical education in English schools, instituted the forerunner of the modern Olympic games 'for the promotion of moral, physical and intellectual improvement'.

Brookes had studied the Ancient Olympics in great detail, and his vision was to revive the ideals of that great competition. The Much Wenlock games were open to sportsmen from all the surrounding

towns and villages, from all classes and professions, involved a variety of sports from quoit throwing to cricket, and were opened with much pageantry as the participants paraded through the town waving banners and flags.

A wealthy Frenchman called BARON DE COUBERTAIN visited the Much Wenlock games as a young man, and was deeply impressed. He had long discussions with Dr Brookes about how to expand the games for the international stage and in 1896, just months after Brookes had died at the age of 86, de Coubertain inaugurated the first modern Olympiad, in Athens. Many of the ideals and ingredients from the Much Wenlock games were incorporated into those first games, and are still present in the Olympic Games of today. In 1994 the president of the International Olympic Committee, Juan Antonio Samaranch, paid a visit to Much Wenlock and laid a wreath on the grave of William Penny Brookes saying, 'I came to pay homage and tribute to Dr Brookes, who really was the founder of the modern Olympic Games.'

Wilfred Owen
◄ 1893–1918 ►

Regarded by many as the finest war poet in the English language, WILFRED OWEN was born in Oswestry. He was teaching English in

France when the First World War broke out, and returned to England to enlist, for although he was a deeply committed Christian who believed war was wrong, he felt ashamed of his inactivity while his own generation were fighting and dying, and he despised what he called 'wishy-washy' pacifism. It was this conflict that inspired his remarkable poetry. A courageous and popular commander, he won a Military Cross for bravery at Amiens, when he single handedly captured a German machine gun and turned it on the enemy. He was shot and killed leading his men across the Sambre canal at Ors, just one week before the end of the war – his parents heard of his death while the Armistice bells were ringing.

Benjamin Britten, who inherited the mantle of Sir Edward Elgar as the great English composer, based his work *The War Requiem* on the poems of Wilfred Owen.

THOMAS MINTON (1765–1836), potter, inventor of the Willow Pattern, was born in SHREWSBURY.

EDITH PARGETER (1913–95), author better known as Ellis Peters, creator of the Shrewsbury-based detective monk Brother Cadfael, was born in HORSEHAY.

> *What passing-bells for these who die as cattle?*
> *Only the monstrous anger of the guns.*
> *Only the stuttering rifles' rapid rattle*
> *Can patter out their hasty orisons.*
> *No mockeries for them from prayers or bells,*
> *Nor any voice of mourning, save the choirs, –*
> *The shrill, demented choirs of wailing shells . . .*
>
> WILFRED OWEN, 'Anthem for Doomed Youth'

Somerset

HOLY GRAIL ✦ HOLY THORN ✦ AVALON
✦ ENGLAND'S SMALLEST CATHEDRAL CITY
✦ OLDEST ENGLISH STREET ✦ UPPITY SWANS

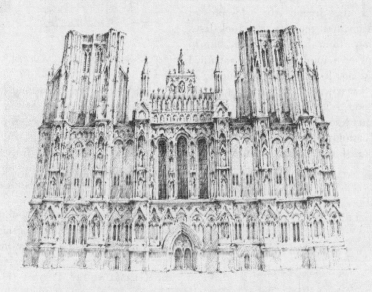

*Wells Cathedral, a prominent landmark in
England's smallest cathedral city.*

◄ SOMERSET FOLK ►

Henry Fielding ✦ John Locke ✦ Richard Lovell Edgeworth ✦ Sir William
Edward Parry ✦ John Edward Taylor ✦ Sir George Williams
✦ John Hanning Speke ✦ Sir Benjamin Baker ✦ Sir Cyril Pearson
✦ Margaret Bondfield ✦ Sir Arthur C. Clarke ✦ John Cleese

[243]

Glastonbury

And did those feet in ancient time
Walk upon England's mountains green?
And was the Holy Lamb of God
On England's pleasant pastures seen?
WILLIAM BLAKE

The words to 'Jerusalem' refer to the legend that Joseph of Arimathea, the man who took Jesus down from the cross and laid him in his own tomb, earlier accompanied the boy Jesus to England, landing in GLASTONBURY, then an island in the flooded Somerset levels. Some years after Jesus's death, Joseph returned to Glastonbury with the Holy Grail, and buried it beneath Glastonbury Tor at

Glastonbury Abbey Kitchen

Chalice Well, where the spring now runs red with the blood of Christ. He also built a church to watch over the Holy Grail, on flat land a short distance from the Tor, and Glastonbury thus became the birthplace of Christianity in England, and Joseph the first Bishop.

When he arrived in Glastonbury, Joseph stuck his staff in the ground at Wearyall Hill, and it blossomed into a magnificent hawthorn tree, the GLASTONBURY THORN (Holy Thorn).

Pilgrims from all over Christendom came to pay homage to the original Glastonbury Thorn, until it was wantonly cut down by a Roundhead soldier, during the Civil War. He was blinded by flying splinters for his trouble. Fortunately, cuttings from the original bush were secretly planted in the abbey grounds and in the

churchyard of St John's – the latter now being regarded as the official Glastonbury Thorn. Every year a sprig is cut from this tree and sent to decorate the Queen's Christmas table, in a custom dating from the reign of James I, when the Bishop of Bath and Wells donated a cutting to James's wife Queen Anne.

The Glastonbury Thorn only grows in and around Glastonbury and, unusually for a hawthorn, flowers twice a year, once in the spring and once on Christmas Eve. Since the revised Gregorian calendar was adopted in 1752, the thorn now blossoms on 5 January, in line with the previous Julian calendar.

At the beginning of the 8th century King Ine put up the first recorded church at Glastonbury, and in the 10th century Glastonbury was expanded by its first great Abbot, St Dunstan, who went on to become Archbishop of Canterbury.

Avalon

Glastonbury has long laid claim to be the fabled ISLE OF AVALON, where King Arthur was taken to die after defeating Mordred at the Battle of Camlann. In 1191, fortuitously for the abbey's finances, monks found a great oak coffin buried 16 ft (5 m) under the abbey's Lady Chapel, bearing the words 'Here lies interred in the Isle of Avalon the renowned King Arthur'. Inside were the bodies of a large, powerful man and a tall woman, assumed to be Arthur and his Queen Guinevere. In 1278 they were moved, in the presence of Edward I, to a specially constructed black marble tomb, which was unfortunately destroyed at the Dissolution of the Monasteries in 1539. A sign now marks the spot where Arthur waits patiently, ready to ride out and rescue his people when peril threatens.

Wells
England's Smallest Cathedral City

The same King Ine who built the church at Glastonbury also founded the Minster church of St Andrew, up the road near the Great Spring at WELLS, in 704. In the 10th century this building became WELLS CATHEDRAL, and in the late 12th century was itself replaced by the present grand cathedral. Wells is ENGLAND'S SMALLEST CATHEDRAL CITY, and because it developed solely as a religious centre (rather than defensive or industrial), provides perhaps the most complete and unspoilt example of a medieval ecclesiastical town in England.

Wells Cathedral is the first all-English cathedral, retaining nothing from its Norman and Saxon predecessors, but using Early English Gothic architecture throughout. The west front is England's finest gallery of medieval sculpture, with nearly 300 mostly life-sized statues set in individual niches, and completed in about 1280.

Inside, extraordinary scissor-style strainer arches were added in the 14th century to take the weight of the central tower, and there is an astronomical clock of 1390, which is unique in that it retains its original medieval clock face showing the universe with the Earth at its centre. On the hour, mounted knights emerge from the castle at the top, while a seated Quarter Jack strikes the quarter hours with his heel.

Wells's special treasure is the set of foot-worn steps that lead up from the cathedral to the Chapter House and

form the loveliest staircase in England, sweeping this way and that, like a mound of windswept leaves or a swirling brook.

To the north of the cathedral is THE OLDEST UNCHANGED ENGLISH STREET IN EXISTENCE, the 14th-century VICAR'S CLOSE, which is slightly tapered at the northern end to make it appear longer. The houses of the Close were built to accommodate the men of the cathedral choir, and the chimneys were made uncommonly tall so that the smoke would not affect the men's voices.

To the south of the cathedral, and accessed from the market-place through a grand 15th-century gateway called the Bishop's Eye, are the gardens surrounding St Andrew's Well, from which the city takes its name. A battlemented gatehouse leads to the moated Bishop's Palace, built in 1210 and one of the few left in England still occupied by a bishop. For centuries, the

mute swans living on the moat have been trained to use a bell-rope attached to the side of the gatehouse to ring for food when they are hungry, a skill still practised by the present generation.

Well, I never knew this about
SOMERSET FOLK

Henry Fielding
———◄ 1707–54 ►———

HENRY FIELDING was born at Sharpham Park, his grandfather's estate near Glastonbury. He is best remembered for his novel *The History of Tom Jones, a Foundling*, which was considered scandalous in some circles for its lusty portrayals. Fielding was the first novelist to write pure fiction, undisguised as letters or memoirs, and to introduce a wide and eclectic range of comic characters, and is regarded as THE FOUNDER OF THE MODERN ENGLISH NOVEL. All his work was bawdy and full of humour, which shocked some and amused others. The government of Robert Walpole brought in the Theatrical Licensing Act as a result of Fielding's satirical plays, while Jonathan Swift admitted that Fielding's work caused him to laugh for one of the only two times in his life.

ENGLAND'S FIRST POLICE FORCE, THE BOW STREET RUNNERS, formed in 1754, were the brainchild of Henry Fielding and his brother John, when they were both sitting as magistrates at Bow Street in London.

John Locke
———◄ 1632–1704 ►———

THE FATHER OF ENGLISH PHILOS-OPHY, JOHN LOCKE, the first English empiricist and libertarian philoso-pher, who believed that human

Born in Somerset

nature is governed by actual experience rather then theoretical laws, was born in a tiny cottage by the church at WRINGTON, in North Somerset. His ideas on the liberty of the individual, and belief in government by consent rather than by the divine right of either the Church or the aristocracy, greatly influenced Thomas Jefferson and the Founding Fathers of America, and helped to create the framework for the American Constitution.

It was Locke's philosophy that 'the ruling body, if it offends against natural law, must be deposed', that legitimised the American Revolution.

'All mankind . . . being all equal and independent, no one ought to harm another in his life, health, liberty or possessions.'

John Locke

RICHARD LOVELL EDGEWORTH (1744–1817), writer, road-making pioneer and inventor of the caterpillar track, was born in BATH.

SIR WILLIAM EDWARD PARRY (1790–1855), rear admiral and explorer whose voyages first located the entrance to the elusive Northwest Passage, was born in BATH.

JOHN EDWARD TAYLOR (1791–1844), founder of the *Guardian* newspaper, was born in ILMINSTER.

SIR GEORGE WILLIAMS (1821–1905), founder of the YMCA (Young Men's Christian Association), was born in DULVERTON.

JOHN HANNING SPEKE (1827–64), explorer who discovered and named Lake Victoria, was born in ILMINSTER.

SIR BENJAMIN BAKER (1840–1907), civil engineer and designer of the Forth Railway Bridge, was born in FROME.

SIR CYRIL PEARSON (1866–1921), founder of the *Daily Express*, was born in WOOKEY.

MARGARET BONDFIELD (1873–1953) one of the first three female Labour

MPs and the first female Cabinet member, was born in CHARD.

SIR ARTHUR C. CLARKE (1917–2008), author of *2001: A Space Odyssey*, was born in MINEHEAD.

JOHN CLEESE, comic writer and actor best known for *Monty Python* and *Fawlty Towers*, was born in WESTON-SUPER-MARE in 1939.

Staffordshire

HORN DANCE ✦ CROOKED HOUSE ✦ ANCHORS AWEIGH
✦ BRANSTON PICKLE ✦ HIGH HOUSE ✦ BULL TERRIER

High House in Stafford, the largest remaining timber-framed town house in England.

◄ STAFFORDSHIRE FOLK ►

Sir Stanley Matthews ✦ Cardinal Pole ✦ Phillip Astley ✦ James Wyatt
✦ Peter de Wint ✦ Robbie Williams

Abbots Bromley Horn Dance

THE HORN DANCE was first performed in the pretty, black-and-white and Georgian village of ABBOTS BROMLEY, at the St Bartholomew's Day Fair in August 1226. It is THE OLDEST SURVIVING FOLK FESTIVAL IN ENGLAND. Based on an ancient pagan ceremony, in medieval times it marked certain rights and privileges of the townsfolk for hunting, trapping and clearing in Needwood Forest, which belonged to the King and was governed by the strictest rules.

Today the Horn Dance takes place each year on Wakes Monday, the Monday following the first Sunday after 4 September. The company, which consists of Robin Hood on a hobby horse, Maid Marian, a boy with a bow and arrow, a jester, two musicians and six men wearing reindeer antlers, meets on the village green beside the 14th-century wooden butter cross, and then sets off to dance at various points around the village, finishing up on the lawns of nearby Blithfield Hall, ancestral home of the Bagots.

When not in use, the antlers, which have been dated to Norman

times, are hung on the wall of Abbots Bromley church.

The Crooked House

Cum in an av sum hum brewd erl
Stop us lung as yom erbul
At a public called the Siden House
Weer the beer runs up the terbul.

Not far from Dudley, on the road heading west to Wales, as it runs by the Himley Hall estate, there stands a most precarious and remarkable hostelry, surely the only pub in England where you feel tipsy before you even enter. One end of THE CROOKED HOUSE, or Siden House

in the local vernacular, has sunk by several feet as a result of subsidence due to mining operations by landowner Sir Stephen Glynne, who removed too much coal from underneath.

The whole building now leans at an amazing 15-degree angle, the windows and the doors are all haphazard, and visitors find themselves staggering across the sloping floor when making their way to the bar, as if at sea in a bad storm. Inside, the furniture doesn't match up to the floors or windows, there is a grandfather clock that tilts alarmingly, and if you roll a bottle down one of the tables it turns around and rolls back up again – and that is nothing to do with a pint of mine host's finest ale.

Anchors Aweigh

The hilltop church at NETHERTON, gazing down across the Black Country near Dudley, was witness a century ago to an early chapter in one of England's most tragic tales. NOAH HINGLEY & SONS of Netherton were the world's premier makers of anchors, and would later equip the British Grand Fleet with anchors during the First World War.

On this day, however, the church watched proudly as the firm's latest and most prestigious project was carefully loaded on to a wagon drawn by 14 horses, and taken away to Dudley. It was the biggest anchor in the world, weighing an astounding 16 tons, and was destined for the biggest ship in the world, the mighty and 'unsinkable' TITANIC, pride of the White Star Line. From Dudley the anchor was taken by train to Holyhead and then shipped across to Belfast, where the *Titanic* was being built. The anchor from Netherton now lies at the bottom of the ocean for, the following year, the *Titanic* hit an iceberg in mid-Atlantic and sank with the loss of 1,500 lives.

One of those who died was a son of Staffordshire, the Captain of the ill-fated vessel, EDWARD SMITH, who was born in HANLEY, Stoke-on-Trent, in 1850. Smith remained on the bridge of the *Titanic* as she sank, leaping into the sea only after the waves had washed her decks clear, but was drawn down into the depths along with his command. The *Titanic*'s maiden voyage was due to be his final command before retirement.

Branston Pickle

Branston Pickle takes its name from the village of Branston, near Burton-on-Trent, where it was first produced by Crosse and Blackwell in 1922.

Stafford

The magnificent High House in the county town of Stafford, built in 1595 for the Dorrington family, is THE LARGEST REMAINING TIMBER-FRAMED TOWN HOUSE IN ENGLAND. Charles I stayed here in 1642 on his way to Shrewsbury.

Staffordshire Bull Terrier

Bull terriers were first bred in the 17th century by crossing English white terriers with fighting bulldogs. Dog fighting was a popular sport in those days, particularly with the miners and colliers of the Staffordshire Black Country, and the owner of a good fighter could make a lot of money. After dogfighting was made unlawful by the Humane Act of 1835, some breeders started to crossbreed their bull terriers with Dalmatians for showing in the ring. These dogs became known as English bull terriers, and in order to avoid confusion the original bull terriers had the name Staffordshire added, since dogfighting had been so closely associated with the origins of the bull terrier.

The Staffordshire bull terrier suffers mightily from being mistaken for the American pit bull terrier, which is bred to be more vicious. In fact the 'Staffy' is one of the safest and most affectionate breeds of dog – it is the only breed to have the words 'totally reliable' in its breed standard, and one of only two breeds, from almost 200 recognised by the UK Kennel Club, to have a specific mention for suitability with children

Well, I never knew this
about
STAFFORDSHIRE FOLK

Sir Stanley Matthews
◄ 1915–2000 ►

STANLEY MATTHEWS was born in HANLEY, Stoke-on-Trent, and grew up to become one of the most renowned English footballers of the 20th century. At the age of 14 he joined his home town football team, Stoke City, straight from school. He stayed with the Potters for nearly 20 years, interrupted only by his service with the RAF during the Second World War.

In 1947 he controversially joined Blackpool, where he stayed for another 14 years. In 1953 he gave his most memorable performance in the final of the FA Cup, which has become known as the Matthews Final, when he inspired Blackpool to a last-minute win over Bolton.

In 1948 he became THE FIRST PLAYER TO WIN THE NEWLY INTRODUCED PLAYER OF THE YEAR AWARD, and he was also THE FIRST TO WIN THE INAUGURAL EUROPEAN PLAYER OF THE YEAR AWARD in 1956. The following year he became THE OLDEST PLAYER EVER TO PLAY FOR ENGLAND when he played against Denmark in a World Cup qualifier at the age of 42.

He rejoined Stoke City in 1961 and played his last game in 1965, five days after his 50th birthday, ending a professional career that spanned 33 years and included 84 England caps.

Stanley Matthews was a brilliant outside-right, known as the 'Wizard of Dribble', and his precision passing created goal-scoring opportunities almost out of nothing. He was also known for his fair play, earning another nickname, 'the First Gentleman of Soccer', and he did not receive a single booking throughout his long career. In 1964 he was THE FIRST PROFESSIONAL FOOTBALLER TO BE KNIGHTED.

His ashes are buried at the Britannia Stadium, home of Stoke City Football Club.

Cardinal Pole
◄ 1500–58 ►

REGINALD POLE was born at STOURTON CASTLE, near Stourbridge. His mother's father was George Plantagenet, 1st Duke of

Clarence, brother of Edward IV and Richard III and, as such Pole was the last of the Plantagenet line.

Pole studied theology at Oxford and travelled widely in Italy. As an important figure in the Church he was approached by Henry VIII, who offered to appoint him as Archbishop of York if Pole would support Henry's divorce from Catherine of Aragon. Pole refused and went into self-imposed exile in France. Henry took revenge on Pole's family, throwing his mother, brothers and other relatives into the Tower of London and executing them one by one – a handy way of ridding himself of the remaining Plantagenets, potential rivals for the throne.

When the Catholic Queen Mary I came to the throne in 1551 Pole, by now a Cardinal, returned to England and was made Archbishop of Canterbury. Over the next two years he presided over Mary's brutal persecution of the Protestants, which turned England violently against the Roman Catholic Church.

Cardinal Pole, THE LAST ROMAN CATHOLIC ARCHBISHOP OF CANTERBURY, died just hours after his Queen and was buried in Canterbury Cathedral. As part of his legacy he planted what is now ENGLAND'S OLDEST FIG TREE in the courtyard of Lambeth Palace in London.

Born in Staffordshire

PHILIP ASTLEY (1742–1814), inventor of the modern circus, was born in NEWCASTLE-UNDER-LYME.

JAMES WYATT (1746–1813), architect known for the Royal Military Academy at Sandhurst, for his neo-Gothic work (Ashridge House, Belvoir Castle, Goodwood House) and for his cathedral restoration work, was born in BURTON CONSTABLE.

PETER DE WINT, (1784–1849), landscape artist known for his watercolours, was born in STONE.

ROBBIE WILLIAMS, pop singer, was born in STOKE-ON-TRENT in 1974.

Suffolk

✦•✦•✦

ROYAL SAXON TREASURE ✦ BENJAMIN BRITTEN
✦ ALDEBURGH FESTIVAL ✦ SUFFOLK PUNCH
✦ AUTHOR OF EMPIRE ✦ OLD ENGLISH ORGAN

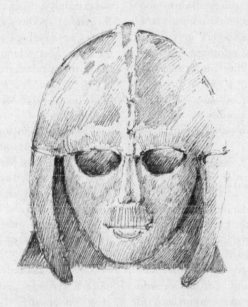

King's Helmet found at Sutton Hoo that
tells us much about our earliest kings.

◄ SUFFOLK FOLK ►

Thomas Gainsborough ✦ Cardinal Wolsey ✦ V.S. Pritchett ✦ Sir Trevor
Nunn ✦ Ralph Fiennes ✦ Humphrey Repton ✦ Sir Peter Hall
✦ Bob Hoskins

Sutton Hoo

◆◆◆◆

In 1939 a startling discovery was made near the Suffolk coast that lit up the Dark Ages and gave us a glimpse into the lives of some of the earliest Englishmen.

During the 1930s Mrs Edith Pretty began to have strange dreams about the mysterious grassy mounds beside the River Deben on her SUTTON HOO estate near Woodbridge. She saw a warrior standing on the largest mound, she saw a funeral procession, and she saw mountains of treasure. So she asked Basil Brown, the archaeologist from Ipswich museum, to have a look.

What he found was one of the most spectacular and important discoveries in the history of English archaeology, the burial place of King Raedwald of the East Angles, ruler of much of England south of the Humber. Brown uncovered a huge ship of the early 7th century, 90 ft (27 m) long and 15 ft (4.6 m) wide, with room for 20 rowers on each side, the first of its type ever to be found in Europe. There were brooches, coins from Gaul dated around 625, gold and silver plate, and a jewelled sword, battle-axe and ornamental helmet that clearly belonged to a powerful king.

There were also some everyday items that the king would need beyond the grave: cauldrons, bowls and, interestingly, two christening spoons. This was a time of transition in England between paganism and Christianity, and this burial would seem to have combined elements of both. To bury a king with his treasure was certainly a pagan custom, but the christening spoons indicate that the Angles were perhaps at least hedging their bets. Sutton Hoo was one of the last barrows raised in England, and has been described by some as the final burial-place of paganism in England.

The finds at Sutton Hoo reveal a huge amount about our earliest English ancestors. We can study the boats they travelled across the sea in, we can work out what they ate and how they hunted and farmed, we can even guess at what they looked like and how they ordered their society.

Raedwald was only the third King of the East Angles, and yet the Sutton Hoo burial site shows that the kingdom was already wealthy and powerful and had well-established trading links with Scandinavia and the Continent. Here, in the quiet pastures of Suffolk, we have been given perhaps the clearest snapshot of life in Angles Land.

Benjamin Britten
1913–76

One of the greatest English composers of the 20th century, BENJAMIN BRITTEN was born in Lowestoft on 22 November – the feast-day of St Cecilia, the patron saint of music. He studied at the Royal College of Music and for some of his early works collaborated with the poet W.H. Auden. In 1936 he met the tenor PETER PEARS, who became his life partner and the inspiration for much of his work. After some time in America, Britten and Pears returned to England in 1942 to live in Aldeburgh, and Britten began work on the series of English operas for which he is best known, beginning with *Peter Grimes*, based on the poems of George Crabbe, an Aldeburgh poet.

Although Britten's operas such as *Albert Herring, Billy Budd* and *Turn of the Screw* were well received by audiences, Britten's politics and his unconventional lifestyle and approach to music were frowned upon by the musical establishment, and he withdrew from the London scene for the more tolerant climes of rural Suffolk.

In 1947 he established the English Opera Group, with a small company of musicians, to present his own operas as well as the new works of other English composers, such as Lennox Berkeley. The cost of touring proved prohibitive and so in 1948 they founded the Aldeburgh Festival, which premiered with *Albert Herring* in the Aldeburgh Jubilee Hall, just yards away from Britten's home in Crabbe Street.

The Aldeburgh Festival has since expanded to other venues in Suffolk such as Orford and Framlingham, and now includes not just classical music and opera but drama, poetry, art exhibitions and lectures. Today it is one of the most popular and influential festivals in the world, while still uniquely English, in part thanks to its location at the Suffolk seaside.

In the mid-1960s the festival was able to make use of a new concert hall at SNAPE, a collection of old malting houses, imaginatively converted into an arts complex, which has now become the festival's main venue. The Snape Maltings burnt down on the opening night of the

1969 festival but were restored in time for the opening of the 1970 festival.

In 1962 Britten introduced what is considered his masterpiece, the *War Requiem*, based on the poems of Wilfred Owen and written for the consecration of the new Coventry Cathedral.

Benjamin Britten and Sir Peter Pears are buried in the churchyard of St Peter and St Paul in Aldeburgh. Nearby lies IMOGEN HOLST (1907–84), daughter of the composer Gustav Holst, and a composer in her own right, as well as a good friend of Britten. She lived most of her life in Aldeburgh, was director of the festival from 1956 until 1977 and contributed many of her father's papers to the Holst Library, based in Snape Maltings.

Set up on the beach at Aldeburgh is a shell-shaped sculpture by Maggi Hambling called *The Scallop*, dedicated to Benjamin Britten and edged with words from *Peter Grimes*: 'I hear those voices that will not be drowned.'

The Horse Before the Cart

The chestnut-coloured SUFFOLK PUNCH is THE OLDEST BREED OF HEAVY HORSE IN ENGLAND and

until the 1930s was bred exclusively in Suffolk. All Suffolk Punches descend from 'Crisp's Horse of Ufford', who was foaled in 1768. Today the Suffolk Punch is an endangered species, as there are only 300 pure Suffolk Punches left in the world, and the Suffolk Punch Trust has been set up to try and preserve and restore the breed.

Richard Hakluyt 1552–1616

WETHERINGSETT is a picture-book Suffolk village hiding amid trees, with pink-and-cream thatched cottages approached by tiny stone bridges that cross a rippling brook. It probably looks much the same as when RICHARD HAKLUYT came to take over the large 14th-century church here, as Rector in 1590.

He stayed in Wetheringsett for the remaining 26 years of his life, and it was there that he wrote his extraordinary masterpiece *The Principal Navigations, Voyages and Discoveries of the English Nation* (1598–1600). Throughout the Elizabethan era, English explorers and adventurers sailed the oceans of the world extending the English horizon across the globe by discovering new lands and civilisations. Gilbert and Frobisher sailed west to look for the Northwest Passage, Grenville explored the South Seas, and Drake had become the first Englishman to sail around the world. But until Hakluyt came along no one had thought to record these voyages, so that others might learn from them.

Hakluyt (his name is of Welsh origin) talked to all the great adventurers and merchants of the time, including Drake, Raleigh and Frobisher. He travelled to the ports and sea towns, where he sought out not just the captains but the crewmen and the sailors, to tell him of strange lands and uncharted seas. In rich, ribald language he recounted not only their tales of bravery and ingenuity and wonder, but also their mistakes and disasters and disappointments. He preserved the logs and the charts they made, and left an invaluable record for the traders, diplomats and merchants who were to follow.

It was Hakluyt who persuaded Sir Walter Raleigh that he should establish a base in America from which to search for the Northwest Passage, and he who first suggested that new-found lands should be colonised to create trading bases and outposts for the spread of the English way of life and language. It was Hakluyt who sowed the seeds of Empire in the minds of his fellow Englishmen.

Hakluyt is the definitive record of this extraordinarily prolific period of exploration and learning, and the Hakluyt Society still exists today to pay tribute to this remarkable man, and to promote the publication of expedition records and travel journals.

The Wetheringsett Organ

I n 1977, during the restoration of a 17th-century farmhouse in Wetheringsett, a large oak service door was removed and put aside to be broken up. It was of unusual shape and construction however, and on inspection, a series of holes and grooves were found that indicated a higher purpose. The door was shown to an expert, Noel Mander, and he recognised it as the soundboard of a very early 16th-century English organ.

Until this exciting discovery very little was known about the inner workings of these rare pre-Reformation English organs, but the Wetheringsett door has enabled a team of organbuilders to reproduce a working version of an Early English organ which now resides in Durham Cathedral and plays music as Henry VII might have heard it.

Well, I never knew this
about
SUFFOLK FOLK

Thomas Gainsborough
◄ 1727–88 ►

THOMAS GAINSBOROUGH, first of the English style of painters, was born in the attractive river port of SUDBURY, where his father was a weaver. He began sketching as a child, and at the age of 13 produced a landscape of such promise that he was sent to London to study art. Landscapes were his first love and he is regarded by many as the first great ENGLISH landscape painter – his contemporary Richard Wilson was Welsh. Like Wilson, however, Gainsborough found that landscapes didn't pay so he reluctantly turned to portrait painting instead, and it was as a portrait painter that he found fame.

After spending ten years in Ipswich, Gainsborough moved to Bath, where he attracted a number of wealthy clients and was able eventually to move to London. In 1768 he became a founder member of the Royal Academy, but later fell out with them and gave private exhibitions at Schomberg House, his home in London's Pall Mall, instead.

His only rival as a portrait painter was Sir Joshua Reynolds, but Reynolds' work was far less adventurous, and

was classically derivative, while Gainsborough developed his own original style. This, along with the fact that Gainsborough could also paint memorable landscapes, supports the claim that Gainsborough can be called the true founder of the English School of Painting.

Unlike most artists of his day Gainsborough never taught students, nor did he make the Grand Tour of Europe, which is perhaps one reason why his style remains so fresh and individual. His best-known work is probably his full-length portrait of Jonathan Buttall, known as *The Blue Boy*, for which he practised by painting his nephew Edward Gardiner in the same blue suit.

Gainsborough's House in Sudbury is now a museum in his memory and is the only English artist's birthplace that is open to the public.

Born in Ipswich

CARDINAL WOLSEY (1475–1530), Lord Chancellor to Henry VIII and builder of Hampton Court Palace.

V.S. PRITCHETT (1900–97), author and critic.

SIR TREVOR NUNN, theatre director (*Cats, Les Misérables*) and Director of the Royal Shakespeare Company and National Theatre, born 1940.

RALPH FIENNES, film actor, best known for *Schindler's List* and *The English Patient*, born 1962.

Born in Bury St Edmunds

HUMPHREY REPTON (1752–1818), landscape gardener (Attingham Park, Woburn Abbey).

SIR PETER HALL, theatre director and founder in 1960 of the Royal Shakespeare Company, born 1930.

BOB HOSKINS (1942–2014), film actor (*The Long Good Friday, Mrs Henderson Presents*).

Surrey

*The Great Seal of King John, attached to England's
earliest defence of human rights, Magna Carta.*

◀ SURREY FOLK ▶

P.G. Wodehouse ✦ Dame Peggy Ashcroft ✦ Sir David Lean ✦ Roy Hudd
✦ Kate Moss ✦ William Cobbett ✦ Aldous Huxley ✦ Mary Wesley
✦ Dame Margot Fonteyn ✦ Delia Smith ✦ Eric Clapton

Kingston-upon-Thames

Set in greenery beside the slow flowing Thames, the bustling Surrey town of Kingston was royal long before its mighty neighbour London. Its regal heritage dates back nearly 1200 years to 838, when King Egbert, King Alfred's grandfather, held a Great Council under the trees here. Kingston's proudest possession can be found in front of the modern Guildhall, set on a crude base, surrounded by ornamental railings and open to the wind and rain: the earliest throne of English kings, the King Stone on which seven Saxon kings were crowned – the first Kings of England.

In 901 King Alfred's son Edward the Elder was enthroned at Kingston, in St Mary's Chapel, then Athelstan

(925), who won Northumbria at the Battle of Brunanburgh, Edmund the Magnificent (940), conqueror of Cumberland, Edred his brother (946), Edgar the Peaceful (958), later confirmed as the first true King of England at Bath Abbey by St Dunstan, and then Edward the Martyr (975), murdered by his own stepmother at Corfe Castle to make way for Ethelred the Unready, crowned at Kingston in 979.

Across the market-place, the dimensions of the Saxon chapel of St Mary, in which the coronations took place, are marked out beside the present church of All Saints. Undermined by grave-digging, the chapel collapsed in 1730, killing the sexton and injuring his daughter Esther.

Encased inside the stone and brick 14th-century tower of All Saints is the original Norman chalk tower, possibly the oldest chalk structure in England.

Kingston hides its ancient heritage well, but in 1977, on her Silver Jubilee, Elizabeth II, Queen of England, the oldest ever English monarch, came to the town where her line began and unveiled a stone commemorating one of the earliest English monarchs, her Saxon predecessor, Edward the Elder.

Kingston grew up on the Hogsmill River where it enters the Thames. The Clattern Bridge over the Hogsmill near the market-place dates from the 13th century and is one of the oldest bridges in Surrey. The medieval name 'Clateryn-

All Saints, Kingston

brugge' is descriptive of the clattering of hooves as horses cross the bridge.

Sir John Millais painted a willow tree growing beside the Hogsmill, upstream at Ewell, for his picture of Ophelia, and Holman Hunt also painted the Hogsmill in *The Light of the World*.

Runnymede

❖❖❖❖

No freeman shall be seized, or imprisoned, or disseised, or outlawed, or any way destroyed, nor will we go upon him, nor will we send upon him, except by the lawful judgment of his peers, or by the law of the land. To none will we sell, to none will we deny, to none will we delay right of justice.

MAGNA CARTA

Spread at the foot of Cooper's Hill, between Egham and the River Thames, are the lush green meadows of RUNNYMEDE which, in the summer of 1215, were witness to the first faint stirrings of English freedom, the first real attempt to limit the absolute power of the King and recognise the rights of ordinary Englishmen. On the 15th day of June, King John, the worst King ever to sit on the English throne, angrily stamped his royal seal on the preliminary draft of the Great Charter that forms the foundation stone of English liberty.

MAGNA CARTA was the result of King John's abject misrule. His arbitrary raising of taxes to pay for disastrous foreign wars, and his extravagant injustices, forced the squabbling barons to unite against him, and in Stephen Langton, Archbishop of Canterbury, they had a brilliant and articulate champion. John was summoned to Windsor, and for several days the King, representatives of the noblemen, the Church and the merchants of London, and even some ordinary English yeomen, gathered beside the Thames on the broad green sward of Runnymede to thrash out an agreement that would answer 49 grievances drawn up by the barons.

Although the Magna Carta is rough and clumsy, and by no means the most effective or far-reaching declaration of basic freedoms and

rights ever written, it is nonetheless the most revered, by virtue of being the first. It is the raw template from which all other charters draw their inspiration, and forms the basis for the constitutions and statutes of countries across the English-speaking world. It underlies the American Constitution and Bill of Rights, and even the European Convention for Human Rights.

Derby Day

In 1618, during a severe drought, an Epsom boy took his cattle to drink from a spring on Epsom Common – and found to his consternation that they refused. Investigations revealed the water to be very salty, but while cows might not have liked it, human folk found that a quick draught relieved all kinds of digestive ailments. EPSOM SALTS became famous, and people from all over Europe flocked to the town, one of the first English spa towns. Hotels and assembly rooms were built, and gipsy fairs and horse races were held on the Downs to entertain the visitors. Attracted by the endorsement of Charles II, it was not long before the Quality came to Epsom, bringing their horses with them.

In 1778, during a raucous dinner party at the Earl of Derby's Carshalton estate, The Oaks, the Earl and his friends came up with the idea of a sweepstake for three-year-old fillies to

be run on the Downs over a distance of one and a half miles. The race was inaugurated the following year, in 1779, and named after the house where it was conceived. The first winner was the Earl's own horse BRIDGET.

Such was the success of the event that during the celebrations afterwards, the Earl of Derby and his friend Sir Charles Bunbury decided to organise a further race the next year, 1780, run over the same distance but this time to include three-year-old colts as well as fillies. They flipped a coin to see who the race would be named after – had it landed the other way up then the most famous and prestigious flat race in the world would be the Bunbury. As

it was, Sir Charles had to make do with having the first Derby winner, DIOMED.

Until recently the Derby was always run on the first Wednesday in June and attracted hundreds of thousands of spectators. It was regarded as 'London's Big Day Out', when Londoners of all classes would take the day off and come to the Downs with their picnics to enjoy the racing and the gipsy funfairs. In Victorian times even Parliament was adjourned for the day. However, in the 1990s it was deemed too difficult for workers to get the day off in the middle of the week, and so the Derby was switched to the first Saturday in June.

Because free access to the Downs

Derby Facts

The Derby and the Oaks are two of the five English 'classics'.

The Derby was THE FIRST EVER HORSE RACE TO BE FILMED, by a chap called BIRT ACRES on 29 May 1895. It was also the first British sporting event ever to be televised, on 3 June 1931.

In 1981 the Derby was won by ten lengths, the biggest winning margin in the history of the race. The horse that achieved this feat was the last odds-on winner, the legendary SHERGAR, who gave the Aga Khan his first English classic triumph. In 1983 Shergar was snatched from the Aga Khan's stud in Ireland and was never seen again.

The most successful jockey in the history of the Derby is LESTER PIGGOTT, with a total of nine wins..

The downhill stretch at Epsom is reputed to be
THE FASTEST RACING STRETCH IN THE WORLD.

is protected by an Act of Parliament, those who want to can see the Derby for nothing, and this has helped to make England's oldest major sporting event also England's most popular major sporting event, with average crowds of well over 100,000.

Chaldon Doom

Lost in the trees on the Surrey Downs, beside an old bargeboard farmhouse, there is a quiet little church of Norman England that hides a startling treasure. In the days when Englishmen could neither read nor write, the stories of the Bible were told to them through pictures, and painted on the west wall of Chaldon's crooked church is the finest and most vivid Norman illustration in England, the CHALDON DOOM. It shows the Ladder of Salvation linking Heaven and Hell. Tormented souls tumble down the ladder to be roasted and boiled in Hell, while Heaven is filled with music and angels. The grotesque figures are full of vitality, picked out in white against a dull red background, and even today the effect remains powerful and terrifying, as it was designed to be.

This amazing medieval gallery was discovered in 1870 under layers of whitewash, which had served to protect its lustre and colour. Chaldon, only minutes away from the noise and stress of modern Croydon and the M25, is one of England's secret glories.

Well, I never knew this
about
SURREY FOLK

P.G. Wodehouse
◄ 1881–1975 ►

PELHAM GRENVILLE WODEHOUSE, known as 'Plum' from his mispronun-ciation of his own name as a child, was born in GUILDFORD, and will for ever be the finest comic writer in the English language. As anyone who has attempted to come up with a

---

'Her face was shining like the seat of a bus-driver's trousers.'

'From his earliest years there has always been something distinctive and individual about Gussie's timbre, reminding the hearer partly of an escape from a gas pipe and partly of a sheep calling to its young in the lambing season.'

'He was a tubby little chap who looked as if he had been poured into his clothes and had forgotten to say "when!"'

'I could see that, if not actually disgruntled, he was far from being gruntled.'

'Memories are like mulligatawny soup in a cheap restaurant. It is best not to stir them.'

P.G. WODEHOUSE

---

comic phrase, metaphor or simile will know, Wodehouse has already written a funnier one.

While Bertie Wooster and his gentleman's gentleman Jeeves are perhaps Wodehouse's best-known characters, all of his comic creations are loved and recognised across the world as affectionate caricatures of the English, set in a timeless England – 'where every prospect pleases and only man is vile'.

He is buried in the Remensburg Cemetery in New York.

Born in Croydon

DAME PEGGY ASHCROFT (1907–91), actress, who won an Oscar for *A Passage to India* in 1984, and for whom Croydon's theatre is named.

SIR DAVID LEAN (1908–91), film director (*Lawrence of Arabia, Bridge on the River Kwai, A Passage to India*).

ROY HUDD, comedian, born 1936.

KATE MOSS, model, born 1974.

Born in Surrey

WILLIAM COBBETT (1763–1835) radical journalist and farmer, was born in FARNHAM. For his *Rural Rides* he rode through much of England and recorded his observations on the English countryside, noting the changes being wrought by the Industrial Revolution.

ALDOUS HUXLEY (1894–1963) author of *Brave New World*, was born in GODALMING.

MARY SIEPMAN, pen-name MARY WESLEY (1912–2002), author of *The Camomile Lawn*, was born in ENGLE-FIELD GREEN.

DAME MARGOT FONTEYN (1919–91), ballerina, was born in REIGATE.

DELIA SMITH, TV chef, England's best-selling cookery writer and Chairman of Norwich Football Club, was born in WOKING in 1941.

ERIC CLAPTON, rock guitarist, was born in RIPLEY in 1945.

Sussex

The End of Anglo-Saxon England ✦ Class ✦ Domesday Book ✦ English Country House ✦ The Waves Rush In ✦ Last Resting Place of the Saxon English

Parham House, a jewel of Elizabethan England.

SUSSEX FOLK

Rudyard Kipling ✦ Richard D'Oyly Carte ✦ Percy Bysshe Shelley ✦ Edward Gibbon ✦ E.F. Benson ✦ Vanessa Bell ✦ Virginia Woolf ✦ Duncan Grant ✦ Enid Bagnold ✦ Vita Sackville-West

Battle Abbey

On the morning of 14 October 1066, Saxon England, that young, fledgeling 'land of the Angles', united and forged with such effort by Alfred the Great and his descendants, was crushed to earth, and Norman England was born. The BATTLE OF HASTINGS, as it became known, was the most important battle in English history and the result changed England and the English for ever.

In 1070 William the Conqueror began building an abbey on the site of the battle, which is in fact some 7 miles (11 km) north of Hastings, both as a celebration of his great victory and a penance for the huge loss of life suffered on that day. The high altar was placed where the Saxon King Harold fell, and although the walls of the abbey church are no more, the foundations are still in place, along with some 13th- and 14th-century remains. To stand where the Saxon army stood, nearly 1,000 years ago, its banners flying in the wind, and to gaze across the valley, now filled with trees, to where the Norman forces were assembled on Telham Hill, is spine-tingling.

English Class

Amongst the most profound effects of the Norman Conquest was the creation of the English class system, which, with a few modifications along the way, has shaped English history ever since. In those days power came from owning land, and so William declared that all land, and hence power, belonged to the Crown. He then handed out parcels of that land to his supporters in return for their loyalty.

The class system that

developed was therefore based on the ownership of land. Most of those who owned the land, the upper classes, were French-speaking Normans, while those who worked the land, the working classes, were dispossessed, English-speaking Anglo-Saxons.

This divide was reflected in both accents and vocabularies. While Royalty and the ruling classes used rounded Norman vowel sounds, as in 'barth', the working classes used short flat vowel sounds, as in 'baath'. English words used to describe culture and lifestyle, food, fashion, furniture and titles tend to be French based, while English words of Anglo-Saxon origin are much more direct and earthy and are used for the basics.

For instance, the fact that the working class handled the live animal while the ruling class ate it, is reflected in words used for food, with Saxon words describing the uncooked and Norman words the cooked.

Anglo-Saxon	*French*
Cow, Ox	Beef
Sheep, Lamb	Mutton
Pig, Swine,	Pork,
Ham	Bacon
Calf	Veal
Deer	Venison

(Deer entrails, which were left for the servants, were called 'umbles' – hence to 'eat humble pie'.)

Domesday Book

In order to find out how much land he did in fact now own, William the Conqueror ordered his officials to travel the length and breadth of England and make an inventory of every landholding and settlement in the country, along with its produce and worth. This survey, completed in two years from 1085 to 1086, is known as the 'DOMESDAY BOOK' and is THE EARLIEST PUBLIC RECORD OF ENGLAND THAT EXISTS.

Although the Domesday Book was a remarkable achievement, the project was rendered a great deal easier by the fact that the Anglo-Saxons left William a kingdom already efficiently divided into a network of shires that would survive, pretty much unchanged, until the clumsy reorganisation of county boundaries in 1974.

The English Country House

'England's most characteristic contribution to European culture'
CHRISTOPHER HUSSEY

The power that was endowed by the ownership of land came largely from the tenants and rents that went with it. Rent was often paid by working and fighting for the landowner as well as through farming, and the estate required a headquarters from where it could be both administered and defended, in other words, a castle.

In more peaceful Elizabethan times, it was no longer necessary to build fortified houses, and the rich merchants began to build vast palaces that visibly proclaimed their wealth and status. Ownership of a country house was a symbol of the fact that you had arrived, and it became the ambitious Englishman's most desired possession – as it still is.

In its heyday, English country house living was possibly the most perfect form of existence invented by man – it provided employment, living accommodation, food, and beauty in architecture and landscape that was limited only by the owner's pocket and his architect's imagination.

Bosham

While the first Norman King of England went on in glory to shape the land of his conquest, the fate of the last Saxon King of England is less clear. Waltham Abbey in Essex has long claimed King Harold's body, but there is evidence to suggest that he may never have left Sussex, the kingdom of the South Saxons where he met his doom.

In the far west of Sussex is BOSHAM, a large and outstandingly pretty village overlooking Chichester Harbour, where gardens and mossy lawns are lapped by the muddy green sea, and artists, sailors and wildfowl are lured by the bracing air. Bosham was one of the few settlements to appear in the Anglo-Saxon chronicles, and therefore must have been a place of some importance in those times. St Wilfred of York was known to have established a small monastery at Bosham in the 7th century on the site of an even earlier cell. The fabric of the ancient church contains Roman fragments, Saxon arches and Norman pillars.

KING CANUTE had a palace at Bosham, and it was here that he went down to the water's edge and commanded the tide to turn back, knowing that it would not, so that he could prove to his fawning courtiers that he was not all-powerful. Canute also met with

tragedy in Bosham, for in 1020 his young daughter drowned in the mill stream and was buried beneath the stone church floor.

King Harold's father, Earl Godwin, made Bosham his home, and Harold later inherited the palace. The Saxon chancel we see in Bosham's church today is much as Harold would remember it, and appears in the Bayeux Tapestry, where Harold is shown at prayer before embarking on the sea voyage that was to seal his fate. His ship was wrecked on the coast of Normandy and he was taken to Duke William in Rouen, where it is believed he made an agreement to support William's claim to the throne of England on the death of Edward the Confessor. When Harold returned and claimed the throne for himself, William felt cheated and came to take his due by force.

After the Battle of Hastings some records state that the bodies of Harold and his father were brought back to their home at Bosham. In the 1950s a tomb was found under the floor of the church containing a corpse with the head, right leg and left hand missing – which corresponds to the injuries that Harold had sustained at his death, according to accounts by the Bishop of Amiens.

Could sleepy, seaside Bosham be the last resting-place of the Saxon English?

Well, I never knew this
about
SUSSEX FOLK

'Oh, East is East, and West is West, and never the twain shall meet.'

'But that's another story . . ,'

'For the female of the species is more deadly than the male.'

The quotes above are from the work of RUDYARD KIPLING, THE FIRST ENGLISHMAN AND THE YOUNGEST PERSON EVER TO WIN THE NOBEL PRIZE FOR LITERATURE, who made Sussex his home from 1897 until his death in 1936. From 1902 he lived at Bateman's, a beautiful 17th-century ironmaster's house in the village of Burwash, but his first Sussex home was a house called The Elms by the village pond in ROTTINGDEAN, near Brighton, where his aunt Georgina Burne-Jones had a holiday home. She was married to the Pre-Raphaelite

Rudyard Kipling

painter SIR EDWARD BURNE-JONES, who is buried in the church-yard at Rottingdean. The church itself can boast a set of stained-glass windows made by William Morris to the design of Burne-Jones, considered to be amongst their finest work.

A frequent visitor to The Elms was Kipling's friend the society portrait painter SIR WILLIAM NICHOLSON, who eventually came to live in The Grange in 1912. He made a woodcut of Rottingdean windmill up on the downs, which was used by the publishers Heinemann as their logo.

Daddy Long Legs

For a few glorious years at the end of the 19th century Rottingdean was

linked to Brighton by an imaginative railway dreamed up by Brighton-born MAGNUS VOLK, the BRIGHTON AND ROTTINGDEAN SEASHORE ELECTRIC RAILWAY, affectionately known as 'Daddy Long Legs'. From a pier at Rottingdean, a tramcar perched on high stilts moved along on rails running under the sea some 100 yards (90 m) offshore, and met up with Volks's land-based railway on the sea-front at Brighton, opened in 1883 as the world's first publicly operated electric railway. The Brighton railway is still in action today, but the Daddy Long Legs had to close in 1901, after a slightly precarious career, when Brighton council wanted to build groynes out into the water for sea defence. Lengths of the track bed can still be seen at low tide,

PERCY BYSSHE SHELLEY (1792–1822), poet, was born in HORSHAM.

Writers and Artists Buried in Sussex

EDWARD GIBBON (1737–94), historian and author of *The Decline and Fall of the Roman Empire*, is buried in FLETCHING.

along with the stumps of some of the posts that carried the power lines high above the water. Magnus Volk is buried in the churchyard of St Wulfstan's, Ovingdean, tucked into the hills behind Rottingdean.

E.F. BENSON (1867–1940), author of the Mapp and Lucia books, is buried in RYE, where his novels are set.

VANESSA BELL (1879–1961), Bloomsbury Group artist and interior designer, is buried in FIRLE.

Looking down imperiously from the cliffs between Rottingdean and Brighton is ROEDEAN, perhaps the most famous private school for young English 'gals' after St Trinian's. Roedean was founded at 25 Lewes Crescent, Brighton, in 1885 by the Misses Dorothy, Millicent and Penelope Lawrence to provide 'young ladies' with an all-round education. The school moved to its present, purpose-built site in 1899. Old girls include the actress Sarah Miles and Dame Cicely Saunders, founder of The Hospice Movement.

VIRGINIA WOOLF (1882–1941), Bloomsbury Group novelist, is buried in RODMELL.

DUNCAN GRANT (1885–1978), Bloomsbury Group painter, is buried in FIRLE.

ENID BAGNOLD (1889–1981), author of the classic girl's story *National Velvet*, is buried in ROTTINGDEAN.

RICHARD D'OYLY CARTE (1844–1901), Gilbert and Sullivan's patron and impresario, is buried in the church at FAIRLIGHT.

VITA SACKVILLE-WEST (1892–1962), gardener, poet and novelist, is buried in WITHYHAM.

Vale of The White Horse

---◆◆◆---

ENGLAND'S OLDEST HILL FIGURE ✦ DRAGON HILL
✦ WAYLAND'S SMITHY ✦ ENGLAND'S OLDEST ROAD
✦ FIRST TRUE KING OF ENGLAND ✦ ENGLISH BEGINNINGS

King Alfred, the first true 'Great' King of England.

◄ WHITE HORSE FOLK ►

George Orwell ✦ Agatha Christie ✦ Thomas Hughes ✦ Lester Piggott

Uffington White Horse

High up on the Berkshire Downs lies the oldest hill figure in England, the UFFINGTON WHITE HORSE. Roughly 365 ft (111 m) long and 120 ft (37 m) high, it is the largest of all England's White Horses.

Over the years there have been many theories about the origin of the White Horse: that it was carved in celebration of King Alfred's victory over the Danes at the Battle of Ashdown in 871, or cut in the 5th century by the first Saxon invaders Hengist and Horsa, whose emblem was a horse. However, the White Horse has recently been dated to around 1200 BC, making it over 3,000 years old. It is now believed that the figure might have had religious significance, as it was created in the late Bronze Age when horses were revered.

Religious festivities associated with horse worship also probably account for the celebrated 'SCOURING OF THE WHITE HORSE', when the trenches are weeded and edged, and crushed chalk is added to keep the shapes true and clearly visible. This has been going on for centuries, although it was not recorded until the 17th century. Without the 'Scouring' the horse would have long since been overgrown and disappeared. The festival used to take place every seven years and latterly was accompanied by great celebrations and merrymaking, with feasting and games such as cheese rolling down the steep sides of the Manger, a deep valley scooped out of the hillside beneath the horse.

Today the Horse is maintained by the National Trust and English Heritage.

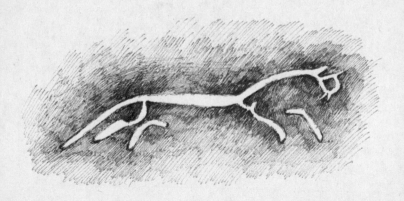

Dragon Hill

····

J ust below the White Horse is a small, flat-topped hill crowned with a bare patch, devoid of grass. It is known as DRAGON HILL, because it was here, according to local legend, that St George slew the dragon – and where the dragon's blood fell the grass cannot grow. Some say that the White Horse is not a horse at all, but rather a representation of the dragon slain by St George, and certainly the somewhat abstract styling of the creature lends itself to that interpretation.

Wayland's Smithy

····

A bove the White Horse, on the top of the hill, is UFFINGTON CASTLE, an extensive, Bronze Age hill fort covering 8 acres (3.2 ha). A little further west, along the Ridgeway, is WAYLAND'S SMITHY, a neolithic burial chamber surrounded by beech trees. Wayland was the Saxon god of smiths, who forged armour that gave the wearer the wings of eagles, as well as invincible swords. Indeed, it was Wayland who forged King Arthur's sword Excalibur.

Wayland is never seen, but he will shoe a horse if the rider leaves a silver coin on the stones and goes away – on the rider's return the horse will be found newly shod.

All these places give the most glorious views over the countryside that takes its name from its sacred landmark – the Vale of the White Horse.

The Ridgeway

ENGLAND'S OLDEST ROAD runs for 87 miles (140 km) from near the stone circle at Avebury to Ivinghoe Beacon in the Chilterns. For 4,000 years our ancestors have trod this road, carrying their goods or driving their cattle along the high ground – and not much has changed, for the route of England's most ancient trade route is in large part mirrored by one of England's newest highways, the M4. The majority of the mysterious 'crop circles' discovered in recent years have occurred in the vicinity of the Ridgeway.

King Alfred

THE FIRST TRUE KING OF ENGLAND, ALFRED THE GREAT, was born in the Royal Palace at WANTAGE in AD 849, one of four sons of Ethelwolf, King of Wessex. Although the youngest, Alfred was the most learned, and when their mother promised to give an illustrated book to the first of the brothers who could learn to read, Alfred won.

He was also a great warrior and fought alongside his brothers in numerous battles against the invading Danes. In 871 he led the forces of his brother King Aethelred in a great victory at the Battle of Ashdown on the Berkshire Downs.

The Danes kept coming, however, and when Aethelred was killed in one of the subsequent battles, Alfred became King. After being defeated at the Battle of Wilton in late 871, he was forced to negotiate a large payment to secure peace, and for a few years the Danes kept to themselves in eastern England.

In early 878 the Danes, led by King Guthrum, made a surprise attack on Alfred's palace at Chippenham, in Wiltshire, and the Saxon king and his men were forced to flee into the Somerset marshes. After a few weeks they

---

The Beginnings of English

The English language evolved from a mingling of the Old Norse of the east with the Old English of the west, both of which were Germanic in origin. The distinction can be seen in the different kinds of place name found in east and west – names ending in wick (inlet), scar (rock), kirk (church) or thorpe (farm) are Norse, while ham (village), borough (town), bury (fort), hurst (wooded hill) or lee (clearing) indicate Saxon origins.

managed to regroup, and emerging from the wetlands in May 878, routed the Danes at the Battle of Edington.

At the resulting Treaty of Wedmore, King Guthrum agreed to keep within his own lands in the east of England, behind a line that followed the Roman Watling Street. This area was known as the Danelaw, where Danish rule and customs prevailed. Guthrum also agreed to convert to Christianity, and thus Christianity became the prevailing religion in almost all of England.

Alfred moved fast to fortify Wessex against further incursions by creating a series of fortified market places, or 'burghs', and by founding the English Navy to protect the coastline. In the 18th century, the United States Navy commemorated his achievement by naming its first flagship USS *Alfred.*

Alfred introduced new laws based on Christian teachings, and encouraged education and reading, which

had almost ceased since the Danes had sacked the monasteries. He translated many important works from Latin into English and instigated the ANGLO-SAXON CHRONICLES, THE FIRST HISTORY OF ENGLAND WRITTEN IN ENGLISH.

Alfred also began the division of England into counties and hundreds, using natural features such as rivers and hills as boundaries, divisions that lasted almost unchanged until bureaucratic minds began to 'tidy them up' in the 1970s.

After ten years of peace and progress, Alfred died on 26 October 899 and was buried in his capital, Winchester.

Alfred excelled as a military leader and a wise ruler. He set in place a code of law and laid the foundations of a united England. The first true King of England is the only one of all our kings and queens to be honoured as 'the Great'.

Well, I never *knew this*
about
WHITE HORSE FOLK

George Orwell
1903–50

GEORGE ORWELL, author of two of the greatest political novels ever

written, lies in the churchyard at SUTTON COURTNEY, buried under his real name Eric Arthur Blair.

Born in India, he won a scholarship to Eton and joined the Civil

Service in Burma, where his observations of poverty and cruelty turned him against colonialism and his middle-class background. He decided it would do him good to learn about life as a tramp, and he returned to London, where he lived on the streets amongst the poor, recording his experiences in a book, *Down and Out in London and Paris*.

Next came *The Road to Wigan Pier*, written about his time spent amongst the working classes in a northern town suffering from mass unemployment. In 1936 he volunteered to fight in the Spanish Civil War against General Franco, and his left-wing beliefs were severely shaken when he watched how the Soviet-backed Communists turned on his fellow Trotskyites. Orwell was shot in the throat and almost killed by the Communists, and was invalided back to England, where he wrote *Animal Farm*, about what happens when revolution is corrupted. The philosophy of the main character in the book, based on Stalin, is 'All animals are equal but some animals are more equal than others.'

To write *1984*, his masterpiece, Orwell took himself off to a cottage on the Scottish island of Jura, and he just managed to finish it before collapsing with the tuberculosis from which he died in 1950.

The title of *1984* is the reverse of the year in which he wrote the book, 1948. The story tells of Winston Smith, who tries in vain to escape from a totalitarian society where people are always watched and made to conform. 'If you want a picture of the future, imagine a boot stamping on a human face – for ever.'

It is regarded as one of the defining books of the 20th century, and is astonishingly prescient of the society we live in today, as indicated by the terminology from the book that has crept into the language used to describe the modern world: 'Big Brother is watching you', the Thought Police, Doublespeak. Even Orwell's name has become an adjective 'Orwellian' is used to describe the modern surveillance society and authoritarian government, particularly in Britain.

Two television shows take their names from the book, *Big Brother* and *Room 101*.

In *1984*, Room 101 is a torture chamber at the Ministry of Love where a victim is forced to face his greatest fear or nightmare. Orwell took the name Room 101 from a conference room at BBC Broadcasting House where he used to have to sit through mind-numbing meetings.

George Orwell would be amused, or chilled, to learn that today, within 200 yards of the flat where he lived in Islington, and where he began planning *1984*, there are 32 CCTV cameras, monitoring everything that moves. 'Big Brother is watching you.'

AGATHA CHRISTIE (1890–1976), novelist, playwright and poet, is buried in the churchyard at CHOLSEY. She is best remembered for her detective novels featuring Miss Marple and Hercule Poirot and for *The Mousetrap*, the world's longest-running play, with over 23,000 performances so far in London's West End.

THOMAS HUGHES (1822–96), lawyer and author, was born in UFFINGTON. He is best known for his semi-autobiographical novel set at Rugby school, *Tom Brown's School Days*.

LESTER PIGGOTT, the most successful jockey in the history of the Derby, with nine wins, was born in WANTAGE in 1935.

Warwickshire

❖❖❖❖

THE BARD ✦ HIS ANCESTORS ✦ HIS CHILDHOOD ✦ HIS MARRIAGE ✦ HIS RELIGION ✦ NEW PLACE ✦ GEORGE ELIOT ✦ FIRST LABOURING MP

Anne Hathaway's Cottage, England's most famous chocolate box cottage.

◄ WARWICKSHIRE FOLK ►

William Sheldon ✦ Joseph Arch ✦ Sir Frank Whittle ✦ Richard Lindon ✦ Sir Joseph Lockyer ✦ John Wyndham

Meriden

The Warwickshire village of Meriden is reckoned to be the geographical centre of England, and the claim is marked by a stone cross. The village has a memorial to all cyclists who died in the Great War, and cyclists from all over England gather here once a year to pay tribute. Meriden was also home to Triumph Motorcycles from 1942 to 1983.

William Shakespeare
1564–1616

Warwickshire has been described as the most typically English of all the English counties, and so it is fitting that it should lie at the very centre of England and be the home county of the man who has contributed more to the

English language than any other, WILLIAM SHAKESPEARE.

Ancestors

William Shakespeare's ancestors were Warwickshire farmers rooted in the farms and villages of the Forest of Arden, a wild area north of Stratford upon Avon. Shakespeare played and grew up in a forest landscape of trees and plants and animals, and this very English landscape forms the background to many of his plays, such as *A Midsummer Night's Dream* and *As You Like It*.

Shakespeare's family can be traced back to the 14th century, to Oldeditch Farm in Balsall, when the son of Adam of Oldeditch gave himself the name of Shakespeare, or Shakesper, which derives from military usage as someone who wields a spear. It was not an uncommon name in Warwickshire, possibly because many of the yeomanry and squires of the area had fought in the Wars of the Roses, a claim later made by William's father John, when he applied for a coat of arms.

Birthday

William Shakespeare was born in Henley Street in Stratford, and we may still stand in the very room where he first opened his eyes. He was baptised in Holy Trinity Church on 26 April, and as it was the custom in Elizabethan England to have a child

Shakespeare's birthplace

baptised three days after birth, William's birthday is accepted as 23 April – St George's Day.

Childhood

He attended the Grammar School in Stratford, housed in a long, half-

Holy Trinity

timbered building which has remained essentially unchanged since it was erected as the home of a religious guild in 1428. The schoolroom was upstairs, while below was the hall where William saw his first play. From a young age he would have mingled with the various acting companies that came to Stratford, as they would have had to apply for a licence to William's father John when he was Mayor of Stratford.

At the age of 11 William went to see the pageantry surrounding Queen Elizabeth's legendary visit to Robert Dudley at Kenilworth Castle, pageantry that he would later to recreate in many of his plays.

During the holidays Shakespeare would wander through the countryside visiting friends and relatives, including the Shakespeares of Packwood Hall with whom he would sometimes stay, and while there he got to meet the historian RAPHAEL HOLINSHED, who lived at nearby Packwood House. Holinshed was the author of the *Chronicles of England and Scotland*, the source for much of the material in Shakespeare's history plays.

Marriage

When William was 18 he married ANNE HATHAWAY, who was 26 and three months pregnant. Anne lived in SHOTTERY, a small village about a mile (1.5 km) outside Stratford, and the path that William would have taken to visit the thatched cottage where she lived can still be followed. Inside, the cottage is furnished as it would have been in Shakespeare's day.

William and Anne married in the church at TEMPLE GRAFTON in 1582. They chose here rather than Stratford to wed, because the priest at Temple Grafton was sympathetic to a Catholic form of marriage.

Religion

In the days of Elizabeth I the official religion of England was Protestant, and although Catholics were tolerated they were not popular, with the memory of Bloody Queen Mary's persecutions still fresh and England under constant threat from Catholic France and Spain. The Forest of Arden was a strongly Catholic area and both William's parents came from Catholic families, so it is reasonable to suppose that William was privately, if not overtly, Catholic.

Once married, William and Anne moved in to live with William's parents in the house on Henley Street, and his first child Susannah was born there six months later. In early 1590 William began to write his first play, *Henry VI Part I*, and in 1592 he moved to London to try his hand in the theatre as an actor and playwright, leaving behind his wife and children in Stratford.

It has been suggested that Shakespeare fled to London after being caught poaching in the grounds of CHARLECOTE PARK, a magnificent Tudor pile east of Stratford, and got his revenge on SIR THOMAS LUCY, Charlecote's owner, by portraying him as Justice Shallow in *The Merry Wives of Windsor*. It is more likely that the poet ridiculed Lucy, a local Justice of the Peace and prominent Protestant, for his harassment of Catholics in Warwickshire, and in particular for his part in the arrest and trial of Edward Arden, kinsman of William's mother Mary Arden.

New Place

In 1597 Shakespeare returned to Stratford as a rich man and bought NEW PLACE, the second largest house in Stratford, and the only one made of brick. He retired there in 1610.

Gatehouse, Charlecote Park

William Shakespeare died in 1616 on 23 April, his 52nd birthday, apparently after a drinking session with Ben Jonson in the Falcon Inn at Bidford. He is buried in the chancel of Holy Trinity Church, where he had been baptised.

New Place was inherited by William's daughter Susannah, and then passed to her daughter Elizabeth, who married the next-door neighbour Thomas Nash. The house was eventually purchased by a disagreeable parson called FRANCIS GASTRELL, who became so infuriated by people gawping over the wall that he went out into the garden one night and chopped down the mulberry tree that Shakespeare had planted, reducing it to a pile of logs. The inhabitants of Stratford were so incensed that they flung stones through Gastrell's windows until, driven to madness by a tax demand, he finally lost his temper and razed the whole house to the ground. The eccentric clergyman was run out of town, and no one of that name may ever live in Stratford again. On the site of New Place there is now a replica of an Elizabethan knot garden.

George Eliot
1819–80

GEORGE ELIOT, one of the greatest English novelists, was born Mary Anne Evans at ARBURY

FARM (now South Farm), set in the middle of the Arbury estate near Nuneaton, where her father was the estate manager for the Newdegate family. The farmhouse in which she was born is still there, lived in by the present estate manager. Mary was christened in the church at Chilvers Coton, where her parents are now buried, and grew up in nearby Griff House, which appears as Doricote Mill in *The Mill on the Floss*. It is now a hotel.

When her father retired to Coventry, Mary began to move in intellectual circles, and their lofty disdain caused her to reject her religious upbringing, much to her father's bewilderment. After he died she moved to London, where she became editor of the *Westminster Review*, working under the first of her many assumed names, since editing was not considered women's work. She also embarked on an affair with the philosopher Herbert Spencer, the founder of socialism, which she hoped might lead to marriage, but Spencer discarded her, commenting cruelly that she was too ugly. She then met the true love of her life, an already married man called George Henry Lewes, and they started to live together as husband and wife. He encouraged her to write and this she did, hiding behind the name George Eliot lest her scandalous live-in relationship with Lewes should affect how her books were received.

Two of her celebrated novels, *Adam Bede* and *Middlemarch*, are based on her early life in Warwickshire, and in much of her work she includes references to North Warwickshire locations she knew and loved as a child. Her novels are renowned for their psychological insight and realism.

Well, I never knew this
about
WARWICKSHIRE FOLK

William Sheldon

WILLIAM SHELDON WAS THE FIRST ENGLISH TAPESTRY MAKER. Through marriage, he inherited the Manor of BARCHESTON, near Shipston-on-Stour, and set up England's first tapestry workshop in the manor house barn, in about 1560. He learnt the technique from Flemish weavers brought to England by his manager Richard Hickes, and Sheldon tapestries are now regarded as some of the finest in the world. Particularly sought after are his tapestry maps of English counties such as Warwickshire, Gloucestershire, Oxfordshire and Worcestershire. A number of these were purchased by Horace Walpole. They are very rare now, but a Sheldon tapestry of Warwickshire, dated 1588, hangs in the Warwickshire Museum in Warwick's market-place.

Joseph Arch
◄ 1826–1919 ►

JOSEPH ARCH, the FIRST AGRICULTURAL LABOURER TO BECOME AN MP, was born in the village of BARFORD, in a tiny cottage that remained his home all his life. Arch came from a family of farm labourers and his early days were spent in the fields, but his mother encouraged him to read at night and he trained to become a Methodist lay preacher. His skill as a speaker enabled him to organise and articulate the local farm workers' protests against the poor wages and living conditions of the 1870s. In 1872 Arch called a meeting in nearby Wellesbourne, held under a chestnut tree and lit by candlelight, where he formed the National Agricultural Labourers' Union to put pressure on the powerful land-owning establishment. As President of the Union he is credited with persuading Gladstone to force through the Reform Act of 1884–5, which gave rural workers the same voting rights as their town counterparts. In 1885 he became Liberal MP for a rural Norfolk constituency.

Arch loved Warwickshire and particularly his home village of Barford, and he is buried in the churchyard across the road from his cottage. He lived his life by his own creed, 'Make a man proud of, and interested in, his birthplace, make him

feel he has a part in it, and you have started him on the road to good citizenship . . .'

Sir Frank Whittle
◄ 1907–96 ►

SIR FRANK WHITTLE, the INVENTOR OF THE JET ENGINE, was born in COVENTRY and grew up in Royal Leamington Spa. He joined the RAF in 1923, became a pilot, and began to think about new ways of powering fighter planes to make them faster and more manoeuvrable. He came up with the idea of combining a gas turbine with rocket propulsion, and in 1930 took out a patent for an engine built along this concept. He received little encouragement from the Air Ministry and was forced to find private backing to set up a firm,

Power Jets Ltd, to design an engine to his specifications. The onset of war in 1939 finally ignited the Air Ministry's interest and they began to back Power Jets' research. On 15 May 1941 the Jet Age was born when the first GLOSTER WHITTLE E28 jet took to the skies and performed flawlessly. 'Frank, it flies!' they cried. 'That's what it was designed to do, isn't it?' he replied.

RICHARD LINDON (1816–87), inventor of the oval rugby ball, was born in RUGBY.

SIR JOSEPH LOCKYER (1836–1920), scientist who discovered helium and founder of the journal *Nature*, was born in RUGBY.

JOHN WYNDHAM (1903–69), author of *The Day of the Triffids*, was born in KNOWLE.

Westmorland

England's Biggest Horse Fair
✦ Smallest County Town ✦ England's Oldest Topiary

Appleby Castle, at the heart of England's highest county town.

◀ WESTMORLAND FOLK ▶

Catherine Parr ✦ George Romney ✦ John Cunliffe ✦ Sir Arthur
Eddington ✦ David Starkey

Appleby-in-Westmorland

THE BIGGEST HORSE FAIR IN THE WORLD takes place every year in June at APPLEBY-IN-WESTMORLAND, the former county town of Westmorland. The fair was established by charter from James II in 1685, and is held on the outskirts of the town at Fair Hill, originally known as Gallows Hill, which gives a small hint as to what went on there before. Gypsy horse traders and Romany families come together from all over the country to conduct their business, and during the fair horses can been seen everywhere in the town, tethered in the high street, trotting through the town centre or just grazing by the side of the road – creating an exhilarating, 'wild west' frontier town effect. Before being put up for sale, the horses are trotted or raced along Flashing Lane and then washed and spruced up by youngsters in the River Eden. Sales are usually sealed with a spit and a hand-shake.

Appleby-in-Westmorland is THE SMALLEST COUNTY TOWN IN ENGLAND, with a population of just 2,600. It used to be simply Appleby, but after local government reorgan-isation in 1974, when Westmorland was abolished as an administrative county, the 'in Westmorland' was added to ensure that the historic county name was not forgotten. Appleby has had as its MP two men who became Prime Ministers, William Pitt the Younger in 1783, the year he became the youngest ever Prime Minister, and Viscount Howick, who became Earl Grey. Ironically, it was Earl Grey's administration that passed the Great Reform Act in 1832, which saw Appleby lose its Member of Parlia-ment, the only county town to be so disenfranchised.

Appleby Grammar School occu-pies a notable place in American history, for amongst its roll-call of old boys are Lawrence and Augustine Washington, half-brothers of the first American President, George Washington. Lawrence would go on to build a fine house in Virginia, which he named Mount Vernon in honour of his commanding officer, English hero Vice-Admiral Edward Vernon, and which eventually became George Washington's home.

APPLEBY CASTLE overlooks the town from behind its curtain wall at the top of the main street. The central keep was built around 1170 and is surrounded by a collection of medieval buildings that were restored in the 17th century by Lady Anne Clifford, who was responsible for preserving many homes and castles across the North.

Levens Hall

❦

The gardens at LEVENS HALL, just south of Kendal, were laid out in 1694 by a French gardener called Guillaume Beaumont. He was already well known in England for his work at Hampton Court Palace and various other English gardens, but the gardens at Levens Hall are the only surviving example of his work. They are an extravagant riot of box, beech and yew, cut into extraordinary shapes, pyramids, columns and displays with names like the 'Judge's Wig', the 'Bellingham Lion', and 'Queen Elizabeth and her Maids of Honour'. One exhibit, the 'Jugs of Morocco', recalls a powerful ale that was imbibed at the convivial annual Radish Festival held at Levens Hall in May. Beaumont's garden survives almost intact and boasts THE OLDEST AND MOST EXTENSIVE TOPIARY IN ALL ENGLAND.

Beaumont was commissioned by James II's Keeper of the Privy Purse, Colonel James Grahame, who had won Levens Hall from a cousin, Alan Bellingham, in a game of cards. Apparently the game was won with an ace of hearts, and in recognition of this the down spouts of the guttering are decorated with gilded hearts.

The hall itself, a glorious Elizabethan house built around a 13th-century peel

tower, is said to be haunted by a gypsy woman who was refused hospitality there. As she lay dying of starvation she put a curse on Levens, to the effect that 'no son should inherit the house until the River Kent ceased to flow and a white fawn was born in the park'. And indeed, Levens Hall was passed down solely through the female line until 1896, when the river froze over, a white fawn appeared in the park and a male heir, Alan Bagot, was born to the owner Sir Josceline Bagot. Levens Hall is still the home of the Bagot family today.

Well, I never **knew this**
about
WESTMORLAND FOLK

CATHERINE PARR, the sixth wife of Henry VIII, and the only one to survive him, was born in KENDAL CASTLE in 1512. Her prayer book, bound in silver, can be seen in the town museum.

The portrait painter GEORGE ROMNEY, who was born at nearby Dalton-in-Furness in 1734, had his first studio in Kendal, where he worked on his portraits of prominent Lakeland families. His name lives on in Romney's Kendal Mint Cake, the Westmorland speciality.

KENDAL MINT CAKE was apparently invented in 1869 by Joseph Wiper, a Kendal confectioner, when he over-cooked a recipe for glacier mints, containing glucose sugar and water, and the mixture started to 'grain' and become cloudy. When the liquid was poured out from the pan and cooled,

mint cake was the result. Wiper set up a factory and began to market his secret recipe, which was an instant success, particularly as a source of energy for those climbing the Lakeland mountains. WIPER'S KENDAL MINT CAKE was supplied to Sir Ernest Shackleton's Antarctic expedition of 1914–16.

ROMNEY'S, founded by another Kendal confectioner Sam T. Clarke, began making Mint Cake in 1918. ROMNEY'S KENDAL MINT CAKE was carried to the summit of Mt Everest in 1953 by the first men to conquer the world's highest mountain, Sir Edmund Hilary and Sherpa Tensing. Tensing left some mint cake at the top to appease the mountain gods.

Kendal is Westmorland's largest town. Holy Trinity Church, begun in the

13th century and added to in the 15th and 18th centuries, has five aisles and is ENGLAND'S WIDEST PARISH CHURCH, 103 ft (31 m) across.

LONGSLEDDALE, near Kendal, was the inspiration for Greendale, the setting for the postal round of the children's television character POSTMAN PAT, and the old Beast Banks post office (now closed) in Kendal was the model for Greendale's post office. Postman Pat's creator, JOHN CUNLIFFE, lived in Kendal while writing the stories.

SIR ARTHUR EDDINGTON (1882–1944), astrophysicist, who introduced Einstein's Theory of Relativity to the English-speaking world, was born in Kendal.

DAVID STARKEY, historian and TV presenter, was born in Kendal in 1945.

Wiltshire

Bridge chapel at Bradford-on-Avon,
one of only four remaining in England.

◄ WILTSHIRE FOLK ►

Thomas Hobbes ✦ Joseph Addison ✦ Joseph Fry ✦ Henry Shrapnel
✦ Henry Fawcett ✦ Robert Morley ✦ Diana Dors ✦ John Francombe

Malmesbury

King Athelstan, who reigned from 925 until 939, was the first king to rule over a united English nation. He won his kingdom at the first English battle to be recorded in epic poetry, the Battle of Brunanburgh in 937, defeating the Vikings and driving them out of York and the North. He is buried in the abbey at Malmesbury, England's oldest borough, which was granted its charter by Athelstan's grandfather King Alfred in 880. In Athelstan's day Malmesbury served as England's capital.

MALMESBURY ABBEY stands on the site of a Benedictine monastery founded in AD 675. One of the early abbots was St Adhelm, a great scholar and teacher, who installed ENGLAND'S FIRST ORGAN in the church in AD 700, 'a mighty instrument of innumerable tones, blown from bellows, and enclosed in a gilded case'.

In 1010 a monk from the abbey named ELMER became the first Englishman to fly, if only briefly. Widely known as a student of astronomy and mathematics, Elmer had observed jackdaws in flight and calculated from them how to use simple aerodynamics. His fame attracted a large crowd to watch as he fastened rudimentary home-made wings to his arms and feet, climbed the tower of the Saxon abbey, posed for a moment on the balustrade, essayed a tentative flap and then, commending his soul to Heaven, launched himself into the Malmesbury sky. For a few magical seconds all appeared to be going well until, as contemporary records have it, Elmer

panicked, stalled, and plunged to earth, breaking both his legs. Even in his agony, Elmer was undaunted. He had flown 660 ft (200 m) and knew where he had gone wrong – no tail! Alas, the abbot banned further experiments and Elmer lived to a venerable, if disappointed, old age. It would be 800 years before another Englishman took to the skies, when inventor Sir George Cayley, inspired by watching seagulls in flight, sent his coachman soaring high above his garden in Yorkshire, the first man in the world to fly in an aeroplane.

The abbey we see at Malmesbury today is the truncated nave of the Norman abbey church built around 1150. While much diminished, what is left still dominates the town and is one of the finest and most impressive Norman buildings in England, with a spectacularly carved outer doorway and, inside, massive round pillars and pointed Late Norman arches. In medieval times the abbey had a stupendous central spire soaring 427 ft (130 m) – 23 ft (7 m) higher than the spire of Salisbury Cathedral, which is England's tallest spire today.

In the churchyard is the grave of HANNAH TWYNNOY, THE LAST PERSON IN ENGLAND TO BE EATEN BY A TIGER. In 1703 she was working as a barmaid in the White Lion Inn, when the travelling circus came to Malmesbury and set up in the pub courtyard. Hannah couldn't resist teasing the tiger, which finally broke free from its cage and mauled her to death.

Just outside the west door of the abbey is the OLD BELL, ENGLAND'S OLDEST HOTEL, which was built around the remains of a Saxon castle in 1220 by Abbot Walter Loring, as a guest-house for important visitors to the abbey. It has been in continuous use as a lodging house and hotel ever since. At the eastern end of the building is a spiral staircase that spirals upwards in an anti-clockwise direction, a sign that it was constructed by the peaceful monks, for men of war made their castle staircases spiral upwards in a clockwise direction so that the defenders could have room to swing their sword arm.

NANCY HANKS, the mother of US President Abraham Lincoln, was born in Malmesbury, to a family that had lived in the town since the days of King Athelstan.

Bradford-on-Avon

The Abbot of Malmesbury, St Adhelm, founded a little chapel dedicated to ST LAURENCE in the Wiltshire town of BRADFORD (Broad Ford), early in the 8th century. The church was nearly lost during the Middle Ages,

being used as a charnel house for the Norman church next door, a workshop, a storeroom, a school and even just a cottage. In 1857 the Vicar of Bradford, Canon Jones, looked down on Bradford from the top of the hill and thought he discerned the shape of a small church amongst the ramshackle cottages below. From his subsequent excavations emerged England's most perfect Saxon church. It is tiny, THE CHANCEL ARCH THE NARROWEST IN ENGLAND. It is also exquisite, with elegant pilasters, beautiful arcading and carved stone panels in the chancel. Most thrilling of all, high up on the east wall of the nave there are two flying angels, the most important Saxon sculptures surviving in England.

Bradford-on-Avon is a gorgeous old mill town with shops and houses that scramble over each other to climb the impossibly steep hillside in a series of terraces. All roads tumble down to the quaint town bridge, originally built in stone by the Normans and widened in the 17th century. The pointed Norman piers can still be seen on the upstream side. The bridge boasts one of the only four bridge chapels remaining in England. Once common, bridge chapels were built for travellers to pray for, or to give thanks for, a safe crossing of the river. This chapel was later used as the town lock-up, where drunks and troublemakers would be incarcerated for the night.

Bradford also possesses one of

England's largest and best-preserved tithe barns, dating from the 14th century. In feudal England it was customary for landowners to give a tithe, or one-tenth of their produce, to the Church, and great barns were built to store these tithes.

A Queen's Retreat

Down in the Avon valley below Stonehenge lies AMESBURY ABBEY, where King Arthur's Queen Guinevere fled after the death of her husband and took up the life of a nun. Her lover Sir Lancelot came to Amesbury to find her, but she refused to give up her life of penance and Lancelot retreated to become a recluse. He dreamt one night of Guinevere's death and returned to Amesbury to carry her body to Glastonbury, where she was laid to rest next to Arthur.

In 979 Queen Elfreda founded a Benedictine monastery at Amesbury, as penance for her part in the murder of her stepson King Edward at Corfe Castle, which placed her own son Ethelred on the throne of England.

Amesbury Abbey today has taken on the form of a classical mansion built by Inigo Jones for the Dukes of Queensberry. The playwright JOHN GAY, a friend of the Queensberrys, was staying here as a guest in 1727 when he wrote *The Beggar's Opera* – the first of what became known as ballad operas, in which original dialogue was set to the tunes of popular ballads and folk songs.

On the Amesbury estate to the west of the house, beside the A303, is a clump of beech trees planted by the Duke some 200 years ago to represent the alignment of the British and French ships at the Battle of the Nile. This was done at the request of Lady Emma Hamilton, Nelson's mistress, who became friends with the Duke after the Admiral's death.

Well, I never knew this
about
WILTSHIRE FOLK

Ancestors of the English Race

Wiltshire is where England's most ancient temples stand, emerging from the mists of time, created by people who shaped this land before it was England, but whose genes run deep through the English race.

AVEBURY, begun around 3,000 BC and surrounded by a ditch a mile (1.5 km) long, covers 28 acres (11 ha) and has at its heart THE LARGEST STONE CIRCLE IN THE WORLD. Here you can wander in amongst the stones and touch the walls of this mighty cathedral where 4,000 years ago families came to worship and wonder, much as Englishmen of all faiths do today.

The largest stone at Avebury is called the Swindon Stone. The Barber's Stone killed a man trying to move it in the 14th century by falling on top of him. Young women used to sit on the Devil's Chair on May Day Eve (Beltane) and make a wish, and even now, if you run round the Devil's Chair 100 times anti-clockwise you can summon up the Devil

himself. Meanwhile the Diamond Stone apparently crosses the road by itself at midnight – many coming out of the Red Lion pub at closing time have witnessed it.

The stone circle at Avebury is so large that an entire village has been built inside it. As well as the Red Lion, there is an Elizabethan manor house and a Saxon church, built to praise the Christian God where pagan gods were once worshipped. There is also a museum founded by the marmalade millionaire Alexander Keiller, who used the wealth of his family marmalade business to purchase Avebury and set about restoring it, excavating the circle and resurrecting the stones that had been toppled and neglected. Avebury is now in the care of the National Trust.

About a mile (1.5 km) from Avebury is the enigmatic SILBURY HILL, THE LARGEST AND TALLEST PREHISTORIC MAN-MADE MOUND IN EUROPE, perhaps the world. It was built around the same time as the later stages of Avebury, and no one knows why. Even modern scientists, who claim to know how the Universe began, are stumped.

Stonehenge

STONEHENGE, the High Temple, is the greatest achievement of prehistoric man in Europe. Now England's most venerable icon, it stands alone on bare Salisbury Plain, a monument to the ingenuity and enquiring minds of our ancestors. Stonehenge is an observatory, built and developed over a period of 1,000 years or more by early men of science, to help them learn the secrets of the seasons and the heavens. The stones are placed to line up with the sun on the summer solstice, and although they no longer match exactly, they would have been accurate in 3,500 BC, which is how we know when they were laid. The bluestones were brought by land and water from the Presceli Hills in Pembrokeshire, while the bigger sarsen stones were dragged overland on rollers from the hills near Marlborough.

Stonehenge may be thousands of years old, but the aura that drew our ancestors there still casts its spell today. New Age travellers, modern pagans, druids and others still descend on Stonehenge on Midsummer's Day every year to celebrate the solstice. In 1985, at the famous Battle of the Beanfield, the travellers battled with police who were trying to prevent them from reaching the stones. Stonehenge is now fenced off, but organised festivals are allowed on the site, which is run by English Heritage.

THOMAS HOBBES (1589–1679), philosopher, was born in MALMESBURY. Celebrated for his book *Leviathan*, which argues that individuals should cede power to a strong central authority in return for protection, and that abuses of that power are the price to be paid for security.

JOSEPH ADDISON (1672–1719), essayist, poet and founder of the *Spectator* magazine, was born in MILSTON.

JOSEPH FRY (1728–87), founder of Fry's, the makers of Fry's Chocolate Cream and Fry's Turkish Delight, was born in SUTTON BENGER. He made THE WORLD'S FIRST SOLID CHOCOLATE and THE FIRST EDIBLE CHOCOLATE BAR.

HENRY SHRAPNEL (1761–1842), army officer and inventor of the shrapnel shell, a hollow cannonball that burst in mid-air and showered the enemy with shot, was born in BRADFORD-ON-AVON.

HENRY FAWCETT (1833–84), Postmaster General who introduced parcel post, postal orders and the sixpenny telegram, encouraged the setting up of public telephone boxes and campaigned for women's votes, was born in SALISBURY.

ROBERT MORLEY (1908–92), character actor, remembered fondly for playing 'pompous windbags', was born in SEMLEY.

DIANA DORS (1931–84), actress, seen as the English 'blonde bombshell', was born in SWINDON.

JOHN FRANCOMBE, jockey and TV presenter, was born in SWINDON in 1952.

Worcestershire

Music All Around Us ✦ Battle of Worcester ✦ Train Sets ✦ Pubs and Pub Signs

Sir Edward Elgar, as English as the Malvern Hills that inspired his music.

◄ WORCESTERSHIRE FOLK ►

Sir Rowland Hill ✦ King John ✦ A.E. Housman ✦ William Richard Morris ✦ Nigel Mansell

The Land of
Heavenly Spring

Sir Edward Elgar
1857–1934

*'There is music in the air,
music all around us . . .'*

Worcestershire's own Prime Minister, Stanley Baldwin, described his home county as 'The Land of Heavenly Spring'. Worcestershire is England's orchard, one of the most English of counties, quiet, beautiful and unassuming. Worcestershire has England's oldest hills, the Malverns, with bubbling spring water fit for a queen. It has the Vale of Evesham, ripe with plums, apples, pears and currants for the fruit baskets of England. Its cricket ground boasts the most perfect setting in English county cricket, set on the River Severn and watched over by King John from Worcester's medieval cathedral.

There is certainly music in the Worcestershire air, for it is the fields and hills of this mellow English county that gave birth and inspiration to that most English of composers SIR EDWARD ELGAR.

Elgar was born in a humble brick cottage called The Firs in UPPER BROADHEATH, near Worcester, on 2 June 1857. His father owned a music shop in Worcester and, as a boy, Elgar would take manuscripts from the shop out into the countryside on his bicycle to study them, and so came to associate music with the scenery around

him. He lived in Worcestershire until he was nearly 30, playing and teaching the violin, composing, cycling along the country lanes and wandering across the Malvern Hills. Perhaps this is why his music manages so powerfully to capture the essence of England and the English countryside.

Any film-maker who wants to establish an English setting will choose Elgar's music for his soundtrack, for it is as iconic of England as a thatched cottage, a red telephone box, a cathedral, a Constable painting, a cricket match or a cream tea.

His music is associated with two great national occasions. 'Land of Hope and Glory', adapted from *Pomp and Circumstance March No. 1*, with words by A.C. Benson, was composed as a Coronation Ode for Edward VII. It is considered to be a National Anthem for the English and is sung lustily amidst much flag-waving at the Last Night of the Proms.

The performing of 'Nimrod', from Elgar's *Enigma Variations*, by massed bands at the Cenotaph in London on Remembrance Sunday is often cited as one of the most moving moments of that reflective day, along with Laurence Binyon's famous poem 'For the Fallen', which Elgar put to music in his *Spirit of England*.

The Dream of Gerontius, Elgar's choral setting of Cardinal Newman's poem about a man's journey into the next world, resurrected the reputation of English choral music and established Elgar as England's foremost composer.

On 12 November 1931, Sir Edward Elgar performed the opening ceremony at ENGLAND'S, AND THE WORLD'S, FIRST CUSTOM-BUILT RECORDING STUDIOS, THE ABBEY ROAD STUDIOS at St John's Wood in London, conducting the London Symphony Orchestra in an historic recording of 'Land of Hope and Glory'.

Sir Edward Elgar died in Worcester on 23 February 1934. He is buried beside his wife in the churchyard of St Wulstan's Roman Catholic Church in Little Malvern.

From 1999 until 2007, Elgar was featured on the Bank of England's £20 notes.

Battle of Worcester

The last great battle of the English Civil War took place in Worcester on 3 September 1651, between Prince Charles (later Charles II) and Oliver Cromwell's troops. Charles watched the battle from the top of the tower of Worcester Cathedral, and when he realised the day was lost he ordered his bodyguard to fight a rearguard action while he escaped. The Prince stopped to have his horse reshod at Ye Olde Black Cross inn at Bromsgrove, now supposedly haunted by a Royalist soldier, and then made his way into Shropshire, where he was forced to spend the night hiding in an oak tree.

Train Sets

The English invented the railways and they also invented model railways, and Worcestershire boasts an exquisite piece of model railway heritage. The railway footbridge used by Hornby train sets is modelled on the wonderfully preserved Victorian footbridge across the railway at Hagley Station, south of Stourbridge, which was built in 1884 and is Grade II listed. Hornby, founded by Frank Hornby in 1901 as a model toy manufacturer, is THE OLDEST MAKER OF MODEL RAILWAYS IN THE WORLD. The engines were originally made with Meccano, which Frank Hornby invented in 1907.

Pubs and Pub Signs

'When you have lost your inns drown your empty selves, for you will have lost the last of England!'
Hilaire Belloc

The origins of the English pub go back to the Roman 'tavernae vinariae', where food and wine were served around a communal table. Later there were hospices, established by monasteries, where pilgrims and travellers could find food and accommodation.

Roman 'tavernae' were identified by hanging vine leaves outside. In Britain, vines were rare and a bush was substituted, hence The Bush, which is the oldest pub sign. Once the Normans arrived in England, most pubs began to hang signs outside for those who couldn't read, which was the majority. Simple symbols were used such as The Sun, The Star, The Plough, The White Horse or The Bull.

In 1393 Richard II made it compulsory for pubs to have a sign, so that they could be identified by his official ale tasters, and many establishments adopted Richard's emblem, which was a White Hart. Religious signs were popular, particularly as many pubs were owned by monasteries. Hence The Cross Keys (of St Peter), The Mitre, The Monk's Retreat and The Bishop's Arms. After the Reformation pubs began to give themselves royal titles – The King's Head, The Crown, or The Rose and Crown – and even the names of the monarchs themselves such as the King George or the Queen Victoria.

Then there are the names of historic figures such as The Duke of Wellington, The Lord Nelson or

The Churchill Arms, and industrial descriptions – The Railway Inn, The Bricklayer's Arms or The Mason's Arms.

The most popular pub name in England is the Red Lion, which comes from James I (James VI of Scotland) who ordered that the heraldic red lion of Scotland be displayed outside important buildings in England, especially pubs.

The story of Charles II hiding in the oak tree is behind the name Royal Oak.

No other country depicts its history and its heroes in such an imaginative and colourful way, and the English pub sign remains a unique and irreplaceable feature of the English heritage.

*Well, I never knew this
about*
WORCESTERSHIRE FOLK

Sir Rowland Hill
◄ 1795–1879 ►

ROWLAND HILL, Inventor of the postal system that changed the world, was a Worcestershire boy, born in Blackwell Street, KIDDERMINSTER, in 1795. His family was not well off, and Hill never forgot the feeling of dread at the sound of the postman's knock, for in those days payment was demanded from the receiver rather than the sender, and often the recipient would be too poor to redeem the letter. The cost also varied according to the distance the letter was carried and the number of sheets of paper, and this all resulted in a postal system that was hopelessly inefficient and accessible only to the rich. Hill, an

educator and inventor, tried for many years to devise a system whereby the postage could be prepaid by the sender, reducing costs and increasing efficiency. Finally, in 1837, a Scotsman by the name of James Chalmers submitted an invention to Parliament which would provide Hill with the means to introduce reform – the adhesive postage stamp.

Hill's vision was for a uniform rate of one penny for a half-ounce letter to anywhere in the British Isles, and on 1 May 1840 THE WORLD'S FIRST OFFICIAL ADHESIVE POSTAGE STAMP, THE PENNY BLACK, was issued by the United Kingdom of Great Britain and Ireland. Because the original stamps were only issued in Britain at the time, there was no need to show the country of origin and the Penny Black showed just a portrait of Queen Victoria. British stamps are still the only stamps in the world not to show the country of origin.

Sir Rowland Hill was MP for his home town of Kidderminster, and in the town centre there is a statue of him by Worcester-born sculptor Sir Thomas Brock, who made the Queen Victoria Memorial in front of Buckingham Palace in London.

KING JOHN (1166–1216), the king who signed the Magna Carta, is buried in WORCESTER CATHEDRAL beneath ENGLAND'S OLDEST ROYAL EFFIGY. Also buried in the cathedral is Henry VII's eldest son PRINCE ARTHUR (1486–1502), who died at Ludlow Castle, shortly after his marriage to Catherine of Aragon.

A.E. HOUSMAN (1859–1936), classical scholar and poet, was born at Valley House in FOCKBURY, near Bromsgrove. His most famous work, *A Shropshire Lad*, was an idealised evocation of rural English life, inspired by the view from his Worcestershire home of 'those blue remembered hills' in Shropshire.

WILLIAM RICHARD MORRIS, 1ST VISCOUNT NUFFIELD (1877–1963), creator of Morris Motors, was born in WORCESTER. His Morris Minor was the first English car to sell a million, and his Mini Minor became an English icon.

NIGEL MANSELL OBE, Formula One World Champion in 1992, was born in UPTON UPON SEVERN.

Yorkshire

HOUSE OF YORK ✦ NORTHERN CAPITAL
✦ LARGEST GOTHIC CATHEDRAL ✦ FIRST SEASIDE
RESORT ✦ ENGLISH TAKEAWAY ✦ FIRST TOURIST
ATTRACTION ✦ CRADLE OF THE ENGLISH CHURCH
✦ OLDEST ENGLISH CLASSIC ✦ PUDDING ✦ TERRIERS

The Shambles, a perfect medieval street.

◄ YORKSHIRE FOLK ►

William Bradley ✦ Thomas Chippendale ✦ Guy Fawkes
✦ Joseph Rowntree ✦ Frankie Howerd ✦ John Barry ✦ Dame Judi Dench
✦ Lord Leighton ✦ Charles Laughton ✦ Sir Ben Kingsley

The House of York

THE HOUSE OF YORK is one of the great royal dynasties that have shaped English history. It descends from Edmund of Langley, fourth son of Edward III, who was the first Duke of York, and gave us Edward IV, Edward V (one of the Princes in the Tower) and Richard III, the last English king to die in battle. The emblem of the House of York was a white rose, still the emblem of Yorkshire today. Edmund of Langley's older brother was John of Gaunt, the first Duke of Lancaster, whose emblem was a red rose.

York

YORK today is one of the oldest and loveliest of English cities, nestling in THE LARGEST ENGLISH VALE, and the crowning glory of THE LARGEST ENGLISH COUNTY. There are wonderful walks along the ancient walls, which almost completely encircle the old city and are pierced by battlemented gates, including THE LAST CITY GATE IN ENGLAND TO RETAIN ITS BARBICAN, the Walmgate. The narrow, overhung Shambles is the most perfect example of a medieval town street, and the Minster one of the world's great medieval treasures.

York (Eboracum) was one of the two capitals of Roman Britain. The Emperor Septimus Severus ruled the entire Roman Empire from York for two years before he died there in AD 211. In 306 the Emperor Constantius Chlorus died in York and his son Constantine was proclaimed Emperor there.

York served as the capital of the Saxon province of Northumbria under King Edwin. In 627 he was baptised in the first York Minster, made of wood, by the first Archbishop of York,

Paulinus, who was a member of Saint Augustine's mission to convert the Anglo-Saxons. York was then considered the ecclesiastical capital of the north, and the Archbishop of York is one of the two Primates of All England, along with the Archbishop of Canterbury. In 2005 JOHN SENTAMU was enthroned as Archbishop of York – ENGLAND'S FIRST BLACK ARCHBISHOP.

In the 9th century York became the centre of the Viking Kingdom of York and was known as Jorvik. Jorvik was the last major town to be freed from Viking rule before England became united under the Anglo-Saxons in 965.

York Minster, begun in 1220, is THE LARGEST MEDIEVAL GOTHIC CATHEDRAL IN NORTHERN EUROPE and boasts ENGLAND'S WIDEST GOTHIC NAVE. THE GREAT EAST WINDOW, which dates from 1408, possesses THE LARGEST EXPANSE OF MEDIEVAL STAINED GLASS IN THE WORLD. It is possible to see in York Minster examples of all the stages of English Gothic architecture from Early English, through Decorated, to Perpendicular. The Gothic style began around 1180 and was originally imported from France, but became blended with the native English Romanesque or Norman style to create the Early English style.

Scarborough
Down to the English Seaside

————◆◆◆————

SCARBOROUGH WAS THE FIRST ENGLISH SEASIDE RESORT. In 1626 a spring was discovered on the edge of the beach to the south of Scarborough, and a book written in 1660 by Dr Wittie, about the medical benefits of the spa waters, attracted people with ailments from all over Yorkshire and beyond. BATHING MACHINES, THE FIRST IN ENGLAND, were introduced in 1735, and in 1845 visitors to the resort were welcomed into one of England's first purpose-built hotels, THE CROWN, overlooking the south bay.

In 1867 Scarborough's most distinctive landmark, the massive GRAND HOTEL, opened for business. It originally had 365 bedrooms, one for each day of the year, 52 chimneys, one for each week, 12 floors, one for each month, and four towers representing the four seasons. In 1914 the hotel was badly damaged and the top two floors were demolished, after Scarborough became THE FIRST TOWN IN ENGLAND TO COME UNDER GERMAN FIRE, bombarded from offshore by four cruisers of the German High Fleet.

A blue plaque outside the Grand Hotel marks the site of Wood's Lodgings, where the novelist ANNE BRONTË died in 1849. Racked with consumption, she came to Scarborough in the hope that the fresh sea air might help her recovery, but she was already too weak. She is buried in St Mary's churchyard, beneath the walls of Scarborough Castle.

For 500 years from 1253 until the middle of the 18th century, Scarborough held one of the largest trading fairs in Europe, attended by merchants from all over the Continent, and commemorated in song by Simon and Garfunkel.

Are you going to Scarborough Fair?
Parsley, sage, rosemary and thyme . . .

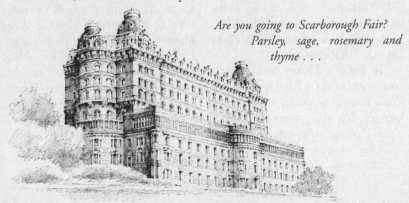

Guiseley

THE BIGGEST FISH AND CHIP SHOP IN THE WORLD is HARRY RAMSDEN'S in GUISELEY, near Leeds.

ENGLAND'S FIRST FISH AND CHIP SHOP was opened in London's East End in 1860 by a Jewish immigrant called JOSEPH MALIN, fried fish being a Jewish custom imported into England with the return of the Jews in the 17th century. Thomas Jefferson records having eaten 'fried fish in the Jewish fashion' on a visit to London in 1786.

Chips were invented in the 18th century by a Belgian housewife who, unable to get any fresh fish, cut a potato into fish-shaped portions and fried them, to satisfy her family. They were introduced into America by Thomas Jefferson as 'potatoes fried in the French manner', which is why they are known as 'French fries'.

Joseph Malin was the first person known to have brought the two dishes together, and the inexpensive but nourishing combination was exported north, where it was an immediate success. In 1863 JOHN LEES began selling fish and chips from a wooden hut in Mossley, in Lancashire, under a sign saying 'This is the first fish and chip shop in the world'.

The favourite fish in the north is haddock or hake, while in the south it is cod, and while oil is used for cooking in the south, beef dripping is preferred in the north.

The traditional way of eating fish and chips from a newspaper was discouraged in the 1980s, when food hygienists began to worry about the food absorbing toxic newsprint.

The Petrifying Well

Near the River Nidd, just outside Knaresborough, is THE PETRIFYING OR DROPPING WELL, ENGLAND'S OLDEST TOURIST ATTRACTION, which opened its gates in 1630. Fed by a spring that has never been known to dry up, a silver curtain of water flows over an overhanging rock face into a huge rock bowl whose sides resemble a giant's face. The water is laced with minerals, and any object that is placed in the rock pool becomes covered in mineral deposits, which slowly harden, making it look as though the object has been turned to stone. The Well is located in an old royal forest that was sold by Charles I in 1630 to Sir Charles Slingsby, who fenced it off and charged visitors to look at it – the first time anyone in England had thought of doing such a thing.

Whitby

WHITBY is a glorious ancient seaport, where English poetry first flowered and the English Church was fashioned.

Cottages laced with narrow alleyways are piled high on the steep banks of the River Esk and tumble down the valley towards the harbour, where fishing boats bob and seagulls squabble. High atop the southern cliffs, and reached by a staircase of 199 steps, are the spectacular 13th-century ruins of WHITBY ABBEY, founded in 657 by St Hilda. It was here, in 664, that the Northumbrian King Oswy held the first Synod, bringing together Christians from the south, who followed the Roman tradi-

tions of St Augustine, and Celtic Christians from the north and west, who believed in a more monastic form of Christianity. Their purpose was to decide which Christian discipline should prevail. King Oswy, pragmatically, chose in favour of the Roman Church, whose leader Wilfred of York claimed his authority came from St Peter, holder of the keys to heaven. As Oswy declared, 'Then I will obey St Peter, lest when I come to the Gates of Heaven there be none to open to me.' This established the supremacy of the Roman Church in England, which lasted for nearly a thousand years until the English Reformation. Another far-reaching issue settled there was the date of Easter – we celebrate Easter when we do because of a decision made 1,300 years ago by those Saxon bishops at Whitby.

Also in those momentous days CAEDMON, an uneducated cowherd at the abbey who tended his cattle on the cliff-top pastures, had a dream in

which an angel commanded him to write a song about the glory of Creation. His 'SONG OF CREATION' was THE FIRST ENGLISH POEM, and Caedmon THE FIRST ENGLISH POET. His vision of Creation influenced Milton's *Paradise Lost* and still resonates today in the bitter, on-going argument between Creationists and Evolutionists. On the cliffs is a monument, in the form of a tall stone cross, commemorating Caedmon, which was unveiled in 1898 by the Poet Laureate Alfred Austin. Carved on the base of the column are the first lines of poetry in the English language:

Now must we praise the Guardian of
    Heaven's realm.
The Creator's might and his mind's
    thought.

St Leger

The West Riding town of DONCASTER is the home of THE WORLD'S OLDEST CLASSIC HORSE RACE, THE ST LEGER, first run on 24 September 1776. The race is named after its founder, Lieutenant-Colonel Anthony St Leger, who established a two-mile race for three-year-olds on Doncaster's Cantley Common. In 1779 it moved to its present home Turf Moor. The St Leger is the longest of the English Classics and has only been cancelled once in its history, in 1939 at the outbreak of the Second World War.

The English Classics are flat races (without jumps), restricted to three-year-olds and each run once a year. The five classics are:

The Two Thousand Guineas (Newmarket in April/May)
The One Thousand Guineas (Newmarket in early May)
The Oaks (Epsom in June)
The Derby (Epsom in June)
The St Leger (Doncaster in September)

Yorkshire Pudding

The most iconic English dish, apart perhaps from fish and chips, is roast beef and YORKSHIRE PUDDING. Yorkshire pudding was invented in Yorkshire as a means of filling out the meal when there was not enough meat to go around. A batter made from flour, eggs and milk is placed underneath the meat as it is cooking, so that the fat and meat juices drip on to it. The pudding was sometimes given to children in place of meat, and today is often served on its own, filled with onion gravy.

Yorkshire Terriers

Two kinds of English terriers hail from Yorkshire. THE AIREDALE, largest of the English terriers, is named after the Yorkshire valley where it was first bred, from an otter hound and a breed of terrier now extinct. At the other end of the scale is the smallest English terrier, the miniscule YORKSHIRE TERRIER or Yorkie, a toy dog bred as a fashionable pet in the 19th century, from a mix of Scottish terriers.

Well, I never knew this
about
YORKSHIRE FOLK

William Bradley – The Yorkshire Giant
◄ 1787–1820 ►

It seems fitting that THE TALLEST ENGLISHMAN was born in England's largest county. WILLIAM BRADLEY was born in MARKET WEIGHTON, in Yorkshire's East Riding. He weighed 14 pounds (6.35 kg) at birth, and reached his full height of 7 ft 9 ins (2.36 m) by the age of 20, by then weighing in at 27 stone (171 kg). While the other 11 members of his family were all of normal height, his father

was just 5 ft 9 ins (1.75 m) tall. For some years William Bradley made appearances at fairs all over England, calling himself The Yorkshire Giant and charging people a shilling for a handshake. When he granted an audience to George III, the King gave Bradley a gold watch on a chain, which he wore for the rest of his life.

Bradley died in Market Weighton aged just 33, and was buried at All Saints Church – inside to deter graverobbers. His house on Market Hill is now a shop. Since 1996, in May every year, Market Weighton has celebrated

Giant Bradley Day, with market stalls, entertainers and exhibitions.

THOMAS CHIPPENDALE (1718–79), English furniture maker, was born in OTLEY, south of Leeds. The two best collections of his furniture anywhere in England can be found in two Yorkshire homes, Harewood House, the home of the Lascelles, north of Leeds, and Nostell Priory, the home of the Winns, near Wakefield. Both houses can be visited.

Born in York

GUY FAWKES (1570–1606), Catholic revolutionary, the foiling of whose plot to blow up the Houses of Parliament on 5 November 1605 is commemorated on Bonfire Night.

JOSEPH ROWNTREE (1836–1925), Quaker philanthropist who developed his father's chocolate factory in York into the biggest in England. Rowntree's merged with Mackintosh's of Halifax in 1969 and was in time taken over by Nestlé in 1988. In 1976 Rowntree brought out the Yorkie Bar, a chunky chocolate bar aimed at men. An ad campaign in the 1970s – 'The Yorkie. Not for Girls' – saw the Yorkie Bar banned from several railway stations for being sexist. The Joseph Rowntree Foundation is today a leading organisation for research into social problems in England.

FRANKIE HOWERD (1917–92), classic English comedian, the Queen Mother's favourite, whose catch-phrases included 'Titter ye not' and 'Oh no, missus, noooo'.

JOHN BARRY (1933–2011), film score composer. Wrote the music for the earlier James Bond films, the most successful English film franchise ever. Winner of five Oscars, two for *Born Free* (1966), and one each for *The Lion in Winter* (1968), *Out of Africa* (1985) and *Dances with Wolves* (1990).

DAME JUDI DENCH, popular English actress who now plays 'M' in the Bond films, born 1934. So powerful is her presence that she won an Oscar for just eight minutes on screen as Elizabeth I in the film *Shakespeare in Love*.

Born in Scarborough

LORD LEIGHTON (1830–96), sculptor and artist, who became President of the Royal Academy and was the first English artist to be made a peer. He died the day after receiving the honour.

CHARLES LAUGHTON (1899–1962), actor. In 1934 became the first English actor to be awarded an Oscar, voted Best Actor for *The Private Life of Henry VIII*.

SIR BEN KINGSLEY, born Krishna Bhanji in 1943. His father was of Indian descent, and Kingsley won a Best Actor Oscar in 1982 for his portrayal of Mahatma Gandhi in Richard Attenborough's film *Gandhi*.

Gazetteer

Interesting places and locations that can be accessed by the public.

NT = National Trust (www.nationaltrust.org.uk)
EH = English Heritage (www.english-heritage.org.uk)
Map grid references are from Ordnance Survey Landranger Series.

BEDFORDSHIRE

Ickwell Green
   Map 153 ref TL 153 454
St Mary's Church, Northill
   Map 153 ref TL 149 466
Elstow Abbey
   Map 153 ref TL 048 474
Cardington
   Map 153 ref TL 086 479

BERKSHIRE

Windsor Castle, Windsor
   Tel: 020 7766 7300
   www.royalcollection.org.uk
Shaw House, Church Road, Shaw,
   Newbury
   Tel: 01635 519804
   www.westberks.gov.uk

BUCKINGHAMSHIRE

Bletchley Park Milton Keynes MK3
   6EB
   Tel:: 01908 640404
   www.bletchleypark.org.uk
Jordans Friends Meeting House
   Welders Lane, Jordans, Nr.
   Beaconsfield HP9 2SN
   Tel: 01494 675280
   www.quakers-chilterns-area.org.uk

Milton's Cottage, Deanway
   Chalfont St. Giles, Bucks HP8 4JH
   Tel: 01494-872313
   www.miltonscottage.org
Hell Fire Caves, Church Lane
   West Wycombe, Bucks HP14 3AH
   Tel: 01494 533739
   www.hellfirecaves.co.uk
Hampden House
   Great Hampden, Bucks HP16 9RD
   Tel: 01494 489042
   www.hampdenweddings.com
Hughenden Manor NT
   High Wycombe, Bucks HP14 4LA
   Tel: 01494 755565
   www.nationaltrust.org.uk
Roald Dahl Museum and Story
   Centre
   81-83 High Street, Great Missenden
   Bucks HP16 0AL
   Tel: 01494 892192
   www.roalddahlmuseum.org

CAMBRIDGESHIRE

Kings College Chapel
   Tel: 01223 331212
   www.kings.cam.ac.uk

CHESHIRE

Little Moreton Hall NT
St Oswald's Lower Peover
  Map 118 ref SJ 743 743
St Cuthbert's, Marton
  Map 118 ref SJ 851 680
Jodrell Bank, Macclesfield
  Cheshire SK11 9DL
  Tel: 01477 571339
  www.jb.man.ac.uk

CORNWALL

Tintagel Castle EH
  Tel: 01840 770328
  www.english-heritage.org.uk
Poldhu Cove, Marconi Monument
  Map 203 ref SW 664 194
Come-to-Good meeting house
  Map 204 ref SW 814 404
Carn Brea, Trevithick Birthplace
  Map 203 ref SW 688 415
Jamaica Inn, Bodmin Moor
  Map 201 ref SX 184 768

CUMBERLAND

Rum Story, Lowther Street
  Whitehaven, Cumberland CA28
  7DN
  Tel: 01946 592933
  www.rumstory.co.uk

DERBYSHIRE

Lea Hurst, Holloway (Private)
  Map 119 ref SK 325 561
Dethick Farm (Private)
  Map 119 ref SK 327 580

DEVON

Hayes Barton Farm (Private)
  Sir Walter Raleigh's Birthplace
  Map 192 ref SY 052 852

Buckland Abbey NT
  Yelverton, Devon PL20 6EY
  Tel: 01822 853607
  www.nationaltrust.org.uk

DORSET

Tolpuddle Martyrs Museum
  Tolpuddle Dorset DT2 7EH
  Tel: 01305 848 237
  www.tolpuddlemartyrs.org.uk
Hardy's Cottage NT
  Higher Bockhampton Dorset DT2
  8QJ
  Tel: 01305 262366
  www.nationaltrust.org.uk
Sherborne Castle
  Cheap Street Sherborne
  Dorset DT9 3PY
  Tel: 01935 813182
  www.sherbornecastle.com

COUNTY DURHAM

Oriental Museum
  Elvet Hill Durham DH1 3TH
  Tel: 0191 334 5694
  www.dur.ac.uk/oriental.museum/
Bede's World
  Church Bank Jarrow
  Tyne & Wear NE32 3DY
  Tel: 0191 489 2106
  www.bedesworld.co.uk

ESSEX

Colchester Castle
  Tel: 01206 282939
  www.colchestermuseums.org.uk
Little Maplestead Round Church
  Map 168 ref TL825 338
Wilkin & Sons Limited,
  Tiptree, Essex CO5 0RF
  Tel: 01621-815407
  www.tiptree.com

GLOUCESTERSHIRE

Berkeley Castle, Berkeley
   Glos GL13 9BQ
   Tel: 01453 810332
   www.berkeley-castle.com
Wildfowl and Wetlands Trust, Slim-
   bridge
   Glos GL2 7BT
   Tel: 01453 891198
   www.wwt.org.uk
Cowley Manor, Cowley
   Cheltenham Glos GL53 9NL
   Tel: 01242 870 900
   www.cowleymanor.com

HAMPSHIRE

St John's Winchester Charity,
   32 St John's South The Broadway
   Winchester SO23 9LN.
   Tel: 01962 854226
   www.cityofwinchester.co.uk
Westgate Museum, High Street
   Winchester
   Tel: 01962 840 222
   www.winchester.gov.uk
Gilbert White's Museum, The Wakes
   Selborne Hants GU34 3JH
   Tel: 01420 511275
   www.gilbertwhiteshouse.org.uk
Jane Austen's House
   Chawton Hants GU34 1SD
   Tel: 01420 83262
   www.jane-austens-house-
   museum.org.uk

HEREFORDSHIRE

Holme Lacy
   Hereford HR2 6LP
   Tel: 01432 870 870
   www.warnerleisurehotels.co.uk

HERTFORDSHIRE

Brocket Hall
   Welwyn, Herts AL8 7XG
   Tel: 01707 335241
   www.brocket-hall.co.uk
Apsley Paper Trail Apsley Mills
   Cottage
   London Road, Apsley
   Hemel Hempstead
   Herts HP3 9RY
   Tel: 0870 950 9272.
   www.thepapertrail.org.uk
The Rhodes Museum
   South Road Bishop's Stortford
   Herts CM23 3JG
   Tel: 01279 651746
   www.rhodesbishopsstortford.org.uk

HUNTINGDONSHIRE

Ramsey Abbey Gatehouse NT
   Ramsey, Hunts PE17 1DH
   Tel: 01480 301494
   www.nationaltrust.org.uk
Little Gidding Church
   Map 142 ref TL 127 817
   www.littlegiddingchurch.org.uk

KENT

Cockle and Winkle Railway
   Tunnel Entrances
   Whitstable end Map 179 ref TR
   134 616
   Canterbury end Map 179 ref TR
   136 610

LANCASHIRE

Cavern Club
   10 Mathew Street Liverpool L2
   6RE
   Tel: 0151 236 1965
   www.cavernclub.org/

Aintree Racecourse
  Ormsirk Road Aintree
  Liverpool L9 5AS
  Tel: 0151 523 2600
  www.aintree.co.uk
Ruskin Museum Brantwood
  Coniston
  Cumbria LA21 8AD
  Tel: 015394 41396
  www.brantwood.org.uk

LEICESTERSHIRE

Belvoir Castle
  Tel: 01476 871000
  www.belvoircastle.com

LINCOLNSHIRE

Epworth Old Rectory
  Tel: 01427 872268
  www.epwortholdrectory.org.uk

MIDDLESEX

Ealing Studios
  Ealing Green London W5 5EP
  Tel: 020 8567 6655
  www.ealingstudios.co.uk
Hogarth's House
  Hogarth Lane London W4 2QN
  Tel: 020 8994 6757

NORFOLK

Custom House
  Purfleet Quay King's Lynn
  Norfolk PE30 1HP
  Tel: 01553 763044
  www.west-norfolk.gov.uk

NORTHAMPTONSHIRE

All Saints, Brixworth
  Map 141 ref SP 748 713
All Saints, Earl's Barton
  Map 152 ref SP 853 638

Holy Sepulchre
  Sheep Street Northampton NN1
  3NL
  Tel: 01604 754782
St Peters Northampton
  www.visitchurches.org.uk
St Mary's Raunds
  Map 141 ref TL 000 731
St Peter and St Paul, King's Sutton
  Map 151 ref SP 498 362
St Peter's Lowick
  Map 141 ref TL 810 977
Canons Ashby NT
  Daventry, Northants NN11 3SD
  Tel: 01327 860044
  www.nationaltrust.org.uk

NORTHUMBERLAND

Lindisfarne Castle NT
  Holy Island Northumberland TD15
  2SH
  Tel: 01289 389244
  www.nationaltrust.org.uk

NOTTINGHAMSHIRE

Edwinstowe and the Major Oak
  Sherwood Forest National Nature
  Reserve
  Edwinstowe Notts NG21 9HN
  Tel: 01623 823202
  www.nottinghamshire.gov.uk
D. H Lawrence Birthplace Museum
  8a Victoria St. Eastwood, Notts
  Tel: 01773 717353
  www.lawrenceseastwood.co.uk

OXFORDSHIRE

Oxford Cathedral
  Christ Church
  Tel: 01865 276155
  www.chch.ox.ac.uk
Botanical Gardens

Rose Lane, Oxford OX1 4AZ
Tel: 01865 286690
www.botanic-garden.ox.ac.uk
Ashmolean Museum
Beaumont Street
Oxford OX1 2PH
Tel: 01865 278000
www.ashmolean.org
Broughton Castle
Banbury,
Oxon, OX15 5EB
Tel: 01295 276070
www.broughtoncastle.com

RUTLAND

Normanton Church
Edith Weston
Rutland Water
Tel: 01572 653026.
www.rutnct.co.uk

SHROPSHIRE

Darwin's Garden, The Mount
Shrewsbury
www.darwincountry.org

SOMERSET

Glastonbury Abbey
Magdalene Street
Glastonbury Somerset BA6 9EL
Tel: 01458 831631
www.glastonburyabbey.com
Glastonbury Tor
Map 182 ref ST 512 386

STAFFORDSHIRE

Abbot's Bromley
www.abbotsbromley.com

SUFFOLK

Sutton Hoo NT
Tranmer House Sutton Hoo
Woodbridge Suffolk IP12 3DJ
Tel: 01394 389700
www.nationaltrust.org.uk
Gainsborough's House
46 Gainsborough Street
Sudbury Suffolk CO10 2EU
Tel: 01787 372958
www.gainsborough.org

SURREY

Runnymede NT
Old Windsor Berkshire SL4 2JL
Tel: 01784 432891
www.nationaltrust.org.uk
Chaldon Doom
Map 187 ref TO 309 557

SUSSEX

Battle Abbey EH
Battle Sussex TN33 0AD
Tel: 01424 775705
www.english-heritage.org.uk

VALE OF THE WHITE HOUSE

Uffington White Horse NT
www.nationaltrust.org.uk
Map 174 ref SU 301 867
Wayland's Smithy
Map 174 ref SU 281 854

WARWICKSHIRE

Shakespeare's Birthplace
Henley Street, Stratford upon
Avon,
Warks CV37 6QW
Tel: 01789 204016
www.shakespeare.org.uk
Anne Hathaway's Cottage

Cottage Lane Shottery CV37 9HH
Tel: 01789 292 100
www.shakespeare.org.uk
Charlecote Park NT
Warwick, Warks CV35 9ER
Tel: 01789 470277
www.nationaltrust.org.uk

WESTMORLAND

Levens Hall
Kendal Westmorland LA8 0PD
Tel: 015395 60321
www.levenshall.co.uk
Kendal Castle
Westmorland LA9
Tel: 01539 725620

WILTSHIRE

Avebury NT
Nr Marlborough Wilts SN8 1RF
Tel: 01672 539250
www.nationaltrust.org.uk
Stonehenge
www.stonehenge.co.uk

WORCESTERSHIRE

Elgar's Birthplace Museum
Crown East Lane Lower Broadheath,
Worcs WR2 6RH
Tel: 01905 333224
www.elgarfoundation.org

YORKSHIRE

Petrifying Well
High Bridge Knaresborough
North Yorks HG5 8DD
Tel: 01423 864600
www.mothershiptonscave.com/
the_petrifying_well.htm
Whitby Abbey EH
Whitby North Yorks YO22 4JT
Tel: 01947 603568
www.english-heritage.org.uk
Nostell Priory NT
Doncaster Road Nostell
West Yorks WF4 1QE
Tel: 01924 863892
www.nationaltrust.org.uk

Index of People

Index of Places